Logotypes & Letterforms

Logotypes &
Letterforms

Handlettered Logotypes and Typographic Considerations

D O Y A L D   Y O U N G

D E L P H I   P R E S S

Sherman Oaks, California

Also by Doyald Young

Fonts & Logos (Delphi Press)
ISBN 0-9673316-0-9

First Edition
2 3 4 5
Copyright © 1993 by Doyald Young
Printed in Hong Kong

Jacket and book designed by Doyald Young

Reproduction or republication of the content
in any manner, without the express written
permission of the publisher, is prohibited.

Library of Congress Cataloging-in-Publication Data
Young, Doyald,
    Logotypes & letterforms: handlettered logotypes and
typographic considerations/Doyald Young,—1st ed.
    p. cm.
    Includes biliographical references and indexes.
    ISBN 0–8306–3956–X
    1. Lettering. 2. Trademarks. I. Title. II: Logotypes
and letterforms.
    NK3600. Y68 1993
    745.6' 1—dc20   91–44288
                                              CIP

Published by DELPHI PRESS
13957 Valley Vista Boulevard
Sherman Oaks, CA 91423
T (818) 788–5562
F (818) 990–1635
e-mail: doyald@pacbell.net
www.delphipress.com

THE TYPES ILLUSTRATED IN THIS BOOK

The following fonts are from *Encyclopaedia of Type Faces*,
fourth edition, by PINCUS JASPERT, W. TURNER BERRY, and
A. F. JOHNSON (London, 1970), and are reproduced by permission
of Blandford Press, an imprint of Cassell: Arrighi italic, Baskerville
bold, Baskerville bold italic, Monotype Bodoni bold condensed,
Bookman old style, Cancelleresca Bastarda, Century expanded
italic, Century Nova, Century old style, Coronet, Empire, Eurostile
condensed, Eurostile bold condensed, Folio bold condensed, Franklin Gothic, Franklin Gothic wide, Futura light, Futura demi-bold
script, Gill Sans bold italic, Gillies Gothic, Hobo, Horizon, Libra,
Microgramma bold extended, Open Roman Capitals, Pericles,
Phenix, Plantin, Times Roman semi-bold, Topic medium, Twentieth Century ultra bold extended, and Stephenson Blake's Vogue.

HAROLD BERLINER'S TYPEFOUNDRY
of Nevada City, California, set the Lutetia Roman.

JACK ROBINSON and PETER ALMADA
set the following fonts from the film library of
Characters & Color Typographers, Los Angeles, California:
Americana extra bold, Basilea, Block, Mergenthaler Linotype
Bodoni bold condensed, Caslon bold condensed, Commercial Script,
ITC Franklin Gothic demi, Frutiger 45, Handel Gothic, Jana,
Michelangelo Titling, ITC Modern No. 216 bold italic, ITC Modern
No. 216 heavy, Murray Hill, Pericles, Radiant medium, Radiant bold,
Radiant bold extra condensed, Serif Gothic regular, Simplex, Snell
Round-hand, Standard extra light extended, Torino, Torino italic,
Trump italic, Univers 63, and Venus extra bold extended.

GERALD LANGE and ROBIN PRICE
of the USC Fine Arts Press, University of Southern California,
Los Angeles, California, set the Optima and the Grayda Script.

ROBERT NELSON
of Gibbs Typesetting, Bell Gardens, California, set the Intertype
Vogue bold condensed.

ROBERT TROGMAN
of Los Angeles, California, set the Firmin Didot and Erasmus light.

Type designers, foundries, and dates of issue, will be found with each
specimen and in the Index of Typefaces Illustrated on page 295.

To my teachers
who taught me how to draw letters

JOSEPH GIBBY

HARRY JACOBS

MORTIMER LEACH

and to

PROF. HERMANN ZAPF

with admiration.

Contents

List of Logotypes and Letterforms Illustrated

Preface

T<small>HIS BOOK BEGAN</small> as a small collection of my handlettered scripts. In winnowing these from other handlettered examples that I had done, it was soon evident that a book covering a wide group of styles could be put together. Except for a few examples, all are my designs, though all have been drawn by my hand. Some were drawn under the aegis of other designers, and they are credited.

Many books have been published on marks and symbols, or how to design corporate identity programs, or how to draw letters. Additionally, there are many books on type and its use. The idea of a book of logotypes as an entity has not been addressed nor, specifically has the handlettered name without a mark or symbol. A logotype may or may not be coupled to a mark for a variety of reasons. While eminently successful logotypes have been designed using only typography, many are expressly *handlettered,* and this book addresses that avenue. It is not a resolute defense of the approach—though I offer explanations for the advantage—but instead is a collection and a record of companies that have made that decision, and one that fits my particular talents.

Instead of grouping the examples by style, I have chosen instead to divide them in chapters that relate to commercial endeavors. This has posed some problems, because some examples can be placed either in "The Company Name" or "The Brand Name," because the product is so strongly identified with the company. The same is true of the chapter "Scripts." Several examples could be included in "The Brand Name." The chapter grouping has a distinct advantage, for it allows me to place them alphabetically (mostly) and not fuss with pairing examples that relate esthetically.

A few examples were drawn in the 1960s—the collection of the Music Center of Los Angeles County shown in the "Entertainment" chapter. I would have preferred to date all of the work, but my records are not complete, and I choose not to date them halfheartedly. However, to satisfy the requirements of Procter & Gamble (owner of some Max Factor and Vidal Sassoon products) for permission to reprint, dates are given to indicate that these are not current products.

In the strongest sense, letterforms do not age but become fixed to a period of time primarily in their application. Longevity is often precluded by blatant design approaches that are banal, modish, and consequently ephemeral. Many products and graphics are designed to seize the moment and cash in on a popular idea.

This book is intended as a resource, but it is also a retrospective of my work because the examples span a thirty-year period, with the major body of the work commissioned in the 1980s. The "Hotels and Resorts" chapter is the most recent, and it dates from 1986 to the present writing. It is my hope that as a compilation of styles, supported by the discussion of letterforms and typography, the information will promote further inquiry.

A knowledge of lettering is helpful in designing logotypes—some say indispensable—but a knowledge of typography is equally important. Here it is my intention to show by example how they are related. This book then is an extension of my teaching: a synthesis of drawing letters and designing logotypes, with comments on typography.

Acknowledgments

Tʜᴇ ᴡᴏʀᴋ that appears in this book has been influenced by the unique talents of Mary Sheridan, Henry Dreyfuss, Sterling Leach, and Mortimer Leach. Their judgment, wisdom, and artistry have been vital to my career and permeate this book in its entirety.

I am indebted to the clients who have granted me permission to reprint their logotypes in this book. Its shape and content are greatly determined by their generosity.

Don Bartels, Colin Brignall, Ray Engle, Allan Haley, Edward Hutchings, Jay Krause, Mari Makinami, and Jo-Ann Stabile—all friends and clients—have generously contributed their professional wisdom to chapter-opening essays, and I thank them especially.

Mari Makinami, friend and valued associate, graciously secured releases to reprint examples for her special clients in Japan, the greater portion of which appear in the "Hotels and Resorts" chapter.

The logotypes that illustrate the opening essay on page 2—from the hands of other designers—have been generously supplied by the companies' public relations departments and sometimes by a company's president.

David Solon, enduring friend, former partner of Mary Sheridan, occasional client, and respected advisor, merits a badge of patience for listening to my litanies on this book's development.

Bob Maile, preeminent lettering artist, friend, and former student, was kind to read the manuscript and offer suggestions. Gerard Huerta, lettering designer, Robert Keene, production designer, and Hal Frazier of Art Center College of Design volunteered reviews of the rough manuscript. James Conner, Niels Diffrient, and George Perkins of the (former) Henry Dreyfuss Pasadena office have been great teachers in learning the complex and important discipline of graphics for industrial design. Ulf Helgesson is a friend and former associate of the Dreyfuss office; examples of our combined efforts appear in "The Company Name" and "Typefaces and Alphabets." The support of Ken Dodge, of Young & Dodge, my partner for many years, was invaluable for projects for Henry Dreyfuss, California Institute of Technology, the Music Center of Los Angeles County, Leach, Cleveland & Associates, Calabasas Park, George Shearing, and Stan Kenton. David Parry, public relations counsel *par excellence,* was responsible for many projects: Knapp Communications Corporation, Milton Meyer & Co., The J. Paul Getty Trust, and Gin Wong Associates. I am indebted to the late E. A. Adams, founder of Art Center College of Design, who hired me to teach there and proved again that teaching is more of a learning experience than teaching. Thanks to Julie Morton for some precise production, and Gregory Ross, who helped in the preliminary stage of this book. Michael Diehl offered suggestions for computer typesetting; thanks to Caesar Chavez of Xerox Corporation for encouragement and for information on Character Code and publishing standards, and to Betty Ishikawa, whose able hand inked some examples. Letitia Burns O'Connor and Dana Levy of Perpetua Press, Vance Studley of Archetype Press at Art Center College of Design, and April Greiman all offered suggestions about publishing. Encouragement was given by Bill Chappell, Jerry Eckert of ABC Letter Art, and Joe Jones. Ramone Muñoz, student and educator, sent research on logo classification; compositor Jack Robinson, and Patrick Reagh, both confirmed type terminology. Randy Tokuda made many photo reproductions, and David Allen of Typecraft Printers in Pasadena contributed the reproduction pages for the UCLA book *Reading Hogarth.* Steel dies were supplied by Don Pennell and Dave Meyer of Ligature. Sandra Hutchins and Jan Zimmerman of Emerson & Stern lent their paper of SignFont text for their important work on the written form of American Sign Language (ASL). Edmark Corporation sent prints of the SignFont alphabet. Jeanne Parry of Art Center College of Design kindly permitted me to reprint the glossary that I prepared when I taught there. Don Dugas proof-read and assembled the many page-dummys. Special praise is extended to Nancy Green, Vice-President Editorial, of Design Press, who introduced clarity and order to my words and brought this book to fulfillment. A key page, "Parts of a Letter," was her inspiration and is vital information to a reader unfamiliar with letterforms. Without the computer instruction, patience, and kindness of Jim Whitney, the task of formatting and writing this book would have been impossible.

Introduction

THE LOGOTYPE examples shown on the following pages are presented as large as possible within this format in order to show clearly the details of the letterforms. With the exception of TV titling, the logotypes are also shown at a small size to illustrate the problems of legibility, spacing, and boldness that occur in reductions. With some examples I have shown a typeface that relates in some manner to the logotype that is discussed, primarily as a frame of reference, and specifically to introduce the reader to a variety of typefaces. Some pairings of logotypes and typefaces are not in total sympathy but are selected as the best approximation either in proportion, weight, or orientation. At times only one family characteristic of a typeface is featured within the logotype design (serif, terminal, swash, etc.). Occasionally I have selected a typeface that acts as a springboard to illustrate a typographic rule, in an attempt to offer information that does not fit neatly into the general description.

The pairing method helps to introduce to a newly interested reader the enormous, complex, and endlessly fascinating world of typography and letterform design. I hope to beguile the reader to explore type books, for to be typographically literate a graphic designer should have a vocabulary of at least twenty or thirty different text and display typefaces.

I gave as a first assignment in my lettering classes the search in periodicals for thirty-five typefaces, collected, identified, and due within six weeks. It is a valuable lesson, for beginners must learn to see for themselves the world of type that surrounds and permeates their lives and to realize that there is a precise distinction between Bulmer and Baskerville. Ideally, lettering and typography should be taught concurrently—for each explains the other.

This book is not an encyclopedia or dissertation on the merits of typefaces, which have been authoritatively covered in a number of titles to be found in the bibliography, but is rather a source book of letterforms and design direction possibilities, with some personal comments on typography. It is not my thesis that each logotype has sprung forth from a redrawing of the typeface that accompanies it, though in some cases this is true. I usually draw from a memory bank of typefaces, because I have studied and loved type for a long time. I do browse on days when ideas are elusive.

Some logotypes in the chapter "Hotels and Resorts" are part of a signature that includes a mark. When the mark is an integral part of the design, I show the total signature; otherwise only the logotype example is presented.

Each logotype is accompanied by a brief text that explains the nature of the company or individual for which the logotype was created, with some occasional comments on related typefaces and a few remarks on the logotype's letterforms. Sketches are helpful in showing a progression of presentation ideas, but in many places they were no longer available because the client kept them or because they were discarded for lack of storage space.

I have always tried to involve clients in the design process, because they help to define the problem. Each commission is laden with complex requirements. These are rarely solved by a single individual. Often the final product is an amalgam of many talents that include a synthesis of varying preferences and experiences. These are not necessarily compromises but, rather, are reconciliations, which means a friendly resolve—a term favored by Gene Fleury, who for many years was a friend and teacher at Art Center College of Design in Pasadena.

The logotypes that appear on the following pages are for a wide variety of clients. Generally they are direct and conservative solutions. Some are refined and delicate, while others are gutsy, sophisticated, mass-market, friendly, austere, middle-of-the-road, flashy, light of heart, exuberant, aggressive, or playful, and many are *very* serious.

The Parts of a Letter

Note—Depending on the source, the usage may vary for terms given here,
which are the ones used in this book. (Set in ITC Baskerville, except where noted.)

 HOTEL Bel-Air
LOS ANGELES

I.magnin

SONY

brother

mazda
IT JUST FEELS RIGHT.

Spode™

GUCCI

Neiman Marcus

TIFFANY & CO.

 Halekulani
On the Beach at Waikiki

SAAB

USAir

John Hancock
Financial Services

SEARS

Yves Saint Laurent

 Hertz

SIEMENS

*These logotypes, created
by other designers, use no marks,
symbols, or illustrations to convey
their message: they rely
only on letterforms.*

The Logotype

DESPITE their great diversity, the logotypes from the hands of other designers on the opposite page share a notable characteristic: they are used in advertising primarily without a mark or symbol. Each is dependent on the successful choice, arrangement, and resolution of letterforms—whether they are handlettered, typeset, bold, narrow, wide, serifed, sans serif, script, italic, stylized, or personal signature. All have enjoyed enormous success—most are known internationally, primarily because of their company's established reputation, extensive advertising, and corporate identity programs. Some have great style—perhaps distinction is the more precise word; others are bold assertive statements. Only a few can be called contemporary, because they are set in typefaces or drawn in styles that are more than fifty years old. Those that appear modern are the most restrained; few are complex. Because they are normally letterspaced, all of them are very legible and are read easily in small sizes. None are cutting edge or avant-garde. Some are "outside of time," to borrow a phrase from Tennessee Williams, and will endure despite the whims of fashion.

Many are widely advertised, some are bolstered by enormous, costly corporate identity programs. Most have been drawn by hand; some, while appearing to be identifiable typefaces, have been slightly modified either in weight or proportion to fit the needs of their owner's preferences and market requirements.

A logotype is a word or group of words that defines an individual, group, product, or company. It may be straightforward type, or it may be a unique design. It originally meant a single piece of type (a metal sort) that contained two or more *separate* letters or figures. *Webster's Third International Dictionary of the English Language Unabridged* (1976) defines logotype as the name of a newspaper, an advertiser's trademark, a company name and address. *Webster's Ninth New Collegiate Dictionary* (1988) defines it additionally as an identifying symbol. Today the shortened word *logo* is commonly used. But this is ambiguous, because a logo can also be a mark, the name and mark, or the name by itself. Landor Associates, one the world's largest industrial design firms, defines a mark and the company name as the "corporate signature." *Wordmark* is used to define a stylized treatment of a word that because of its shape and style is a mark in itself. Seal, monoseal, monogram, signature, abstract, glyph, and alphaglyph are other logo classifications (from *Good Packaging*, November 1975). In this book a logotype may be the name of a company, group, person, or product interchangeably.

The logotype must be effective on stationery, office forms, business cards, and the multitude of applications that reflect and position the company's image. The demands of print media—magazines, newspapers, and direct mail—are rigorous also, because a logo must clamor for attention among a welter of images in both color and black-and-white. The ubiquitous business card is a logo's taskmaster: often the logotype must be reduced to three-quarters or even half an inch, depending on its length and position on the card. With these restraints, legibility and dominance are of paramount importance, for at times the logotype must compete with a product name, division or subsidiary, tag line, address, telephone and fax numbers, name, and title—all within a three-and-a-half- by two-inch space. Some business cards require an E-mail/Ethernet address.

A logotype is its own font, and not the total font of a typeface wherein all letters, punctuation, figures, and special characters must function as a harmonious entity. In a logotype the capital-to-lower-case-height ratio may be drawn to a more favorable relationship. The proportion of one letter to another may be adjusted for more even color spacing, for too often a font must compromise its proportions to fit within a prescribed unit system and to prevent misspacings.

In choosing to use a typeface for a logotype, it must be remembered that all typefaces or fonts are conceived and drawn as individual

A logotype is its own font, and not the total font of a typeface design wherein all letters, punctuation, figures, and special characters must function as a harmonious entity.

letters, then adapted to the compromises of a font, which has been designed to reproduce faithfully at less than 5 points to billboard size. Without modifications, these compromises become an integral part of a logotype's solution. For this reason it is often necessary to hand-letter or modify a typeface to satisfy a set of carefully defined objectives. It can then be designed to reflect its intended use, stylized to present a unique appearance. It is not necessary to handletter a logotype for the sake of originality, but only to improve its legibility and to impart a distinction that makes it individual—setting it apart from its competition. Of great importance is that it will be easy to reproduce in a wide range of sizes. It is often possible to achieve these goals by slightly modifying the letterforms, either by weight, spacing, and/or a change of proportion. As part of a corporate identity program, a logotype and its accompanying typeface should be in harmony with the identity program. Some corporate identity programs specify both a sans serif and a serifed face for use with the logotype. A corporate alphabet based on the original logotype letterforms is sometimes drawn for use in setting subsidiary and division names to strengthen the total graphic image of the program.

First, a logotype must be *legible*—if nothing whatsoever is done to make it distinctive, it must satisfy that requirement. Second, most logotypes must possess a reasonable degree of boldness, simply as a demand to be read or noticed, though there are always exceptions.

Letterspacing alone may constitute the basis for distinction. The basic palette of type is abundant: capitals, small caps, cap and small cap, lowercase, cap and lowercase (five variations), plus the italic version (ten), plus the medium weight (twenty), plus the bold (thirty), plus extra bold, black, or ultra (forty), plus condensed (eighty), plus extended (one-hundred-sixty). These building blocks can be combined in a staggering number of combinations, creating an individual statement without even altering the letterforms. Some typefaces have been drawn in as many as eight weights (Helvetica) and with different proportions. Univers is a family of twenty-two distinct fonts. All too frequently these riches are insufficient. Drawing programs now permit PostScript fonts to be redrawn for a personal esthetic.

I begin a logotype design by drawing it (or setting it in type) in several different weights, in caps, then lowercase, sans serif, serif,

First, a logotype must be legible—*if nothing whatsoever is done to make it distinctive, it must satisfy that requirement.*

italic—extended if it is a short word, condensed if its length is cumbersome—and so on down the list, for in some letter combinations, words often appear more legible or pleasing to the eye in different settings, in caps or lowercase, or in different typefaces.

Within a typeset logotype, only a few letters need to be modified to produce a unique word. But drawing a logotype skillfully by hand based on a predetermined objective imparts a distinction that is often lacking in familiar rigid typeforms, because letters that are contained in a logotype are bound by design rules that apply only to their immediate relationship to each other.

Letters that are contained in a logotype are bound by design rules that apply only to their immediate relationship to each other.

The precise boldness and proportion can be drawn without the distortion that occurs when the logo is manipulated without special computer programs. Without careful redrawing, Helvetica, Futura, and Gill Sans, all monotone faces, are transformed into two-weight letters when they are extended laterally—horizontal strokes become thin; when compressed, the horizontals become bolder and vertical stems thinner, defeating the type designer's premise (figure 1).

Without modification, type can be used in a variety of ways to create a logotype: by a change of size if the logotype contains more than one word; cases may differ; orientation, color, and style all may vary. The most direct approach is to use the same type style and simply reduce the size of the secondary word. Different letterspacing might then be employed (figure 2).

One or more type styles may be married, swash characters introduced, or a design element may be repeated on sympathetic letters for continuity. Ligatures (or overlapped letters) are sometimes appropriate either to correct a misspacing or for use as a design element (figure 3). A combination of roman and italic forms may be combined in one word; typographic ornaments, rules, or flowers may be added to the surrounding field or between words. Letters may be outlined, possess a shadow, or be hand-tooled.

If the logotype is more than one word, it is possible to change type styles, particularly if one word is secondary or if it modifies (figure 4). Scripts may be used with either serif or sans serif—depending on the nature of the logo, this could be any of the basic script styles: single- or two-weight, brush or pen, casual or formal, restrained or expressive, upright or sloping (figure 5). The most subtle modification of a

EOS *a.* EOS *b.*

EOS *c.*

HILTON
INTERNATIONAL
J A P A N

Narita
GOLF CLUB

Figure 1 — a. *Helvetica bold caps, designed as a monotone sans serif face.*

b. *The same type condensed 50 percent set width shows the thinning of the vertical stems when the type is squeezed. It has lost its monotone quality and the designer's original intent.*

c. *A more comfortable distortion—150 percent set width—because bold letters often require a nominal amount of horizontal thinning when they are extended.*

Figure 2 — a. *A logotype of three lines of handlettered generic sans serif justified caps that illustrates a variation of two different weights and three point sizes. Each has different letterspacing to create a specific emphasis for each word.*
*Note that the tail of the **J** extends to the left of the two top lines in order to create a more optically justified alignment.*

Figure 2 — b. *A handlettered logotype with strong influences of Perpetua drawn in two even lines (justified): a large word of cap-and-lowercase, contrasted to a line of smaller-sized caps, letterspaced to exactly control the desired emphasis. The serifs of the example are more generous in length than their type counterpart. (See page 107.)*

Los Angeles Philharmonic Orchestra The Music Center

Figure 3 — *Overlap letters or serifs to improve letterspacing. Useful when a word must be tightly spaced for greater impact or when it must fit within a narrow space. Also employed to nest a cumbersome group of words to create a tighter unit. When strokes or serifs overlap, avoid small areas of white space that tend to fill in. (See page 71.)*

Figure 4 — *A loose pencil sketch of three lines of contrasting styles, weight, and orientation, each for a particular emphasis: Helvetica bold roman caps, Adobe Garamond roman caps, and a smaller size Adobe Garamond italic cap-and-lowercase, separated by a ¼-point hairline to allow the name to read as one unit. The city name, while third in importance, has a slight emphasis supplied by the italic. (See page 34.)*

Figure 5 — *Roman (vertical) sans serif caps paired with a word of small florid, formal script used as an elegant embellishment to a large condensed, two-weight, crisp sans serif. The sans serif may be monotone or two-weight: i.e., Franklin Gothic. The script can be single-weight or two-weight, casual or formal, brush or pen. (See page 96.)*

The history of type design is ultimately the marriage of two or more type forms with modifications.

serif can change the quality of a word. Soften with a bracket (Caslon, Garamond), and soften more with a larger bracket (Baskerville). Right angles are pristine (Bodoni, Walbaum), and sturdy, thickened serifs are assertive (Beton, Stymie). Tapered, chopped-end serifs are crisp (Trump, Augustea), and subtle concave stems with gently flared endings are classic (Jan van Krimpen's Open Roman Capitals and Herbert Post's Post Roman). Variations of these can be mixed with discretion on dissimilar typefaces, for the history of type design is ultimately the marriage of two or more type forms with modifications (figure 6). Stretch, blunt, square-off, point, or cup for different effects. Shorten serifs for a tight bold statement (figure 7).

Terminals are refined beginning or ending strokes found on the roman lowercase letters **a**, **c**, **f**, **g**, **j**, **r**, **y**, **s**, and alternately on some cap and lowercase italics. There are four basic shapes: teardrop, circle, triangle (also beak), and rectangle. Most old-style lowercase faces (Garamond, Janson, Caslon) use the teardrop; modern faces may use the circle or oval (Bodoni, Americana, and Modern 216) or the triangular shape (Egmont, Litho, and Fenice). The rectangle is found mostly on the Egyptians or slab serifs (Beton, Stymie, Graph, and Serifa), though some of these use a chopped triangular terminal for the *c*, *s*, and *z*. The capitals *C*, *D*, *E*, *F*, *G*, and sometimes the *J*, *S*, and *Z*, follow the same scheme. These triangles are easily modified in the same manner as the serifs (figure 8).

The calligraphic structure of letters may be varied. Calligraphic fonts are often "humanistic," *i.e.*, with slight contrast between the thick and thin strokes, and a diagonal axis for all curved forms. Their proportion is derived from the classic roman (see the British Standard type-style classification from Jaspert, Berry, and Johnson's *Encyclopaedia of Type Faces*, page 286). They are based on forms produced with a flat instrument, either pen or brush. When the flat-edged writing instrument is held at an angle approximately 15 degrees from the horizontal, it produces vertical strokes that are thinner than diagonal strokes. A diagonal drawn from top left to bottom right is the same width as the curved stem at its widest point. The diagonal drawn from top right to bottom left will be thinner, as in the capital *A*. The horizontal strokes are a middle weight (figure 9). The angle can be increased or decreased, greatly changing the look of the letter.

Bodoni **M**

Century **M**

Garamond **M**

Serifa **M**

Trump **M**

MONSIEUR

Handlettered Baskerville

MONSIEUR

ITC Baskerville

Garamond **a**

Bodoni **a**

Fenice **a**

Serifa **c**

Figure 6 — Serifs may be lengthened, tapered, blunted, chopped at right angles, or might end with a radius. The radius of the bracket may increase, or the serifs may be exchanged from one face to another—but should be consistently applied.

Figure 7 — To gain a size advantage, the serifs have been shortened in the hand-lettered Baskerville to prevent the serifs from overlapping (top). These proportions differ from the ITC Baskerville font (bottom). (See page 183.)

Figure 8 — The terminals may vary in shape. The four common shapes are teardrop, circle, triangle, and rectangle, sometimes drawn in a slightly triangular manner on very bold Egyptian faces.

Baskerville **h u**

Garamond **h u**

Optima **h u**

Bodoni **h u**

Century **h u**

Trump **h u**

Figure 9 — Calligraphic letters based on humanistic letterforms drawn with a flat instrument held at roughly a 15-degree angle to produce a diagonal axis.

Figure 10 — Branches may change shape. The arch may be more pronounced, symmetrical, angled, flattened, thickened, or tapered. The joining or departure position height can change— it may be tangent or join obliquely.

Branches are the strokes that depart from lowercase letters or that are joined to a vertical stem: *h*, *m*, *n*, and *u* (figure 10). Altering them also changes the visual effect of a word. The joining position may be changed and its weight lessened or increased. A mix of italic and roman lowercase forms lends a softer look to a word because many italic forms have more curves and different skeletal shapes than the upright roman. The combination can be either vertical or slanted.

Whether the word alone or the combination of a mark and logotype is used is determined by complex factors: corporate philosophy, market research, advertising, design consultants, and, at times, public relations counsel. When a design project is initiated, it is often to update an existing logotype or to incorporate an acquisition. The information will determine a general area of design direction—hard sell, elegant, sophisticated, masculine or feminine, for the mass market or for precise target groups. Is a contemporary effect indicated? If not, will old-style letterforms be appropriate? Should the typeface relate historically or geographically—is it necessary to use Caslon or Baskerville type to say "Stilton Cheese"? Logotypes for children's products lean toward the bold and spirited, particularly for toys, while restaurant and hotel logos, especially resorts, are often elegant, fanciful, "romantic" letterforms. Appliance model designations for home or industrial products are generally sober and forthright, often using sans serif or mechanical-appearing type styles. Without the aid of elaborate and costly market-testing programs, the basic rule for logotype design is simple: do your homework. Look at traditional responses, and then determine if innovation is required, and remember that the avant-garde appeals only to a few.

Contemporary typography does not necessarily require new and original letterforms but, more often than not, is the use of classical or familiar typeforms in new surroundings and arrangements that strive to usurp the familiar. The logotypes that survive for the longest time are legible, appropriate, straightforward, and are eminently easy to use in a wide variety of reproduction techniques.

These are general guidelines that only suggest design direction, for a thorough knowledge of typefaces is required to enable a designer to create logotypes of lasting authority. There is a two-thousand-year legacy of roman letters from which to choose and reinterpret anew.

The logotypes that survive for the longest time are legible, appropriate, straightforward, and are eminently easy to use in a wide variety of reproduction techniques.

The Company Name

The Company Name

DONALD BARTELS

Director, Corporate Identity Europe
Landor Associates
London, England

THE PRIMARY GOAL of a corporate identity program is to fuse the positive attributes of a company with its name into a single memory. In this definition, the verbal component of the program, the company name, is cast in the central role because the verbal process—selecting and sequencing words—is critical to everyday life, the arena in which a corporate identity takes root and thrives. Just as recognizing and communicating anything in daily life depend on this verbal activity, so remembering a company requires remembering its *name*.

The positive attributes instantly summoned up with the company name in a successful identity program mix those demanded by today's fiercely competitive global market (dynamic, innovative, agile, assertive, responsive, proactive, aware—"lean, mean, and clean"), those representing traditional values (proud and "statureful," solid and reliable and, of course, quality! quality! quality!) with those describing the company's particular competencies, capabilities, values, products, and/or services. In the design development phase of a corporate identity project, a list of all desired positive attributes (complemented, sometimes, with a list of negative attributes to avoid) sets the basic criteria against which alternative identities are evaluated, so its precise definition is critical to the ultimate success of the program.

Because of its primacy, the company name itself, devoid of visual detail, should communicate as many positive attributes as possible. Although a new appellation bestows upon the company a fresh opportunity to communicate these attributes, often an existing name must be retained, saddling the program with whatever positive and negatives values have come to be associated with it.

Whether the name is old or new, it remains the graphic designer's role to instill into the *display* of the name as many as possible of both the general and specific attributes.

To visually enunciate these positive attributes, the designer can choose from a continuum of forms bracketed by two fundamentals, the *logotype* and the *symbol +*. Each possesses distinct communication limitations and opportunities.

The logotype. In this form, the name stands alone without support from any separate visual device, and the name is thereby emphasized. The designer relies solely on a *distinctive drawing* of the letterforms, each considered as a constituent, to communicate positive values.

This is the simpler, subtler, and more direct of the two fundamental forms. Because of its visual terseness and elegant efficiency, the logotype is a favored competitor in the world of modern corporate communications; it is trim and taut and, when successful, works with a minimum of effort to achieve its goal while commanding attention and achieving memorability with skill and grace.

The limitation of the logotype as a form of company identification is its lack of imagery, with a resulting reliance up-

Opposite—
Detail of Gin Wong Associates
monogram mark
(see page 29).

on the name itself to communicate specific attributes.

The Symbol +. Imagery plus, usually a typeset name or series of names, is the other fundamental form of corporate identification. Literal or representational, abstract or nonobjective, imagery confers the distinct advantage of communicating specific meaning absent or latent in the company name. When successful, a symbol adds a richness to the communication of positive attributes and, at most, empowers the identity with a uniqueness of expression and roundness of definition never available to the logotype alone.

The disadvantage of the symbol is that, because it adds information many people have difficulty remembering; it can encumber communication. Since memory of the company *name* is the primary goal of a corporate identity program, additional visual data such as a symbol can appear superfluous, can distract and dilute, and thus can relegate an identity to the great abyss of the lost and forgotten.

Attesting to the central role borne by the company name in an identity program is the fact that a corporate symbol *rarely* stands alone, not even after decades of use. It almost always requires that the company name, typeset or hand-drawn, be displayed with it.

Although a symbol can replace a name after the two have been long associated, in the only instance in which this has happened in the United States, the role of *words* in the memory process is patently clear: the generic name of the symbol is identical to the proper name of the company, "Shell."

To find symbols that communicate meaning by themselves, one must look outside the area of corporate identity to either religious or national icons, representing all-inclusive concepts or systems of belief (the cross: Christianity; the eagle: the United States and its founding principle of freedom-through-democracy), or to pictograms, where images either depict basic categories of products or services (the customs area at an airport) or provide simple instructions ("No Smoking"), in both cases relying on well-established or obvious images.

Within the continuum of forms of corporate identification are found hybrids in which the characteristics of the fundamental forms are mixed. An example is the "wordmark"—a logotype containing an element integral to its structure that, because of its inherent strength, also may be extracted and used as a separate identification device. Another example is the symbol plus a logotype instead of typesetting. In each, the relative dominance of the custom-drawn letterform vs. imagery varies, relating one hybrid more closely to one fundamental form than the other, and conferring different advantages and disadvantages.

Presented on the following pages are examples from across this continuum.

1234567890

GILL SANS BOLD ITALIC — ERIC GILL, MONOTYPE 1928–30

Top—*Art director's*
preliminary sketch.
Bottom—*An ink comprehensive*
with adjusted weights
and proportions.

125th Anniversary Logo—Arco

Corporate Headquarters, Los Angeles

David Bilotti, Director of Design/Designer
Doyald Young, Artist
Anniversary Banner

Figures designed for a three- by six-foot Arco anniversary banner. The bounced figures are jubilant, festive, and decorative with an inline that adds a special element of texture. Each figure is stag-gered to visually interlock with the previous one, allowing them to be more tight-ly spaced, and the interlocking helps to create a strong, identifiable shape.

Inline, outline, outline drop sha-dow, gravure, tooled, open, or shaded—all are decorative treatments of alpha-bets for both serif and sans serif and add interest to sometimes pedestrian shapes. They are rich special display faces, and restraint should be exercised in their use. It was Voltaire who observed that "constant pleasure is not pleasurable."

These figures, related to Gill Sans, are not of the same weight or width. Gill Sans, in turn, bears strong resemblance to Edward Johnston's 1916 sans serif face for the London Underground. Here a serif has been added to the fig-ure *1* in the style of Futura for greater legibility; the open bowl of the *5* is over-balanced, and the *2* curves more crisply.

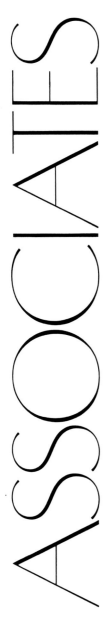

&TOBACK

ASSOCIATES

ASSOCIATES &TOBACK

*Two ampersands whose forms
clearly illustrate their derivation
from the Latin word* et. ***Left***—*Trump Mediaeval italic.*
Right—*Baskerville italic.*

Associates & Toback

Hollywood, California

Norman Toback, President
Tom Kakos, Art Director
Doyald Young, Designer/Artist
Corporate Logotype

The art director of this commercial TV production company had admired an announcement that I designed for a La Cienega gallery and wanted the same type style though more crisply drawn. The exuberant design filled the greater part of the width of the letterhead, and because of its generous size it was possible to draw the letterforms as a light face and with true hairlines. The letters are a slimmed-down version of Optima based on classical proportions.

The corporate name makes use of an ampersand—a contraction of *per se and*—and the character itself: **&**. The shape is a stylized version of the Latin word *et,* meaning "and." Type designers often depart on flights of fancy *and* poetic license upon encountering ampersands. Georg Trump's italic version illustrated here is one of the most spirited and innovative shapes in typography. It is a lowercase *e* instead of the traditional cap *E*. In comparison, the very handsome Baskerville italic *&* is more romantic, with its distinct cap *E* and *T*.

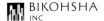

ABCDEFGHIJKLMNOPQRSTUVWXYZ

TRAJAN REGULAR — CAROL TWOMBLY, ADOBE ORIGINAL 1989

Bikohsha Inc.
Tohru Uraoka, President
Osaka, Japan

Mari Makinami, Executive Creative Director,
International Design Associates, Tokyo
David Solon, Designer/Artist, Skyline mark
Doyald Young, Designer/Artist, Logotype
Corporate Logotype

The classic roman letter has been drawn over and over. The hallowed inscription on Trajan's column in Rome that glorified his accomplishments has served as a model. Others have found constant challenge in Nicolas Jenson's wondrous type forms from his tract on Eusebius in 1470.

This ritualistic redrawing is for a very old and highly respected manufacturer of signs, both interior and exterior, with major emphasis on hotel signage. It is a letterform that I have been drawing for a long time in efforts to create a new font. It is both classic and contemporary because of its restraint and simplicity. It is similar to Optima. It does somewhat follow the Trajan proportions, but the serifs have been reduced, the *A* is wide, the *C* narrow, the thick/thin ratio is less, and it is more mechanical. The *N* has a squared-off upper left diagonal joining. The lower lobe of the *B* is pronounced, and the open *K* is yet another obeisance to Hermann Zapf's Michelangelo titling.

BUSHNELL

BUSHNELL

BUSHNELL

ABCDEFGHIJKLMNOPQRSTUVWXYZ

HANDEL GOTHIC — DON HANDEL, VGC 1965

Bushnell
Division of Bausch & Lomb
San Dimas, California

Art Direction: Claus Huckenbeck,
Industrial Design, Tehachapi, California
Doyald Young, Designer/Artist
Corporate Logotype

Bushnell established itself after the Second World War as a merchandiser of optical instruments. It has been so successful that it now designs and sells a wide range of fine optical instruments manufactured to its specifications.

The logotype style is an amalgam of several faces: Radiant Bold, Venus, and characteristics of Handel Gothic. The design intent is precision and quality, with a more contemporary look than Bushnell's previous modified Century Schoolbook logotype. It is a biform, because both the *u* and the *n* are lower-case. The biforms are used to repeat the curved top and bottom of the *S* and the round lobes of the *B*. The *E* and the *L* resemble Handel Gothic, and the softened corners are a *leitmotif* that unifies otherwise disparate shapes. The middle horizontal strokes are drawn above center for an optical balance. There is a generous amount of letterspacing to maintain legibility in reductions when the name is applied to small products.

Connoisseur Antiques

Jeffrey Klawans, President and CEO

Los Angeles, California

Robert Keene, Art Director

Doyald Young, Designer/Artist

Corporate Logotype

For a sumptuous shop on Melrose Place with a pure Georgian façade, the logotype had to function also as a twenty-five-foot exterior sign on the façade of the mansard roof. The sunburst was used only on stationery and collateral items

Long logotypes are best kept simple, because echoed design elements can become excessive. The caps are kept simple—even their size is modest in proportion to most script types, though a bit of ornament should be allowed to reflect the baroque period. The *r*'s terminal is a crossbar for the cap *A*. The sunburst, long identified as the logo of Louis XIV, dates from the middle of the eighteenth century and was probably designed by Louis Luce.[1] It is a fleuron, used for ornamentation on bindings. The piece of metal is one-quarter of the design, with multiple pieces used to create the final sunburst.

1. From a most prized and delightful possession, John Ryder, *A Suite of Fleurons; or, A Preliminary Enquiry into the history & combinable natures of certain printers' flowers conducted by John Ryder.* (Liverpool: Tinlings of Liverpool; London: Phoenix House Ltd., 1956).

Dillingham

Dillingham

ABCDEFGHIJKLMNOPQRSTUVWXYZ
abcdefghijklmnopqrstuvwxyz

VENUS EXTRA BOLD EXTENDED — BAUER 1907–27

Ulf Helgesson Industrial Design

Woodland Hills, California

Ulf Helgesson, Design Director/Consultant
Dillingham Corporate Identity Program
Doyald Young, Designer/Artist
*Dillingham Corporation**
Honolulu, Hawaii
Corporate Logotype

---

* Now Dillingham Construction Corporation,
based in Pleasanton, California.

With divisions and subsidiaries sprinkled on the Pacific Rim, Dillingham's major thrust has been construction—the shape of Honolulu's skyline owes much to their expertise. Their interests include large construction projects in the far east, oceanographic equipment, natural gas, tugboat fleets, land development, and construction in northern California.

This version is bolder than the corporate alphabet, which matched the former logotype (see page 250). Tests for legibility were made by Perceptronics Corporation (opposite). Cap-and-lowercase was found to be the most legible, but the repetition of the straight forms *illin* was hard to read. Increasing the height of the double *l* made for easier reading. Legibility at a distance was critical for viewing at construction sites. The bowl of the *g* is small and above the baseline to prevent the tail from descending excessively.

Dillingham

Dillingham

Dillingham

Dillingham

DILLINGHAM
(Original corporate logotype.)

DILLINGHAM

DILLINGHAM

DILLINGHAM

A series of comprehensive logotypes, used to test legibility at an early stage in the design program. The test included a range of proportions and weights, using different observers from varying vantage points. From this test, a sans serif cap-and-lowercase scheme was chosen.

In a separate study, Teletype Corporation had found that caps and lower-case are approximately 15 percent more legible than all-cap lettering, though this premise is dependent on a medium-to-bold weight for distance viewing, with ample letterspacing. Additional designs were explored in sans serif only, again using a range of weights, proportions, cap height, and letterspacing. Other test examples were purposely misspelled to test the validity of the test and legibility.

A corporate alphabet was created especially for all of the divisions and subsidiaries in the original logotype weight.

eklektix

C.J. Welch, President

Los Angeles, California

Doyald Young, Designer/Artist

Corporate Logotype

Contemporary, futuristic, progressive, avant-garde, cutting edge, leading edge, postmodern, deconstructionist, reductionist—lingo for the latest. This logotype was designed for a company whose select contract furnishings defied tradition.

eklektix is handlettered Futura extra light, with skyscraper ascenders that suggest urbanity and elegant Dunhill accessories. The coined name is derived from the adjective *eclectic*, providing two additional ascenders with triangular shapes that are repeated in the *k*s and the *x*. For balance the *x* has been crossed above center, establishing a grid or line-up for the horizontal bar of the *e*s and the diagonal convergence of the *k*s.

Sans serifs have become synonymous with that which is contemporary, despite examples of pure geometric sans serif inset lead letters found on a marble fountain at Pompeii (*c.* A.D. 79).

In the wake of *die neue Typographie* (the new typography) begun by the Bauhaus—who were really minimalists—Paul Renner's Futura was introduced in 1929 and became one of the most widely used sans for the next twenty-five years, until Helvetica was introduced in 1957. Earlier, in 1916, Edward Johnston, a master calligrapher, designed a geometric sans serif for the London Underground. Still in use, its style greatly influenced Eric Gill in his drawing of Gill Sans. In the United States several faces were designed to catch the competition: Intertype's Vogue, designed for the fashion magazine; Metro, designed by W. A. Dwiggins (designer of Caledonia); and a series by Lucian Bernhard that included a light, quaint font named Bernhard Fashion, used extensively by the cosmetics and fashion industry.

Sans serifs are malleable because their minimal structure allows for extreme weights. Without fussy serifs and terminals, the letterforms can be extended or compressed with extreme amounts of weight for display use. Some of the blackest are Futura extra bold extended, Monotype Twentieth Century extra bold, Helvetica black, and Adrian Frutiger's superb Frutiger 85.

Some display sans serifs are weighted so excessively that the counters of the troublesome letters—*B, E, G, S, K, R, g, e, s,* and the two-story **a**—almost fill when printed (as in Gill Kayo black). To color evenly with the font, the horizontals of these letters must be thinned—the center horizontal is frequently the thinnest.

FUTURA LIGHT — PAUL RENNER, BAUER 1927–30

ABCDEFGHIJKLMNOPQRSTUVWXYZ
abcdefghijklmnopqrstuvwxyz
1234567890

ABCDEFGHIJKLMNOPQ_RSTUVWXYZ

OPEN ROMAN CAPITALS — JAN VAN KRIMPEN, ENSCHEDÉ 1929

Richard Lee Emler Enterprises

Beverly Hills, California

Richard Emler, President
Doyald Young, Designer/Artist
Corporate Monogram

Sagacious, trustworthy, thoughtful, diplomatic, and rock solid. Mandatory qualities in a personal manager and ones to be reflected in the logo—in this case a three-letter monogram.

The letterforms borrow from Buti and Aldo Novarese's Augustea, and Jan van Krimpen's unequaled Open Roman Capitals (designed as a companion face to his Antigone Greek).[1] The serifs are not as pronounced, the proportions are

slightly narrow, and the stems are rigid lines where van Krimpen's appear freely drawn. The *R* tips its hat to Hermann Zapf's Palatino. The bars of the *E* are equal in length. All three letters assume their hierarchical importance in size and proportion. The monogram was two-level, and blind-embossed on stationery.

1. John Dreyfus, *The Work of Jan van Krimpen* (Haarlem: Joh. Enschedé en Zonen, 1952).

THE ENRIGHT

COMPANY

❖

A REAL ESTATE ORGANIZATION

ABCDEFGHIJKLMNOPQRSTUVWXYZ

FRIZ QUADRATA — ERNST FRIZ, VGC 1965/ITC 1974

The Enright Company

Los Angeles, California

Timothy Enright, CEO/Art Director
Doyald Young, Designer/Artist
David Parry, Consultant
Corporate Logotype

A full-page ad in *Architectural Digest* magazine defined The Enright Company as "a comprehensive real estate organization that is as personal in its service as it is professional in its performance." A logotype that reflected those qualities was needed. What better way to express this than with sturdy, no-nonsense classic roman capitals. While the logotype has many qualities of and resembles Friz Quadrata, it borrows its form also from van Krimpen's Open Capitals (opposite page). The logotype is loosely spaced to be read quickly on outdoor billboards and real estate post signs. The large cap *E* is used to enhance legibility. *Company* is more widely spaced and extended, for it assumes a greater reduction. The serifs are more pronounced than the opposite example, and the stems are rigid with a generous flaring that begins deeply. Proportions, except for the *E* and *R*, are more even than the classical roman. The third line is Baskerville, which is used on all collateral items. The dividing rule is a *dash* variation (see "Scripts," page 237).

FEDCO

FEDCO

ABCDEFGHIJKLMNOPQRSTUVWXYZ

AMERICANA EXTRA BOLD — RICHARD ISBELL, ATF C. 1966

Fedco Inc.

Los Angeles, California

Harvey Thompson,
Art Director/Designer
Doyald Young, Artist
Corporate Logotype

Harvey Thompson chaired the advertising department at Art Center College of Design for a great number of years. Always sartorially correct, Harvey sought to update the image of Fedco, a chain of membership discount stores.

This logotype design of his replaced a very comfortable and unsophisticated outline drop shadow script contained in an ellipse. It is an extended Bodoni extra bold, akin to Richard Isbell's Americana

extra bold. Its hairlines are longer and beefier than most Bodoni specimens in order to hold in reduction. The *C*'s ending is widened to color the space that its counter creates and to replicate the mass of the triangular serifs in the *F* and *E*.

Standard rules of lettering and type design demand that the curved stems of two-weight letters be wider than straight vertical stems so to appear optically the same weight (note *D*, *C*, and *O*).

Floorplex

Above—Handset Torino (metal type).
Below—Handlettered version with less angular shapes.

Floorplex

ABCDEFGHIJKLMNOPQRSTUVWXYZ
abcdefghijklmnopqrstuvwxyz

TORINO (ROMANO MODERNO) — NEBIOLO C. 1908

Shafer and Shafer
Santa Ana, California

Joseph Duffy, Designer/Senior Art Director
Doyald Young, Designer/Artist
Floorplex Corporate Logotype

For a manufacturer of contemporary floor coverings, the signature designed by Joseph Duffy includes a stylized tile and brush stroke. The name was presented to me set in Torino type (top), with a request to adjust the proportion and spacing and to redraw some of the angular and abrupt transitions from the hairlines to the weighted curved stems. The drawing effort was to be restrained.

Torino is classified as modern. In its hairlines and general shape it is like countless romans of the late nineteenth century that were overly refined with brittle hairlines that were tiresome to read. This version is from the foundry that issued it in 1908, and it was known then as Romano Moderno.

The *F* is narrowed, and the blending of the brackets on the beak and vertical serif more abrupt. The transition from weighted stroke to hairline is more subtle, and the counters of the lobe more curved. This gentle adjustment is repeated on the *x*'s serif. The top of the *r* and *p*'s stem is reduced in width to allow for a rounded curve at the lobe's joining.

We bring good things to life.

Landor Associates

San Francisco, California

GE Project Design Team:
Donald Bartels, Design Director
Karl Martens, Senior Designer
Rebecca Livermore, Designer
Randall O'Dowd, Designer
Doyald Young, Designer
General Electric Company Monogram
Merle Bonthuis, Manager, Corporate Identity

The hundred-year-old General Electric monogram was modified to become the primary element in the GE Identity Program designed by Landor Associates. The design team headed by Don Bartels developed the program for over a year before I was asked to draw the finished art. They simplified the original monogram drawing, reduced the four border whorls and the ending letter volutes. The top loops were redrawn with parallel axes, the joining stroke was modified with a gentle ogee curve, and subtle weight adjustments were made. The stroke thickness was left unchanged.

In the GE Identity Program, the monogram is used within a specific visual environment, the graphic signature, as shown in the typical example above. This device is used to identify the company, its operating components, licensed affiliates, and the GE brand in all media.

GWA

ABCDEFGHIJKLMNOPQRSTUVWXYZ

BLOCK — H. HOFFMANN, BERTHOLD 1908

Gin Wong Associates

Gin Wong, A.I.A.

Los Angeles, California

Art Direction: Gin Wong, CEO, and
David Parry & Associates, Public Relations
Doyald Young, Designer/Artist
Corporate Monogram

Gin Wong Associates are architects and
planners of many international commissions, including some of southern California's most distinctive silhouettes: Four
Seasons Hotel, Los Angeles, the Meridien
Hotel in Newport Beach, the Twin Towers
at Century City, and the upper-level road-
way at Los Angeles airport.

Their logotype is a monogram of
extra-bold sans serif letters whose greatest usage is on construction site signs
and the countless sheets of plans used to
create each project. The initials of the
name are designed as one unit, with the *A*
as a separate element. The *G*, with its flat
top and bottom, is derivative of some
German typefaces designed around the
turn of the century (*e.g.*, Block). Futura
display and Handel Gothic, while a bit
flat-sided, use the same design element.

It is difficult to join a curve to a
straight line in a flowing transitional
manner without a trace of a corner. This
is accomplished by introducing an additional compound curve between the two.

DEBATES, CONTROVERSIES & CONCEPTS IN THE MANAGEMENT OF HIGH RISK PATIENTS

Cedars-Sinai Medical Center

Los Angeles, California

Donald Lackey, MD,
Director of Medical Education
John De Angelis, MD,
Director, High Risk Symposia
Doyald Young, Designer/Artist
High Risk Symposium Logotype

A direct-mail expert once said that to be effective, a mailer must tell the story on the envelope. Encyclopedic in length, the condensed logotype/message letters were reversed out of a solid red background and were designed to fill the rectangular space as much as possible. The logotype was used on the self-cover of a direct-mail brochure and application form for the symposium.

I have never been fond of tightly spaced roman letters because the serifs become troublesome, partially because they overlap. The weighted stems attract each other and create counters of gaping maws. I prefer instead to condense the letters so that they will color and space evenly. Condensed letters are normally used when space is at a premium or when a stronger statement is needed. I have shortened the serifs to overcome the tight spacing of the title. The letterforms have characteristics of several traditional faces: one is Bauer's Horizon, a handsome face that has not enjoyed much popularity in the United States.

The letters are drawn with many of my favorite conceits: modest serifs, chunky thins, an open *P*, *K*, and *R*, a wide *E* with a high center bar, a *B* with a generous lower lobe, and a splayed *M*. The *S* and the *B* are overbalanced. All thin strokes widen to create evenly colored letters. Multiple prints were made from key letters and assembled.

These subtleties are used to impart style and distinction to letters without exceeding the boundaries of good taste. A good friend of mine, an architect of impeccable taste schooled in the classics, once remarked that "a good building does not offend its neighbors." The same rule applies to many areas of design, including logotypes and letterforms.

ABCDEFGHIJKLMNOPQRSTUVWXYZ
abcdefghijklmnopqrstuvwxyz

HORIZON — KONRAD F. BAUER AND WALTER BAUM, BAUER 1925

ABCDEFGHIJKLMNOPQRSTUVWXYZ
abcdefghijklmnopqrstuvwxyz

FRANKLIN GOTHIC — MORRIS F. BENTON, ATF 1902

David Solon, Graphic Design

Los Angeles, California

David Solon, Designer/Art Director
Doyald Young, Artist
Hughes Aircraft Company Corporate Logotype

David Solon designed the corporate identity program for Hughes, one of the world's most respected manufacturers of satellites, radar, missiles, and highly sophisticated electronic components. They

sought a new corporate logotype that would reflect their conservative and long-established reputation. Never was there a thought or suggestion that the logotype should be innovative. After a series of presentations, this conservative letterform was developed. It resembles Franklin Gothic, one of the most often used sans serifs of the twentieth century, and a face that has enjoyed almost ninety years of consistent use. It is one of Morris Ful-

ler Benton's great achievements. ITC has issued their version with a larger x-height. The proportions here have been narrowed slightly; the small spur of the *G* eliminated and its crossbar raised; the *U* uses full weight on both strokes. The top and bottom arms of the *E* end with an angle; overall the style has more contrast between the bold stems and the lighter strokes. Helvetica black is used as a corporate font for the division names.

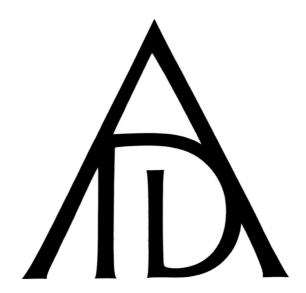

ABCDEFGHIJKLMNOPQRSTUVWXYZ

BASILEA — MARKUS J. LOW, VGC 1965

International Design Associates

Tokyo, Japan

Mari Makinami, Executive Creative Director
International Design Associates
Doyald Young, Designer/Artist
Corporate Monogram

Prestigious graphic designers in Tokyo, International Design Associates are expert in many areas of design—corporate identity programs, hotel graphics, pack-

aging, jewelry design, and department store interiors—with a roster of international clients that includes All Nippon Airways (ANA), Baccarat, Dentsu Advertising, Guerlain, Hilton International Japan, Max Factor Japan, Pioneer Electronics, Royal Copenhagen, and Shu Uemura (see "Hotels and Resorts," page 93).

Corporate signatures that include a monogram and the corporate name are popular in Japan. It is helpful in this

instance because the shortened IDA is easier to use, verbally and graphically. It was necessary to emphasize *Associates* with a dominant *A*. The round stem of the *D* completely overlaps the weighted stroke of the *A* to avoid a massing of weight. The top horizontal stroke of the *D* is soft, curving at the point of departure from the stem of the *I*. The style has influences of Basilea and Optima. The company name is set in Friz Quadrata.

International Design Associates
Tokyo, Japan

Mari Makinami, Executive Creative Director
Ken Nakata, Project Art Director
Doyald Young, Designer/Artist
Dentsu Inc., Tokyo, Japan
JCB Plaza, Corporate Logotype

One of the world's largest credit card companies, JCB has offices in twenty-one major cities worldwide. A new format was needed to accommodate the addition of *PLAZA* and the name of a city. Interest was also expressed in the design of a new monogram. Of the six designs shown on this page, number five found the greatest acceptance. But management opted for their original design placed in a square that has reference to a plaza (bottom left). The monogram was modified by adding weight to the curved hook of the *J*, the top right curve of the *C*, and the convergence of the *B*'s lobes. Additional shoulder was added to the top and bottom-left side of the *C* for a fuller curve. The vertical stem of the *B* was trimmed to lessen the massing of weight that occurs when three horizontals are joined to a stem. *PLAZA* is handlettered in a generic sans that avoids the narrow-proportioned Helvetica *A*. To minimize the space below the lobe of the *P*, its lobe was lowered slightly. The diagonals, the horizontal strokes, both straight and curved, have been thinned to optically match the vertical stems. To overcome the difficult and awkward *LA* spacing combination (the alphabet's worst), the horizontal stem of the *L* was shortened.

JCB *PLAZA*
ROME

1.

2.

JCB
Plaza HONOLULU

3.

JCB *Plaza*
BEIJING

4.

JCB PLAZA
Honolulu

5.

6.

Above—*Presentation comprehensive designs that depart from the Helvetica logotype.*

Opposite page—*Studies of different line arrangements, supporting type styles, and placement of city name, used with the original Helvetica logotype.*

Paris

JCB

Above—*The original logotype set in Helvetica medium.*
Left—*Final art of corporate logotype*

Jurgensen's

Jurgensen's

ABCDEFGHIJKLMNOPQRSTUVWXYZ
abcdefghijklmnopqrstuvwxyz

BODONI BOLD ITALIC — BAUER 1926

Jurgensen's Grocery Company
Pasadena, California

William Jurgensen, President
Doyald Young, Designer/Artist
Corporate Logotype

Jurgensen's is a chain of gourmet food markets in southern California. For many years they used a rather heavy formal script as a logotype both for their signage and on products packaged es-pecially for the company. I was asked not to stray too far from the original image. A formal script logo was requested, but it should be drawn more crisply and with more finesse.

This example is a combination of script and italic forms. In many fonts there is little difference between the two: the distinction is that pure scripts are con-nected letters. Its slant is slight. The *r* and *n* are a two-weight italic sans serif, similar to Hermann Zapf's Optima, while the *es* are Bodoni italic, and the *g* is a mélange of several faces. The serif of the original script *J* was retained, but the curve of the stem was radically changed.

For consistency I wanted to repeat the weighted pen-stroke returns of the *J* and the *g* on the top and bottom of each *s*, but Henry Dreyfuss, who was a benev-olent advisor on the project, preferred the teardrops, citing greater legibility.

**Knapp Communications
Corporation**

Los Angeles, California

Cleon T. Knapp, Chairman and CEO

Originally commissioned by
David Parry & Associates, Public Relations
and Philip Kaplan, Art Director,
Architectural Digest
Doyald Young, Designer/Artist
Corporate Signature

Architectural Digest, the ultra-classy interior design magazine, is among the many publications of Knapp Communications Corporation. This signature was designed in 1979 under the aegis of a former *Architectural Digest* art director in cooperation with a public relations firm.

A mirror of the magazine's formality, the narrow lowercase *k* and rectangular shape complement many of the magazine's elegant subjects. The serifs are heavily bracketed in the style of Caslon. The x-height is two-thirds cap height, and both diagonals are separated from the stem to avoid the visual congestion that normally occurs when these strokes converge. The upper thin diagonal is similar to Palatino, the editorial typeface used in *Architectural Digest.*

The logotype is Basilea, a classically proportioned roman Typositor face, and winner of a 1965 VGC competition.

MADELEINE'S

ABCDEFGHIJKLMNOPQRSTUVWXYZ

CENTURY NOVA — CHARLES E. HUGHES, ATF 1964

Madeleine and Alfred Barnett

Beverly Hills, California

Ron Collier, Art Director
Doyald Young, Designer/Artist
Corporate Signature

Modeled on private restaurant clubs in England where members are enveloped in a cocoon of service, including Rolls Royce livery, the Palladian interior of Madeleine's was designed by Ron Collier.

The monogram *M* is designed with opposing loops and a swooping finishing stroke in much the same style as the spirited example of George Bickham's florid penmanship (right). In printed usage for collateral items, the large opulent form of the cap *M* is subordinate to the name, achieved by blind embossing or printing in a muted color. *Madeleine's* is a slightly bolder hand-drawn, condensed version of ATF's Century Nova.

A traditional letter **M** *from George Bickham's* Universal Penman, *a writing manual for eighteenth-century bookkeepers, and valuable resource for unequaled formal script letterforms.*

Tohru Uraoka
Tokyo, Japan

Mari Makinami, Executive Creative Director
International Design Associates, Tokyo
Doyald Young, Designer/Artist
PAX, Corporate Logotype (unpublished)

PAX, designed for a contemporary gift boutique in Tokyo that planned to specialize in eclectic international gifts. Intended for a Christmas Day opening, it was named for the Latin word for peace.

The design embodies the persistent idea that sans serif designs with a preponderance of circular forms are contemporary statements—they are also reminders of art-deco-styled faces. With the exception of the *X*, the letterforms are reduced to their barest essentials. The *P* and the *A* are formed by a single stroke, instead of traditional double- and triple-stroke forms. Only the *X* is a portion of a circle—the tops of the *P* and *A* are oblate as a personal preference, rather than drawn as a part of a circle, and join the vertical stems smoothly with compound curves. The horizontal curves have been narrowed so as to appear optically the same dimension as the vertical stems.

St. LUKE'S
INTERNATIONAL HOSPITAL

St. LUKE'S
INTERNATIONAL HOSPITAL

St Luke's
International
Residential Park

St Luke's
International Hospital

St. LUKE'S
International
Hospital

St. Luke's
INTERNATIONAL
HOSPITAL

St Luke's
International
Business Plaza

St Luke's
International Hospital

St. LUKE'S
International
Hospital

St. LUKE'S
INTERNATIONAL
HOSPITAL

St. LUKE'S
INTERNATIONAL
HOSPITAL

St Luke's
International
Residential Park

St Luke's
International Hospital

St.
LUKE'S
INTERNATIONAL
HOSPITAL

St Luke's
International Hospital

*Above and right—
Indentification studies for
individual sections of the
complex, with different weights
and proportions of
sans serif letterforms.*

*Left—Some of the initial
studies exploring different
proportions and weights of
traditional letterforms.*

St. LUKE'S

St Luke's
International Hospital

St Luke's
International
Hospital

AABCDEEFGHIJKKLMMNNOPQRSTUVWWXYZ
abcdefghijklmnopqrstuvwxyz

TOPIC MEDIUM — PAUL RENNER, BAUER 1953–55

International Design Associates

Tokyo, Japan

Mari Makinami, Executive Creative Director

Hideo Hosaka, Art Director

Doyald Young, Designer/Artist

St. Luke's International Hospital

Corporate Logotype

An important multi-use complex in Tsu-kiji district, that includes the hospital, chapel, nursing college, office buildings, retirement housing, a small hotel for pa-tient's families, and a shopping mall.

Presentations were made in stages over a two-year period to the large board of directors. The strong and simplified sans serif was selected over the original presentation of very traditional and clas-sic forms. The sans serif gained favor be-cause the lowercase *t* was seen as a posi-tive symbol for the project. The smaller size of *St* permitted the word to be nes-tled between the cap *L* and the *k*. The *e* is drawn not with straight sides but with an extremely subtle arc. Both diagonals of the *k* taper at convergence, and the lower diagonal extends to the right of the upper. Their tips at the baseline and x-height are wider than the vertical stems. The apostrophe is a simple paral-lelogram. From the reverse curve of the diagonal, the left and right curves of the *s* blend smoothly into the horizontals.

ABCDEFGHIJKLMNOPQRSTUVWXYZ

BODONI BOLD CONDENSED — SÒL HESS, MONOTYPE 1934

Mary Mauldin Brown

Encino, California

Mary Mauldin Brown, Owner and Editor,
Showcase Magazine
Doyald Young, Designer/Artist
The Orange County Register
Showcase Masthead

Winner of a LULU award and honored by New York's National Communications Media Association, the tabloid supplement to the Sunday edition of *The Orange County Register* newspaper focused on fashion, trends, and personalities.

With the masthead occupying the full width of the page, it was possible to draw a very classy, fashion-oriented logotype using the Didot type style that *Vogue* magazine and Diana Vreeland estab-lished as *haute couture* for Condé Nast Publications.

Its capitals and condensed proportions lend the utmost formality to the word. Because of the grand scale, the hairlines are drawn as though engraved. The style is a mixture of Bodoni and Didot. One principal distinction between the two faces is the carriage of weight from the vertical beaks of the *E, F, L,* and *T* to the hairline arm. Didot distributes

The Register

WCASE

weight along the arm, diminishing to a hairline at the point where it joins the stem. After bracketing the serif, Bodoni reaches its hairline quickly and reveals a long horizontal line. The terminals of the *c, f,* the ear of the *g, j,* and *r,* are circular in Bodoni and teardrops in Didot. The *E* of the masthead is more Didot than Bodoni, but the *S* and *C* are pure Didot.

For maximum impact the letters are tightly spaced, which permits a gen-erous letter size in a confined space. The piper must be paid for such extrava-gance. The tight fit works and colors well, except for the *CAS.* To make it work, the *C* and *S* were redesigned. The lower beaks of the letters were eliminated and the letters joined to the *A.* This is allow-able depending on use, the client's es-thetic, and the designer's sense of purity. The ligature satisfies a logotype and ty-pography's first requirement—legibility.

Thiem Industries, Inc.

Thiem Industries, Inc.

Thiem Industries, Inc.

Torrance, California

Albert Zukas, CEO

John Springer, Sales Manager

Doyald Young, Designer/Artist

Corporate Signature

An illustrative monogram/mark that describes the path of a router, designed for manufacturers of sophisticated electro-mechanical devices, sheet metal, and machined assemblies. Thiem is contracted by the United States Navy to produce the milled housing for electronic navigational equipment on its destroyers.

The horizontal lines are thinned to achieve equal reading with the vertical lines; in addition, the positive lines are heavier than the negative areas to avoid a visual vibration. For a smooth transition, compound curves were used to join curves to straight lines.

The logotype that completes the corporate signature is not hand-drawn—it is Helvetica black, one of the most popular sans serifs of the past thirty years, designed in 1957 by Max Miedinger for the Haas typefoundry in Switzerland. It was chosen for its compatibility.

THE TIMES MIRROR COMPANY

THE TIMES MIRROR COMPANY

ABCDEFGHIJKLMNOPQRSTUVWXYZ
abcdefghijklmnopqrstuvwxyz

OPTIMA — HERMANN ZAPF, STEMPEL 1958

Mary Sheridan & Associates

Los Angeles, California

Mary Sheridan, Executive Creative Director
Doyald Young, Designer/Artist
The Times Mirror Company
Corporate Logotype

This is one of the largest and most influential publishing empires in America: newspaper, book, and magazine publishing, cable and broadcast television, with a highly respected network of foreign correspondents reporting to their crown jewel, the *Los Angeles Times* newspaper.

The example is part of a former corporate signature and corporate identity program which included a mark made from their historical emblem, a stylized eagle with the corporate initials. Hermann Zapf's Optima has been used as a model. The logotype is straightforward, with only minor adjustments made to the designer's original font. The letters are drawn freehand, and stems, as in the original, are concave, with a slight flaring at the endings. Additionally weighted, the letters are slightly wider.

The classical proportions of the type are modified to modern, or even, widths.

TYPE
Incorporated

ABCDEFGHIJKLMNOPQRSTUVWYXZ

TWENTIETH CENTURY ULTRA BOLD EXTENDED — SOL HESS, LANSTON MONOTYPE C, 1941

Type Incorporated

Los Angeles, California

David Bartlett, Creative Director
Doyald Young, Designer/Artist
Art-Spec, Auckland, New Zealand

A typophile's dream assignment—the logotype for a typographer, in this case one located in the advertising enclave of 5900 Wilshire, Los Angeles. Perhaps the ideal situation for the use of type, but the

client preferred a handlettered version. The word *TYPE* is an unusual combination of letterforms, with each letter a unique shape, admitting almost an equal amount of negative space between them. To make it a tough, punchy, advertising logotype, it was necessary to narrow the proportions of the *Y* and *P*. The lobe of the *P* was shaved considerably to reduce the white space at the bottom right of the letter. A *TY* ligature was used to provide

a greater unity to the word. The style is an amalgam of Lanston Monotype's Twentieth Century ultra bold extended, and Koloss, designed by J. Erbar for Ludwig & Mayer in 1923.

With a large cap *I*, the light formal script *Incorporated* is straightforward—no tricks, drawn as legibly as possible, and used in a contrasting manner of size, weight, and angle to illustrate the opposing qualities of type: tough and classy.

Entertainment

Entertainment

E. JAY KRAUSE

Member of the Academy of Television Arts and Sciences,
Art Direction/Production Design.

THE VISUAL SOPHISTICATION of television today was not there in the 1950s. The networks were *all,* and their experience was radio. The infant industry drew professionals mainly from the theater to design its sets, with little emphasis on the shows' title graphics. Main titles were produced by the studio's graphic arts department, whose font catalogs consisted only of a sans serif named Standard, which was used primarily for impact; the ubiquitous Times Roman to suggest class; and the typeface Hobo, as a catch-all for character. All were hurriedly "hot pressed" on individual cards and televised.

Freelance art directors of the 1960s and 1970s, contracted by independent producers, were sometimes free to commission graphic designers. Producers and directors then began to appreciate what these designers could contribute to their completed products. Even today, for budget reasons, it can be difficult to *sell* the need for a title especially designed, independent of a network art department. When that need is sold, the title designer must work closely with the production designer or art director so that a concerted presentation can be made to the producers and directors.

All too frequently, too many title designs are presented, and the designer's third or fourth choice will be chosen, leaving the designer dissatisfied with his own accomplishment.

While production and graphic designers spend their time frantically working to meet deadlines for shows that are seen once and disappear forever—like writing in the sand—their efforts are indispensable. A *graphic look,* whether it is for a special or for a series, must be presented quickly, boldly, and simply if the design concept is to register. Screen time does not allow the viewer to peruse leisurely a complicated presentation. Technical limitations prevent refinements of thin lines, close spacing, or ornate scripts, which tend to be difficult to read on a rapidly moving list of credits. Titles for many specials are superimposed over complex live action that creates even more competition for the viewer's attention.

Game-show titles tend to offer greater challenges for the graphic designer because game-show sets are usually flamboyant abstract designs. The titles should generate excitement, but when the game starts, simplicity is the imperative. The viewer must be able to follow the game and scoring without being distracted by unnecessary graphic embellishments.

With specials, which are seldom repeated, graphics are often more trendy and showy than weekly sit-com titles, which need a simple recognizable identity, week in and week out.

All elements of the graphics must meld and reflect the mood of a production design, requiring the utmost cooperation of the production designer, art director, costume designer, lighting director, and graphic designer. Then the camera director must bring the concept to fulfillment on the television screen.

Opposite—
Detail of The Tony Awards
(see page 90).

Irving Berlin's 100TH Birthday Celebration

ABCDEFGHIJKLMNOPQRSTUVWXYZ
abcdefghijklmnopqrstuvwxyz
1234567890

CENTURY EXPANDED ITALIC — MORRIS F. BENTON, ATF 1900

Don Mischer Productions
Beverly Hills, California

Robert Keene, Production Design
Doyald Young, Designer/Artist
Irving Berlin's 100th Birthday Celebration
Main Title Graphics

A birthday party held at Carnegie Hall, where a lifetime of his songs had been heard, this was a celebration to honor Irving Berlin's enormous contribution—writing songs that captured the spirit of the American people for over eighty years, songs that will continue to be standards wherever pop music is played.

I have used italics here for their spirited quality, and because swash endings seem to my eye to fit more naturally on leaning letterforms. The swash endings are derived from Moorish arabesques that were originally created by flexible writing instruments. Italics were origi-nally designed as narrow letters that would enable printers to use fewer pages, to produce cheaper books. At first only the lowercase slanted—the caps were not italicized until a hundred years later.

Italics have many uses: book titles, periodicals, works of art, names of ships, stage directions in plays, foreign words, and for emphasis within a text.

I drew the title all by hand because it allowed more design control. It is a Century expanded of indeterminate weight, somewhere between a demi-bold and bold (one of the luxuries of handletter-ing is that you get what you want). Any number of typefaces would answer the needs of the title, but the extra-long words of this title required carefully de-signed shapes at judicious locations to create the organized layout.

The title's *R*s are similar to Palatino. The rest of the forms follow the original premise of the type, but with a slightly enhanced thin stroke and lowercase lobes that are more rounded than the Century typeface. Unlike faces for ma-chine composition, the ciphers are wide and generous. General text composi-tion demands figures that are nearly the same width, fitted into equal areas so that they will tabulate. Handset faces were often accompanied by naturally proportioned figures. The suffix *TH* has been widened and weighted to relate to the larger letters both in weight and mass. The underscore, instead of a nor-mal horizontal dash, is a *swung dash*, a symbol used in typography, particularly in dictionaries to indicate the repeti-tion of a word or a portion of a word. (The same shape used at a smaller scale is called a *tilde* and is used over the n in Spanish to denote the sound *ny*. It has several uses in mathematics and logic.)

Irving Berlin's 100th Birthday Celebration

Preliminary pencil sketch (slightly reduced) for client approval.

The 22nd Academy of Country Music Awards

Academy of Country Music
Hollywood, California

dick clark productions, inc.
Burbank, California

Robert Keene, Production Design
Doyald Young, Designer/Artist
The 22nd Annual Academy of
Country Music Awards
Main Title Graphics

The Academy of Country Music prefers to change its main title graphics for its annual awards, sometimes adopting very different themes, which are sometimes more urban than country.

This is a very vigorous condensed script style, used to accommodate the extremely long title. It is a newly drawn and narrowed version of Éclat. The caps have been redrawn with greatly extended strokes, as evidenced by the *A*s. The same basic upstroke has been shortened on the *M* to allow for tighter word spacing. The ascenders are short and, like Éclat, are not looped. A swash ending has been added to the *s* to fill out the bottom line. For a more emphatic beginning the caps descend. A *Th* ligature solves the problem of the *T*'s crossbar when it is adjacent to an ascender. It would otherwise be necessary to cross the ascender with the

reverse curve, or it would have to be drawn at a higher level. The straight stems of the *a, m,* and *n* are narrowed at the top where the curved lobe joins to allow a deeper join, which prevents a massing of weight.

Purists maintain that type that is designed at a particular size should never be reduced. The small sizes of many metal machine fonts are bolder than the larger sizes, have wider proportions, and are more widely spaced.

From a previous show, three title cards are shown: Reba McEntire, the hostess, and two special guests (below). Key letters were drawn and multiple photostats used to assemble the names.

The original extended version of Éclat Script is distributed by Esselte Letraset in their Premier series; see page 252 in the chapter "Typefaces and Alphabets" for a showing of the complete font.

Reba McEntire

Mac Davis

John Schneider

Names for the hostess and two special guests from a previous annual "Academy of Country Music Awards" drawn in Éclat condensed script.

Bob Hope's Funny Valentine

Hope Enterprises

Burbank, California

Robert Keene, Art Director
Young & Dodge, Graphic Design
Doyald Young, Designer/Artist
Bob Hope's Funny Valentine
Main Title Graphics

One of the many TV specials for Bob Hope, always produced at the last minute, with changes occurring constantly until the cameras rolled—including the main title graphics.

The title has both script and italic forms. It is a hybrid, part Bodoni, part Baskerville, and part pure formal script.

The *H* employs a dot for its crossbar—a decorative Victorian idea.

When lines of type are tightly spaced, the ascenders and descenders pose problems. The *F* and *l* have been joined as a compromise for tight line spacing. The capitals are swash roman forms that are drawn in homage to Jan van Krimpen, one of the luminaries of twentieth-century type design. His extravagant *tour de force,* Cancelleresca Bastarda, was designed in 1934 for the Enschedé typefoundry at Haarlem, Holland. Designed expressly as a script type for the Romulus family, it is more cursive than script. After vainly trying to connect the letters, Stanley

Morison advised him that the scriptorial qualities of the first and last letter of a word would suggest a script style. The font contains two hundred and ten characters, many of them designed expressly for ending a line with grace. In 1939 Will Carter designed an edition—set in 16-point Cancelleresca Bastarda—of Elizabeth Barrett Browning's *Sonnets from the Portuguese,* poems expressing love for her husband.[1]

What better type choice for a main title TV special on a St.Valentine's day?

---

1. John Dreyfus, *The Work of Jan van Krimpen* (Haarlem: Joh. Enschedé en Zonen, 1952), page 39.

ABCDEFGHIJKLMNOPQRSTUVWXYZÆŒ
abcdefghijklmnopqrstuvwxyzæœç
1234567890&

CANCELLERESCA BASTARDA — JAN VAN KRIMPEN, ENSCHEDÉ 1934

CARNEGIE

1891 HALL 1987

The Grand Reopening

A CELEBRATION OF AN AMERICAN TREASURE

Don Mischer Productions

Beverly Hills, California

Robert Keene, Production Design

Doyald Young, Designer

Carnegie Hall,

The Grand Reopening 1891–1987

Main Title Graphics

In the lambent surroundings of marble, crystal, and gold leaf, Leonard Bernstein, The Peter Duchin Orchestra, Lena Horne, Marilyn Horne, Robert Klein, Yo-Yo Ma, Zubin Mehta, Liza Minnelli, Jessye Norman, John Rubinstein, Frank Sinatra, Isaac Stern, Benita Valente, James Wolfensohn, and The New York Philharmonic Orchestra paid homage to the grand old lady in all of her new finery. Private and public donations had been raised to completely recapture the hall's past grandeur.

This is one of the few examples in this collection that does not rely on hand-lettered forms, because the director wanted the main title card to relate exactly to the other titles (and there were many). Any number of bold, dignified roman faces would be appropriate: Baskerville, Bembo, Caslon, Centaur,

Garamond, Palatino, Sabon, or Times Roman. Baskerville seemed direct, legible and with just the right amount of boldness for the numerous words in the title. Its descriptive subhead could have been set in the corresponding Baskerville italic, but its letters are a bit narrow with complex shapes that make it difficult to read as a TV title card. Matthew Carter's Snell Roundhand seemed to have just the right amount of weight, formality, and legibility, with its round letters and generous fit. It is available in several weights, and the medium weight was employed.

The complete title has many words, but it demonstrates a design relief in the change of type size and style. The combination of words is fortuitous because it allows each unit of information to maintain its specific importance, and a change of sizes creates an organized copy block.

center theatre group

center
theatre
group

ABCDEFGHIJKLMNOPQRSTUVWXYZ
abcdefghijklmnopqrstuvwxyz

BOOKMAN OLD STYLE (1860) — C. H. GRIFFITH, LINOTYPE C. 1936

Mary Sheridan & Associates
Los Angeles, California

Mary Sheridan, Executive Creative Director
Doyald Young, Designer/Artist
Music Center of Los Angeles County
Center Theatre Group Logotype

Under the aegis of its artistic director, Gordon Davidson, the Center Theatre Group brought innovative and often controversial theater to Los Angeles.

The logotype was intended to reflect the experimental, while also pleasing Dorothy Chandler, who almost single-handedly raised the funds for the Music Center complex. It was designed to be compatible with the Mark Taper Forum logotype. Its bow to experimentation is the less than daring use of all lowercase letters. Though there are six separate ligatures within the three-line logotype, the letterforms are conservative and rely on their extended proportion, leading, and flush-left arrangement to create an identifiable image.

The *r* and *a* lack the normal teardrop terminal and end abruptly. The face is a blend of Bookman and Clarendon, with stems topped with triangular serifs.

DOROTHY CHANDLER
PAVILION

DOROTHY CHANDLER
PAVILION

ABCDEFGHIJKLMNOPQRSTUVWXYZ

FRIZ QUADRATA — ERNST FRIZ, VGC 1965 / ITC 1974

Mary Sheridan & Associates

Los Angeles, California

Mary Sheridan, Executive Creative Director
Doyald Young, Artist
Music Center of Los Angeles County
Dorothy Chandler Pavilion Logotype

Mary Sheridan established the logotypes and graphics for the grand opening of the Music Center of Los Angeles County. The multipurpose theater was named for Dorothy Buffum Chandler, considered the founder of the Music Center complex, which includes the Mark Taper Forum and the Ahmanson Theatre. The Dorothy Chandler Pavilion and the Music Center logotype were designed to function as a banner in advertising. The pavilion serves as a residence for the Los Angeles Philharmonic, Los Angeles Music Center Opera, and Los Angeles Master Chorale. The logotype had to meet stringent criteria: both dignity and longevity. Legibility was paramount, for one of its major uses is newspaper advertising. This focuses the design direction, for dignity implies conservatism, and newspaper use demands sturdy letters that will hold their own in a one-column ad.

The logotype is a roman with slightly extended proportions; the *N* is faithful to the original Trajan roman, which is a forerunner of Ernst Friz's Quadrata.

MGM/UA Home Video Library
Culver City, California

Bob Hardenbrook, Creative Director
Sam McCay, Art Director
Doyald Young, Designer/Artist
Elvis Collection Video Logotype

Designed as a "header" for the MGM/UA collection of *Elvis Presley Home Video Movies,* the logotype had to compete with the individual movie titles within the confines of an area less than an inch tall, at the top of the package. An extreme slope accomplished this. It was written quickly with a soft, blunted pencil at a small size, then enlarged and retouched, retaining as much of the original's spontaneity as possible. (For other free-style brush script examples, see pages 181, 228, and 236).

Free-style western scripts strive to define and enhance the meaning of a word, phrase, or sentence, either with letter size variation, weight, angle, contrast of up- and downstrokes, alignment, spacing, a smooth crisp execution—or with a brutal attack of brush to paper. The writing speed, the relationship of brush size to letter size, the angle at which the brush is held, the manner in which the word is broken, and most important, the pressure of the brush—all are brought into play. The qualities may be very restrained or flamboyant, depending on the meaning and formality of the word or sentence, or its context.

These methods or techniques of writing western scripts, the chancery hand, or the more stylized script forms for commercial applications, borrow some of the tenets of the Japanese calligraphic art, *Sho.*

Many cultural and artistic aspirations are not easily translated, and some may be ineffable. With this cautionary observation, *Sho* can be described as writing with the mind, and *Shodo,* as an extension of the human mind and spirit.

"Construct," the vigorous example of modern Japanese calligraphy (right) written by Sterling Leach,[1] embodies one of the most important underlying tenets of *Shodo*—a single spontaneous gesture, perfectly performed.[2]

It is written with the brush held in a vertical position, with flowing, sequential movements, in an elaborate series of formal, premeditated paths conceived in intense artistic expression. As part of the brief performance, the brush does not always touch the paper, and that unwritten space is integral to the composition.

1. Recipient of many calligraphy awards, including the Award of Excellence from the 1988 "Sankei International Calligraphy Exhibition," Tokyo, Japan.

2. From *Words in Motion: Modern Japanese Calligraphy* (exhibition catalog), an exhibition sponsored by Yomiuri Shimbun and the Nippon Television Network, with essays by Aoyama San'u, Stephen Addiss, Barbara Rose, Schaarschmidt-Richter, and Yanagida Taiun (Tokyo: Yomiuri Shinbun, 1984).

"Construct" (105 by 136 cm)
Sterling Leach—1991
Tarzana, California

Written with a large brush (fude) *on traditional Japanese white writing paper.*

Full House

1.

Full House

2.

Full House

3.

Full House

4.

Full House

5.

Full House

6.

Full House

7.

Full House

8.

Full HOUSE

9.

Miller·Boyett Productions / Lorimar
Culver City, California
Thomas Miller and Robert L. Boyett,
Executive Producers

Lynn Griffin, Consulting Art Director
Doyald Young, Designer/Artist
Full House Weekly Sit-Com
Main Title Graphics

These were preliminary designs for the pilot show. The Clarendon design (2) was chosen for its playful stance, for the program involves bachelor fathers, a couple, a house full of kids, and one dog.

The letters are condensed to create a shape that fits comfortably within the four-to-three ratio of a TV monitor. The letters vary in height; they tumble in different directions, and some are overbalanced. These designs are straightfor-

ward, casual, bold, relaxed, and carefree. Consciously designed not to be sophisticated or trendy, both lines of the title are positioned to create a shape that is legible and has a strong identity. Acceptable in handlettered forms are serifs that vary in length, overlapping at times—in efforts to create more even color spacing. The nine presentation comprehensives were drawn as dissimilar as possible, yet all were within the demanded casual stance.

ROBERT KEENE *& ASSOCIATES INC* ART DIRECTION

ABCDEFGHIJKKLMNOPQQRRSSTUVWXYZ

MICHELANGELO TITLING — HERMANN ZAPF, STEMPEL 1950

Robert Keene & Associates, Inc.

Burbank, California

Robert Keene, President and Executive
Creative Director
Doyald Young, Designer/Artist
Corporate Logotype

Bob Keene is the Emmy-winning art director/production designer for whom many of the titles in this chapter were designed. He has a keen appreciation for architecture, and this logotype possesses architectural qualities, with its carefully justified lines and the square with softened corners that houses them. Even the classic letterforms reference architectural inscriptional details.

The reversed logotype is the identification component of a title block that appears on working drawings for set designs. A positive version of this appears on a raised panel for the stationery and business cards. The name is a handlettered version of Hermann Zapf's classic titling face, Michelangelo, a sister face to Palatino. The proportions have been modified to carefully fill an allotted space and letter height. Serifs are minimized. The lobe of the *R* is high with an assertive diagonal tail. Similarly, the *B*'s lobe is high. The two lower descriptive lines are photographically weighted versions of the type with hand-sharpened corners.

THE 30TH ANNUAL GRAMMY AWARDS

Pierre Cossette Productions

Los Angeles, California

Robert Keene, Production Design
Doyald Young, Designer/Artist
The 30th Annual Grammy Awards
Main Title Graphics

The Grammy Awards address a variety of musical tastes, which allows a wide array of choices for the title design direction. The style should, however, be fashionable and, in this instance, was art deco revival. The choice was valid because the program emanated from one of the great art deco shrines—Manhattan's fabled Radio City Music Hall. The design char-

acteristics of type that we now call art deco were evident in many of the faces of the 1920s and 1930s: Broadway, Chicago, Vogue,[1] ATF's Hollywood and Newport series, and Lucien Bernhard's quaint but stylish Bernhard Fashion. Many are characterized by highly joined diagonals, circular forms, overbalanced lobes, erratic proportions, and crossbars that are higher or lower than standard practice and often escaped their boundaries.

This "special" title closely follows those shapes with a *Y* that is a lowercase form. The converging pointed diagonals of the *M*s that do not reach the baseline are similar to fixed-proportion faces (see

Teletype 12 fixed pitch, page 269, "Typefaces and Alphabets" chapter). The *A*, *M*, *N*, and *W* are pointed, and the rigid, single-weight script suggests many of the showcard lettering styles of the period that I choose to call Zephyr script, popularized by the Lincoln Zephyr, a forerunner of the classic Lincoln Continental automobile. The four-line title nestles a literal drawing of the Grammy Award.

1. Created for the Condé Nast publication *Vogue* in 1930 and also made available to the general printing trades. See Mac McGrew, *American Metal Typefaces of the Twentieth Century*, preliminary edition (New Rochelle, New York: The Myriade Press, 1986), page 353.

ABCDEFGHIJKLMNOPQRSTUVWXYZ

VOGUE — STEPHENSON BLAKE 1929

ABCDEFGHIJKLMNOPQRSTUVWXYZ
abcdefghijklmnopqrstuvwxyz
.,:;?-()"!1234567890$&*.—..

VOGUE BOLD CONDENSED — INTERTYPE 1930

Photo: Chris Fifthian

*Camera-ready art reduced
to actual size for blind-embossed,
three-level beveled-edge
brass die.*

Fred Harpman

Hollywood, California

Doyald Young, Designer/Artist

Ligature Engravers

Los Angeles, California

Monogram

Production design credits for George Cukor's *Rich and Famous,* John Boorman's *Deliverance,* and Hallmark Hall of Fame TV specials establish Fred Harpman as a master of the medium. This blind-embossed monogram was designed for his stationery and business cards.

Initial tests were cut from heavy paper to determine if the *H* would read more easily as an intaglio image or as bas-relief. The simple, optically single-weight sans serif form required only minor thinning adjustment of the *F*'s horizontals to relate them to the vertical stroke. The height of the *F* was dictated by the horizontal bar of the *H*. Camera-ready art was presented as a fine inked outline for the engraver to sculpt the beveled three-level brass die.

The name was not handlettered but was typeset with generous letterspacing, in Adrian Frutiger's 8-point Univers 75.

Krofft Entertainment, Inc.

Los Angeles, California

Steve Ehlers and Fred Harpman,
Creative Directors
Doyald Young, Designer/Artist
The World of Sid & Marty Krofft Logotype

Famous for many years for their puppet shows in Las Vegas, the Krofft organization also designs very sophisticated amusement parks worldwide. This was designed for an indoor amusement arcade in the Omni International complex in Atlanta, Georgia. It featured a sparkling Lucite carousel of prancing horses.

The outline drop shadows and freestyle sans serifs contain many references. They are playful, fun, amusing, relaxed, informal, carefree, jubilant. For many years toy manufacturers have packaged their wares in boxes adorned with this style. In more extreme versions the style is humorous, for it is still seen in comic strips and books. The logotype is reversed from a colored background to enhance its legibility. The drop shadow and very tight line leading create some complex negative shapes between the letters. At points where these could impair the legibility, they are filled in.

There are no straight lines, vertical or horizontal; all curve slightly, and the horizontal lines have a slight uphill cant.

IN LONDON

**Liza Minnelli Concerts, Inc.
in Association with
Don Mischer Productions**
Beverly Hills, California

Robert Keene, Art Director
Doyald Young, Designer/Artist
Liza in London
Main Title Graphics

A special TV program edited from Liza Minnelli's performance at the London Palladium. Some of the first sketches for the title were done in an exuberant script style in an effort to capture the style and verve of her performance, including the design below—a strong formal design that uses caps similar to Onyx and Bodoni Campanile.

The winning design (opposite) was chosen for its bolder and more dynamic statement. Ms. Minnelli requested that I borrow a design element from the title of the London performance. The element is a dramatic stretched-out dot above the *i*, written with great flair and suggesting haste. The final title design employs separate brush letters based on capital block letters, which were written hurriedly with a brush, as opposed to connected brush script lettering.

These kinds of casual brush letters may touch and overlap to improve an awkward spacing combination, though the ending stroke is best defined to maintain legibility—note the *LI* combination. Letter sizes may change and the horizontal strokes can be stretched to fill an unwanted space or to give the word a cohesive quality—the strokes are often drawn with a tapering uphill slant. With the exception of the righthand stroke of the *A*, each stroke end is swollen and textured, connoting a heavily loaded brush.

A very rough comprehensive design with a more static and formal choice of type forms and layout.

LOS ANGELES PHILHARMONIC ORCHESTRA

ABCDEFGHIJKLMNOPQRSTUVWXYZ
abcdefghijklmnopqrstuvwxyz
1234567890

BODONI — BAUER 1926

Mary Sheridan & Associates
Los Angeles, California

Mary Sheridan, Executive Creative Director
David Parry, Public Relations
Doyald Young, Designer/Artist
Los Angeles Philharmonic Orchestra
Souvenir Program, The Music Center

Drawn in my youth, this remains one of my unabashed favorite lines of lettering. It was drawn about twice this size, reversed out of black, and ran vertically as a banner on a program guide.

It is modeled after a roman designed by Giambattista Bodoni in 1818 in Parma, Italy. Slightly lighter in color and more narrow than the original, except for the *A*, its counters are more oval than elliptical, with a gradual blending of the mass into the hairline. It is similar to the Bauer typefoundry version. I have drawn more weight around the curves of the *S*, increased its diagonal, and softened the shape so that it is not so angular. The straight stem of the *G* has been raised and a pointed spur introduced. The *L* has been narrowed, the bowl of the *P* lowered to fill the the space, the tail of the *R* softened, and more weight carried on the vertical beaks. The letterspacing is rather snug because Mary Sheridan preferred it that way. It is drawn simply, with adjustments made only to enhance its spacing.

$$A\,B\,C\,D\,E\,F\,G\,H\,I\,J\,K\,L\,M\,N\,O\,P\,Q\,R\,S\,T\,U\,V\,W\,X\,Y\,Z$$

$$abcdefghijklmnopqrstuvwxyz$$

TORINO ITALIC (ROMANO MODERNO) — NEBIOLO C. 1908

Mary Sheridan & Associates
Los Angeles, California

Mary Sheridan, Executive Creative Director
David Parry, Public Relations
Doyald Young, Designer/Artist
Los Angeles Philharmonic Orchestra
Souvenir Program, The Music Center

A letterform inspired by the elegant Torino italic, though in this case drawn with opulent swash letters for a gala occasion. It was created for the program for the long awaited premiere of the Los Angeles Music Center, with Zubin Mehta conducting.

The style is both italic and script, though it must be categorized as an italic because the letters do not join. Both the *P* and *L* have been shortened to achieve a very tight line leading—especially the cap *L*. A normally drawn script *L* would create a tangle of lines through the *P* and the ascenders of *Philharmonic*. The *O* descends and overlaps the *T* to ensure a generous cap. Pothooks and ending strokes of the lowercase are shortened for closer spacing. This is evident in the troublesome *rm* combination. Serifs on the caps are eliminated except for the *P*, where a serif at the baseline helps to fill the space. An *h* with a serifed ascender has been used in *The* to avoid the long crossbar of the *T*.

M·B

1.

M'B

5.

MB

9.

M/B

2.

M·B

6.

M·B

10.

M·B

3.

MB

7.

MB

11.

MB

4.

MB

8.

M·B

12.

M/B

Miller·Boyett

PRODUCTIONS

M/B

Miller·Boyett

PRODUCTIONS

ABCDEFGHIJKLMNOPQRSTUVWXYZ
abcdefghijklmnopqrstuvwxyz

MODERN 216 BOLD ITALIC — ED BENGUIAT, ITC 1982

Miller·Boyett Productions

Culver City, California

Thomas Miller and Robert L. Boyett,
Executive Producers

Doyald Young, Designer/Artist

Miller·Boyett Corporate Signature

Tom Miller and Bob Boyett, mavens of comedy, are phenomena in the television industry, with five successful weekly sitcoms to their credit—all in prime time.

This wide range of corporate logotype presentation designs includes a conservative Bodoni, an ultra-bold Franklin Gothic, and an elaborate Bodoni swash version, plus some more informal approaches presented as explorations in an effort to narrow the design direction. The very reserved choice is based on the modern faces from the late nineteenth century, which have their heritage in Bodoni. The **M/B** is a wider handlettered version of Ed Benguiat's Modern 216 bold italic, which was chosen to accompany the monogram/logo.

The virgule, or slash, is usually drawn at a greater angle than the type it accompanies; but as part of the monogram, in this case it is parallel to the capital letter's diagonal. (It is used additionally as an indicator of poetry breaks.) Called a center dot, the dot between the two names centers within the x-height.

MOTOWN

Yesterday, Today, Forever.

25

Motown Productions in Association with Don Mischer Productions

Beverly Hills, California

Robert Keene, Production Design
Doyald Young, Title Design
Motown 25—Yesterday, Today, Forever
Main Title Graphics

A ninety-minute birthday jubilation for Berry Gordy's Motown Records and its legendary stars that made Motown the most important and innovative force in contemporary music. The pantheon is impressive: The Commodores, DeBarge, Four Tops, Marvin Gaye, The Jacksons, Jermaine Jackson, Michael Jackson, Rick James, The Miracles, Martha Reeves, Lionel Ritchie, Smokey Robinson, Diana Ross, The Temptations, Mary Wells, Mary Wilson, and Stevie Wonder. The Motown logotype, not my design, is the basic ele-

ment of the main title graphic. Originally set in Futura extra-bold condensed caps, the logotype required a slight amount of thinning to compensate for the halation that occurs when letters are reversed out of a darker background. Additionally, the letterspacing was increased for legibility. The title was superimposed over a wide shot of live action. The inner diagonals of the *M* and *W* and the diagonal of the *N* were thinned to let more air into the letters without destroying the basic logotype design.

The figures were especially drawn: note that the beginning curve of the *2* is clipped at an angle and repeated on the crossbar of the *5*. The script type was chosen to contrast and soften the mainly rigid letters of the logotype, though the choice of handsome optically single-weight scripts is limited. The slogan is set

in the Bauer typefoundry's Gillies Gothic bold (designed by William S. Gillies, in 1936). Both the *T* and *F* were redesigned for more flair and legibility.

The odds are incalculable for the script slogan to break right, permitting *25* to be placed on the vertical center line.

Gillies Gothic is one of many monotone scripts designed in the mid-1930s. These were popular display faces, and there were many versions, all very similar: ATF's Kaufmann Script is almost a dead ringer for Gillies Gothic, and Monotype's Swing bold and Berthold's Signal are similar. Intertype's Futura demi-bold script, designed by Edwin W. Shaar in 1954 (and not readily available for this assignment), is the most admirable of the lot, though it is more italic than script, with cursive letters whose endings are vertical and touch more than join.

ABCDEFGHIJKLMNOPQRSTUVWXYZ
abcdefghijklmnopqrstuvwxyz   1234567890$

FUTURA DEMI-BOLD SCRIPT — EDWIN W. SHAAR, INTERTYPE 1954

ABCDEFGHIJKLMNOPQRSTUVWXYZ
abcdefghijklmnopqrstuvwxyz Th
1234567890

GILLIES GOTHIC (FLOTT) — WILLIAM S. GILLIES, BAUER 1936

MOTOWN
Returns to the
APOLLO

APOLLO
Backstage

APOLLO
Memories

Motown Productions in Association with Don Mischer Productions

Beverly Hills, California

Robert Keene, Production Design
Doyald Young, Title Design/Artist
Motown Returns to the Apollo
Main Title Graphics

A blockbuster TV musical special about the most famous of all vaudeville theaters in Harlem, with Motown celebrating the grand reopening of the theater which had long been in desuetude. From its very beginning, every major entertainer of color had auditioned at the Apollo, and it became a springboard to legend.

The show starred the luminaries Bill Cosby, host, with Debbie Allen, James Brown, The Commodores, Sammy Davis, Jr., DeBarge, The Drifters, Billy Eckstein, Al Green, Gregory Hines, Thelma Houston, Patti LaBelle, The Manhattans, Lou Rawls, Smokey Robinson, Diana Ross, Little Richard, The Temptations, Sarah Vaughn, Stevie Wonder, and many more.

Motown's logo is Futura extra bold condensed and was redrawn as part of the set design with gently thinned letters and more open spacing for greater legibility. It was necessary to use the name of the theater as it appeared on the marquee as part of the main title graphics. The Apollo logo is a simple sans serif with an unforgettable Hobo-style cap *A* and *L* s with curved main stems. It was drawn from a photograph of the marquee with the weight of the letter balanced against the weight of the Motown logotype. A simpler two-line version was presented (below) but rejected by the committee, because all the emphasis was on Motown.

The brush script is almost single weight and drawn heftily to compete with the two bold logotypes. It was drawn by quickly writing the words at a small size in pencil and retouching them enlarged to a size that exceeds the line-up of Motown and Apollo to gain a size advantage, with an exuberant cap *R* that lends shape to the title.

The title was superimposed over on-rushing dancers at Manhattan's 125th Street subway station, made famous by Billy Strayhorn's song "Take the A Train."

A more simple arrangement, though rejected for lack of emphasis on the theater name.

ABCDEFGHIJKLMNOPQRSTUVWXYZ
abcdefghijklmnopqrstuvwxyz

HOBO — MORRIS F. BENTON, ATF 1910

Mizuki Ohura

Natsume

MIZUKI OHURA

Natsume

Mitzuki Ohura

Natsume

Mizuki Ohura

NATSUME

Natsume

Presentation sketches in 2H pencil.
Note that on the final art (opposite) the
*swash of the **T** has been enlarged*
*and crosses the weighted diagonal of the **N***
lower than on the comprehensive
to avoid trapping a small amount of white space.
A bracket has been added to the top left
*serif of the **N** and **M** as*
*a subtle repeat of the **E**'s spurs.*

NATSUME

ABCDEFGHIJKLMNOPQRSTUVWXYZ&
abcdefghijklmnopqrstuvwxyz
1234567890

BODONI BOLD CONDENSED — MORRIS F. BENTON, MERGENTHALER LINOTYPE C. 1939

Mari Makinami

Tokyo, Japan

Mari Makinami, Art Director
Doyald Young, Designer/Artist
Natsume Logotype
(Mizuki Ohura)

Mizuki Ohura is the stage name of Natsume Sakata, the internationally famous singing and dancing star of the Takarazuka Revue Company.

Ms. Sakata was initially undecided on which name to use, so pencil comprehensive designs for both names were shown. The professional name (opposite, left) has a good mix of ascenders and decenders from which to design an interestingly shaped logotype. The *z*, whether it is a looped descender or a capital, lends itself easily to display. Even Times Roman—the world's most ubiquitous face—has a generous swash on its lowercase italic *z*. The *N, s,* and *e* in *Natsume* are natural shapes for emphasis.

It is important in an initial presentation to show a wide variety of designs (within a general direction). If none of the designs presented is selected, at least a preference for a style may be indicated.

THE LATE SHOW

STARRING

Joan Rivers

Fox Square Productions, Inc.
Los Angeles, California

Vicki Baral and Jerry Hariton,
Art Directors
James Carhart, Assistant Art Director
Doyald Young, Designer/Artist
The Late Show Starring Joan Rivers
Main Title Graphics

Drawn as part of a title for a nightly talk show, this stylized signature evolved into a lengthy job involving several presentations of preliminary directions, with a final presentation of twenty-six separate tight comprehensives—many of the designs reflecting management alterations or design explorations.

Joan Rivers's ballpoint signature was the starting point of the design. Like the signature of many celebrities, it was hurriedly written from the long practice of giving autographs (see page 174). Only the identifying shapes of the signature were used, in an effort to capture its individual qualities: *J, R, n, s*, and the underscore. The rest of the forms were drawn more legibly because of the demands of resolution, and the addition of computer color (known as "paintbox") to the final camera-ready art. The size rela-

tionships, including the cap to lowercase ratio, were changed, and the line thickness beefed up, but the lighter weight difference was kept on all upstrokes.

Personal signatures are often difficult to read, because of the frequent haste in which they are written. When they are used for advertising, they often require a typeset repetition of the name for clarity. Rarely are they written in a legible, clear manner that allows them to stand alone.

The use of a signature projects integrity—one of the most famous is the John Hancock signature, which implies that the company stands behind it. Signatures are valuable in fashion advertising, for they denote originality and exclusivity. Department-store logotypes often employ a form of script that is reminiscent of a signature; one of the more famous is that of Lord & Taylor.

RoMart, Inc.

Dan Rowan, Dick Martin

Burbank, California

E. Jay Krause, Art Director

Young & Dodge, Graphic Design

Doyald Young, Art Director/Artist

Nelson Davis, Designer

Corporate Logotype

Commissioned by production designer E. Jay Krause, multiple Emmy-award recipient, and art director for this long-running series. This signature logotype was used for the credits of "Rowan & Martin's Laugh-In," a weekly show created by a host of geniuses who established a new genre of TV comedy variety.

The style belongs to the sans serifs designed in the late 1920s and 1930s that tried to express the new modernity of towering skyscrapers and sleek streamlined passenger trains, which seventy years later we define as art deco. (The period is named as an afterthought from an arts and industrial exhibition, *Exposition International des Arts Decoratifs et Industriels Modernes,* held in Paris in 1925.)

Herbert Bayer designed the original face, Universal, as lowercase only in 1925 when he was a professor at the Bauhaus in Dessau, Germany. The style was revived in the late 1960s, and Letraset introduced a version with caps named Pump in 1970, and followed with differ-

ent weights, the latest version introduced in 1980. In 1976 ITC introduced their font named Bauhaus, drawn by Ed Benguiat and Vic Caruso of Photo Lettering. As in many contemporary display faces, the x-heights are large. In a related design, Lance Wyman designed a straight-sided, multilinear, biform alphabet for the nineteenth Olympiad in Mexico City.

Compared to Pump, the lobe of the cap *R* of RoMart is smaller and more elliptical. The abbreviated word *INC* was a requisite. To prevent it from assuming too much importance, it is employed as a device for the crossbar of the *t.* Run as the closing program credit signature, the logo was shown in white on a red field.

ABCDEFGHIJKLMNOPQRSTUVWXYZ

abcdefghijklmnopqrstuvwxyz

PUMP DEMI-BOLD — LETRASET 1972

SINATRA

The Man and his Music

ABCDEFGHIJKLMNOPQRSTUVWXYZ
abcdefghijklmnopqrstuvwxyz

FOLIO BOLD CONDENSED — KONRAD F. BAUER / WALTER BAUM, BAUER 1956

Sinatra Enterprises

Hollywood, California

Robert Keene, Production Design
Doyald Young, Designer/Artist
Sinatra, The Man and his Music
Main Title TV Special

(A Man and His Music, *Courtesy Reprise Records and Sue Roberts at Warner Bros. Records*)

A banner statement for one of pop music's dominant figures, derived from an album issued in the late 1960s.

The sans serif caps are generic. They are part of the long history of narrow flat-sided bold caps that were popularized in the nineteenth century, first used on handbills. Most of these were crudely drawn, ill-proportioned, and poorly fitted. Around the turn of the century American Type Founders introduced a titling face, Railroad Gothic,[1] that was part of this heritage, and it became a mainstay for newspaper headlines. During this century the sans have grown up, and there are many sophisticated versions from different foundries to choose from: Eurostile, Folio, Gill Sans, Helvetica, Frutiger, Futura display, Impact, Standard, Topic, Trade Gothic, Univers, and Venus.

The title has some attributes of Folio bold condensed. Both the *A*s and the *N* are widened generously where the two stems join, in order to create a bolder mass for the word, and specifically drawn to minimize the space around the top of the *A*. The crossbar of the *TR* ligature is shortened for a more even color spacing.

When letterforms are used in negative form, halation creates the illusion of bolder letters, tighter spacing, and smaller counters. For this reason the crossbars of the *A*s have been lowered to keep them open. Instead of the ogee curve of the Folio *R*, the tail has been straightened.

The script is a weighted-up version of a freely written pencil writing with overly generous beginning and ending flourishes that add shape to the image.

---

1. *Gothic* means flat-sided, after the black letter. Updike suggests "unless it hints at the artistic abilities of its inventors . . . [Gothic] is nothing but a diagram of a letter—all qualities of design having been left out." D. B. Updike, *Printing Types: Their History, Forms, and Use*, vol. 1 (Cambridge, Massachusetts: Harvard University Press, 1937), page 60.

This caused Frank Merriman to remark, "*Gothic* is the chief offender which during the day, in the shop, we understand to mean a sans serif form; but which after dinner, [over cigars and brandy] with our Updike, we understand to mean black letter (and have no trouble at all in making the switch)." Frank Merriman, *ATA Type Comparison Book* (New York: Advertising Typographers Association of America, Inc., 1965), page xiii.

Original rough comprehensive.
***Sinatra** is ink, and script is in pencil.*

**Robert Henry Productions/HBO
in Association with
Gladys Knight Productions**
Los Angeles, California

Robert Keene, Production Design
Doyald Young, Designer/Artist
Sisters in the Name of Love
Main Title Graphics

A soft, feminine, and above all friendly look was needed for this main title, because the show's format was love songs, interspersed with conversations among the stars. Each took her turn with a song, and then they all rapped a bit about life and love. These women are formidable talents, each a legend—Gladys Knight, Patti LaBelle, and Dionne Warwick.

The title accompanied a very feminine set with a proscenium trimmed with over-scale cutout lace. With a stretch of imagination, a script *S* can double for a treble cleft, for it is a mirror image of the same shape though not quite as complex.

Sisters is essentially a single-weight script with traces of thinning on the upstrokes. It is a reminder of handwriting that is written with a blunt felt-tip pen. Intimate, unsophisticated, empathetic, and pretty, the word is soft and flowing despite the break between the *s* and *t*. The cap is over-scale and slightly condensed. The ogee curve of the *t* crossbar is repeated in the ending stroke of the *s*.

The balance of the title is set in Herb Lubalin and Antonio DiSpigna's Serif Gothic, a minutely serifed face reminiscent of Frederick Goudy's Copperplate Gothic, designed in 1901 for ATF. The serifs have a softer bracket than the Copperplate, and the *E* is a semi-uncial form dating to the fourth century, a style characterized by capitals with an abundance of curves. The *O* is a circle, the *M* is splayed, and the proportions are even.

DANCE
in America
With
GREGORY HINES

ABCDEFGHIJKLMNOPQRSUVX
abcdefghijklmnopqrstuxwxyz
1234567890

PLANTIN 110 — F.H. PIERPONT, MONOTYPE 1913

**Don Mischer Productions for PBS
In Association with WNET New York**
Beverly Hills, California

Robert Keene, Production Design
Doyald Young, Designer/Artist
*Tap—Dance in America With Gregory Hines
Main Title Graphics*

A main title comprising three separate title cards: (1) Tap, (2) Dance in America, and (3) With Gregory Hines. Each appeared successively over live action. A script was requested for the word **Tap**. The balance of the title is a handlettered version of one of the world's most ubiquitous typefaces—Times Roman. In fact, it is the generic serif face, appearing as the resident face in many a laser printer. Here it is dressed up a bit with some swash caps to liven things up. Times Roman has sturdy thins designed to reproduce well on newsprint, because it was originally designed for the London *Times*. The thins have been beefed up even more on this example and the proportions narrowed a bit. The crossbar of the *A* has been lowered for a more open counter. The *R*s in *Gregory* are similar to Baskerville.

Times Roman was designed at Monotype Corporation under the supervision of Stanley Morison in 1931 and was modeled after a Flemish face named Plantin. Earlier, Monotype had issued a version of this designed by F. H. Pierpont, named Monotype Plantin 110. [1]

Morison reputedly had made a set of pencil drawings, which were given to Victor Lardent, a draftsman at Monotype, who made the final drawings. He liked the sturdy qualities of the Plantin but wanted to sharpen the serifs so that they would be crisp after repeated copyings. Another story is that Lardent was given a drawing of Granjon's Gros Cicero type to follow. More likely the model was the Plantin 110, for the similarities are more than striking. It is interesting to compare some of the letters that make up one of the most successful types of the twentieth century. Its proportion is almost modern—the *C* is wider than the *O*, and its proportion is exaggerated by the loss of the bottom serif in Plantin. The abrupt turns of the *g* tail are unlike any other curve in the lowercase and stand out because of it. The *c* appears wider than the *e* where normally the proportions are reversed for optical similarity, and the tail of the *a* appears unnecessarily angular, tight, and abrupt. Both the *E* and *F* are wide in a proportion much favored by the Dutch type designers Jan van Krimpen and S. H. de Roos.

There are many cuttings and drawings of the font, and when the caps are well spaced, they continue to impress with their legibility, beauty, and sparkle.

---

1. For a lively, learned, and mathematical discussion of this, see Walter Tracy, *Letters of Credit* (Boston: David R. Godine, 1986), and Stanley Morison, *A Tally of Types*, edited by Brooke Crutchley (Cambridge: Cambridge University Press, 1973).

ABCDEFGHIJKLMNOPQRSTUVWXYZ&
abcdefghijklmnopqrstuvwxyz
1234567890
ABCDEFGHIJKLMNOPQRSTUVWXYZ&
abcdefghijklmnopqrstuvwxyz
1234567890

TIMES NEW ROMAN — STANLEY MORISON, MONOTYPE 1932

The 1988 TONY AWARDS

Tony Awards® Productions in Association with Don Mischer Productions

Beverly Hills, California

Robert Keene, Production Design
Doyald Young, Designer/Artist
The Tony Awards®
Registered by the American Theatre Wing
Main Title Graphics

Broadway's annual elegant toast to itself dressed to the nines in black-tie type. The Tony Awards were named for Antoinette Perry, a famous Broadway angel.

The title is a handlettered marriage of R. H. Middleton's Radiant and ATF's Empire. More condensed than Radiant and wider than Empire, the title relies on two different weights, two different proportions, and two different sets of letterspacing. It favors the rigidity of Empire, but forgoes the idiosyncratic *N* with its two-weighted verticals and mid-spaced hairline diagonal. The *A* follows the Radiant design, and the tail of the *R* produces a wider shape than the lobe.

Narrow letters often suggest a sense of formality and, depending on their weight, elegance. They are valuable when impact is needed in a narrow measure and are frequently used in decorative letterspaced arrangements. For fine and sensitive typography, select a proportion that will satisfy the demands of importance, without squeezing the letterspacing or the letters themselves. Even color spacing is interdependent upon the relationship of proportion and letterspacing.

Some programs for the computer now allow a font to be squeezed, with disastrous results in the hands of novices. When letters are only slightly compressed, the diagonals and horizontals of a font increase in weight far beyond its designer's thoughtful intentions and hours of meticulous drawing and labor.

ABCDEFGHIJKLMNOPQRSTUVWXYZ

EMPIRE — ATF C. 1937

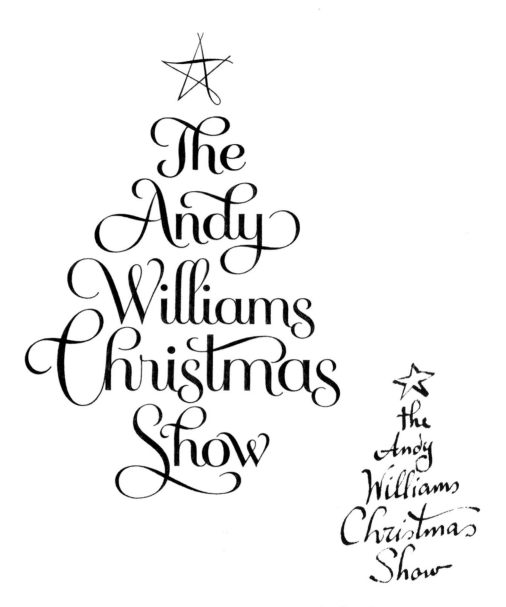

Art director's actual-size comprehensive.

Barnaby Productions

Los Angeles, California

Andy Williams, President
René Lagler, Production Designer
Doyald Young, Artist
The Andy Williams Christmas Show
Main Title Graphics

Because the scanning resolution of a TV screen is so forgiving, a very careful pencil drawing will often suffice for the final art.

Adapted from a calligraphic pen script written by Emmy-award winner René Lagler, this lettering was used as the main title for his production design of an annual Andy Williams old-fashioned Christmas show at grandma's house.

The original design was written with a flat-nibbed pen, angled to produce calligraphic letterforms. The interpretation here is more modern. **The** was reduced and ***Christmas*** enlarged to help define and elaborate the Christmas-tree shape. The volutes of the caps, looped ascenders, and the crossbar of the *t* all were designed for a festive look. The swash of the *S* underscores and completes the base. It is a connected script, though the *e, s,* and *w* are italic forms.

The weight distribution follows Bodoni. The style is similar to ATF's Typo Upright Script, a "social" face used for formal announcements and invitations.

Hotels and Resorts

The logotypes contained in this chapter were designed by the author as an associate of International Design Associates, Tokyo. IDA is a graphic design firm specializing in corporate identity and package design. Their roster of clients includes Baccarat, Dentsu Inc., Georg Jensen Denmark, Guerlain, Max Factor Japan, Mikimoto Cosmetics, and Pioneer Electronics.

English name logotypes are favored in Japan for reasons of international commerce. They are usually accompanied by the name spelled in Japanese.

Except where noted, IDA's staff of designers designed the collateral symbols and marks shown in this chapter.

Hotels and Resorts

MARI MAKINAMI

Executive Creative Director
International Design Associates
Tokyo, Japan

To CREATE the right logotype for a hotel or resort, the graphic designer must prepare a three-pronged attack on the subject. The design must be attractive, must address the desired market, and must be usable in a surprising variety of applications.

A logotype that accurately reflects the character of a hotel or resort will appeal to the customer it is trying to reach. A business traveler looking for service, comfort, and convenience might be drawn to a simple, straightforward look. The light, casual touch would be directed toward the vacationer.

Specific letterforms seem to convey certain qualities. A bold sans serif face tends to look serious, positive, professional—a point of view that could appeal to the busy executive. At the other end of the spectrum, a light, free brush script might suggest carefree good times.

No hotel or resort logotype should overemphasize any single aspect of a facility. The logotype design cannot become so severe, so no-nonsense business oriented, that it looks cheerless, impersonal, and indifferent to its clientele. Sometimes the addition of a small decorative element or symbol will be sufficient to soften the look and reassure the viewer that the personal touch has not been forgotten; from a practical standpoint, this symbol of the hotel is also useful in repeat-pattern textures applied to bags, wrapping papers, and other collateral items.

On the other hand, the resort logotype cannot be so lighthearted as to suggest that its management might be frivolous or unprofessional. Very casual logotypes may be reversed out of a shape or underlined; such simple devices as these can add the missing quality of stability to an informal design. In any case the logotype should convey the impression that the individual's needs have been thoughtfully considered.

Beyond the esthetic and marketing aspects, there still remain the practical considerations.

The hotel or resort logotype must be attractive on a large building sign and still be pleasing and legible when reduced to fit on the manager's business card. To further the initial impression that is created, it must be possible to apply this one logotype to a multitude of items within the hotel. It will be printed on computer forms, embossed on stationery, foil-stamped on menu covers, etched on glassware, and even woven into towels and bathmats. The Hotel ANA in Tokyo applies its signature to nearly three hundred separate uses.

The right logotype for a hotel or resort will initially invite the guest, and beyond that, the logotype's constant presence will support the impression of a well-organized and well-run establishment.

Hotel management has learned that the logotype can continue to function beyond the borders of the hotel property, because expendable items that are saved as souvenirs—menus, matchbooks, coasters, etc.—become valuable advertising pieces that travel the world over.

Opposite—
Detail of
Pacific Star Hotel logotype
(see page 111).

International Design Associates

Tokyo, Japan

Mari Makinami, Executive Creative Director
Hideo Hosaka, Project Designer
Doyald Young, Designer/Artist
ANA Hotel Tokyo, Ark Hills, Akasaka
Atrium Lounge Logotype

The logotype style of this elegant lobby
lounge is an ideal example of contrast:
light and medium weight; all caps against

caps and lowercase; roman sans serif
forms versus an elegant florid script; and
a dominant word against a slighter word.
The sans serif does duty for attention,
and the script adds the "jewelry."

Atrium is a condensed and evenly
proportioned two-weight letter that is a
distant relative of Franklin Gothic extra-
condensed, married to a crisply drawn
Optima. The lobe of the *R* is high and
open, thinning perceptibly as it joins the

diagonal. Its tail has a softened ending.
The *M* is splayed as in Michelangelo. The
thick/thin stem weight ratio is almost
monotone. The deletion of the *A*'s crossbar is an echo of the *M*'s open counters.

Lounge is a traditionally weighted
Spencerian formal script of normal proportions with a dramatic beginning swash
L and a *g* with an ending swash stroke
whose looped descender almost equals
the volume of the cap *L*'s lower loop.

(Menu designed by IDA)

International Design Associates

Tokyo, Japan

Mari Makinami, Executive Creative Director
Hideo Hosaka, Project Designer
Doyald Young, Designer/Artist
ANA Hotel Tokyo, Ark Hills, Akasaka
Cascade Coffee Shop Logotype

Always important in a script form is the flowing quality of the letters. This is a brisk write-out that suggests casual din-

ing, light menus, and crisp, efficient service for travelers on the run. The letters are almost monotone, as though they were written with a round-tipped brush or a round-nibbed pen, though around some of the bottom loops there is evidence of the slight thinning produced by pointed brushes. Ascenders may be slim filled loops, or the loop may be open, as the *d* appears here. The loop may balance other forms in proportion, or it may be

even wider, to suggest spontaneity. Both filled and open loops are permissible; they occur frequently in hurried writing. The ascenders may vary in height: here the *d* is taller than the cap *C*. The lobes of the *a*s are open, and these too may vary— open or closed.

Depending on the word's style, syllables may stand unconnected, and often the beginning letter of the syllable may be larger for easier reading and variety.

International Design Associates
Tokyo, Japan

Mari Makinami, Executive Creative Director
Hideo Hosaka, Project Designer
Doyald Young, Designer/Artist
ANA Hotel, Ark Hills, Akasaka, Tokyo
Le Patio Restaurant

For an elegant light-filled dining room, lush with pendulous ferns, Le Patio's logotype relies on a formal script whose capitals and ending strokes produce its distinctive shape and basic refined form.

The baseline of the *e* is higher than *Patio* for a more snug arrangement, and the bottom loop of the *L* aligns with the baseline. While crossbars of *t*s are usually straight, this one departs from the norm with a weighted, reverse ogee curve that

ends with a small teardrop shape that is repeated on the lower loop of the *L* and *P*. The carefully aligned joinings of the lowercase letters are at a third of the x-height, to make the word light and airy.

When a script word is normally spaced, it is possible to achieve smooth, flowing, tangent joinings. In tighter and bolder versions, it is often necessary to join them obliquely to the more tightly spaced lobed forms: *a*, *d*, *e*, *g*, *p*, and *q*.

Top—*Breakfast menu.* ***Below left***—*Luncheon menu.* ***Below right***—*Wine list.*
(Designed by IDA)

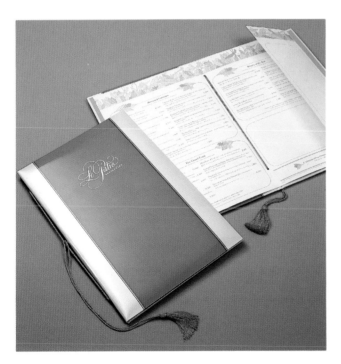

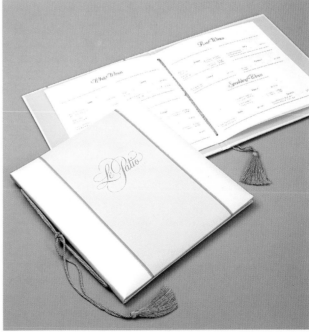

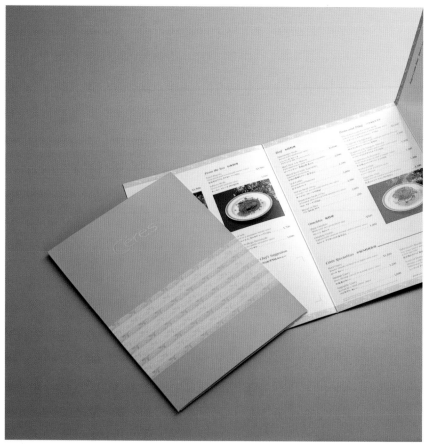

(Menu designed by IDA)

Cérès

International Design Associates
Tokyo, Japan

Mari Makinami, Executive Creative Director
Hideo Hosaka, Project Designer
Doyald Young, Designer/Artist
ANA Hotel Narita
Cérès Coffee Shop Logotype

The hotel's coffee shop is appropriately named Cérès, after the Greek goddess of grain, the classic metaphor for abundant and bountiful food.

The over-scale cap centered on the x-height and the extended, freely drawn lowercase defines the image. The branch of the *r* departs deeply from a softly curved stem. Both the grave accent (`) and the acute accent (´) are pronounced and are used as texture for the logotype.

The style is based on the handsome and classically proportioned Typositor face named Basilea, designed by Markus J. Low, the winner of a 1965 Visual Graphics Corporation typeface competition.

A subtle two-weight roman with a slight widening of the stems, Cérès is in this respect more akin to Optima than Basilea. Because its thins are sturdy, it can be classified as a light classic old style, despite its modern weight distribution.

(Menu designed by IDA)

International Design Associates

Tokyo, Japan

Mari Makinami, Executive Creative Director
Hideo Hosaka, Project Designer
Doyald Young, Designer/Artist
ANA Hotel Narita
Étoile Main Dining Room Logotype

Étoile is the French word for star, with connotations of evening, of romance, and, in this case, elegant dining. The pen script's skeletal form is casual, loose, and spontaneous, drawn with an uneven baseline to convey style and flair. In essence, the script suggests casual elegance. The acute accent has been used as a pronounced design element, and it is curved to be in sympathy with the arc of the script forms. The weight distribution of the letters is pure formal script. A more formal version was considered and is shown above.

The casual style has had many typeface variations from the 1920s through the 1950s. One of these types, Murray Hill, a free style drawn by Emil Klumpp for American Type Founders, is casual in its approach, with more characteristics of the brush than pen writing, with unconnected letters (see page 171 for the font).

Hilton
International JAPAN

International Design Associates

Tokyo, Japan

Mari Makinami, Executive Creative Director
Doyald Young, Designer/Artist
Hilton International Japan
Corporate Logotype

Hilton International Japan is a quartet of hotels: Tokyo, Tokyo Bay, Osaka, and Nagoya. This was the umbrella logotype that carried each hotel's symbol. Each hotel also used a separate logotype. This corporate signature was used on all expendable items for all four hotels, which created savings in printing costs. Because of corporate reorganization, a new logotype superseded this design.

The name is long and cumbersome, and a different emphasis was wanted for each word. The internationally recognized name *Hilton* is a strong and conservative roman with sturdy thins and sharp bracketed serifs that follow the scheme of Times Roman. It is distinguished also as an old style, partly because the ascending *l* is taller than the cap, in the fashion of the Venetian old styles. The calligraphic *t* is similar to Palatino.

The description line is lettered in a widened version of Morris Fuller Benton's Century expanded, updated from a face developed by his father and T. L. De Vinne in 1894 for the *Century* magazine.

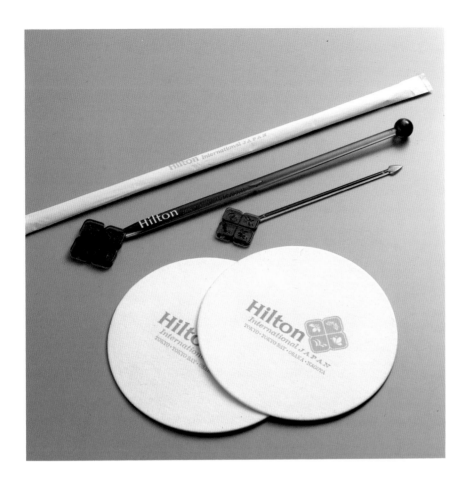

Expendable items with the corporate signature, used for all four hotels, Tokyo, Tokyo Bay, Osaka, and Nagoya.
Top—Straw wrapper, cocktail stirrer, garnish pick, and coasters.   **Below left**—Chocolate candy box.
Below right—Take-out box. (All items designed by IDA)

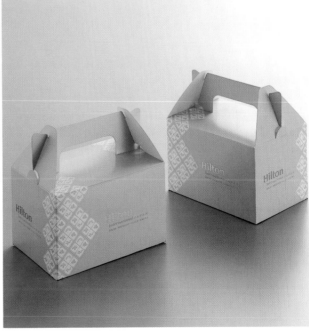

(Menu designed by IDA)

International Design Associates

Tokyo, Japan

Mari Makinami, Executive Creative Director
Doyald Young, Designer/Artist
Osaka Hilton International
Genji Japanese Restaurant

Genji is the hero of *The Tale of Genji*, Japan's oldest novel, which dates from the eleventh century in the Heian period.

A rich and ornate chronicle of Prince Genji's court life, it is valued as the most important work in Japanese literature.

The IDA menu design won a gold medal at the International Menu Competition. The logotype is an extra-bold extended Bodoni italic without serifs. Swash strokes add shape to the word, ensuring a degree of recall, one of the prime assets of any logotype. The names of restaurants have a romantic quality—

each in its own way hopes to invoke a mood, whether of place *(La Serre)*, a period of time *(The Four Seasons)*, a cuisine *(The Epicurean)*, or romance *(Genji)*. Because they avoid the mundane, design liberties are welcome; note the surprise swash ending of the *n*, which is a repeat of the *j*'s descender. Dots of the *i* and *j* are parallelograms. The top left stem of the *n* is angled to allow a deeper join. All of the stroke endings are slightly flared.

(Menu designed by IDA)

International Design Associates

Tokyo, Japan

Mari Makinami, Executive Creative Director
Doyald Young, Designer/Artist
Osaka Hilton International
The Seasons Restaurant

Emphatic beginning and ending caps are from romantic periods of design. They are a Victorian idea that also gained favor in the graphics of the early west. Even the flower-child generation of the 1960s used the conceit on psychedelic posters to rebel against typographic conventions of their day. Here the caps have opulent spiral devices designed to suggest that living well is the sweetest revenge.

It is a standard rule of typography that a word should never be set in all script caps, because it impedes legibility. There are always exceptions—if the caps are simple and the word is familiar and not too long. Except for the the *S*s and the *E*, these letters are mainly italic forms. The ligature **EAS** helps simplify and hold the word together. The last *S* was drawn first, carefully shaping the volute to exactly divide the *O* and to cross the *N* at the desired height. It was then repeated at the beginning with an extended volute to fill the outer shape. All of the hairline strokes are ended with an elongated pear shape to suggest finesse and elegance.

Above—Personalized Narita Golf Club stationery for each club member. (Designed by IDA)

Below—Pencil sketches shown to IDA. Ink comprehensives were then made for full-color client presentation. (Reduced approximately 25 percent.)

International Design Associates

Tokyo, Japan

Mari Makinami, Executive Creative Director
Hideo Hosaka, Project Designer
Doyald Young, Designer/Artist
Aoki Construction Co.
Narita Golf Club Signature

Notable for its million-dollar-plus membership fee, Narita Golf Club has been widely imitated in its approach to elegance and exclusivity for corporate board members only. This logotype perfectly illustrates the design restraint of the club's board of directors, and Ms. Makinami. Chosen from eight final presentation sketches, it is the one that is the most quiet and reserved.

The lettering style is reminiscent of Eric Gill's Perpetua, a typeface with inscriptional qualities that mirror some of Gill's incised letterforms. It is more extended, and the diagonal of the cap *N* does not have the type's extreme overhang; the beginning arc of the *a,* with its heritage of Jenson, begins higher and is drawn more tautly. The stroke that forms the terminal of the *r* has been simplified, and is similar to S. H. de Roos's Egmont, though drawn with a sturdy arc. There is a diagonal to the top right of its stem to allow a deeper, more graceful curve to the departing branch.

Above—*The roman serif cap from the logotype used with script caps, plus variations of script forms exploring different angles and ligature combinations.*

Below—*Menu for Narita Golf Club main dining room. (Menu designed by IDA)*

International Design Associates

Tokyo, Japan

Mari Makinami, Executive Creative Director
Hideo Hosaka, Project Designer
Doyald Young, Designer/Artist
Aoki Construction Co.
Narita Golf Club, Narita, Japan
Monogram

Monograms, somewhat like printer's colophons, echo coats of arms and are used to personalize possessions. The gilded monograms of Louis XIV, and of Marie-Antoinette, are displayed at Versailles as opulent royal imprints.

This monogram for the Narita Golf Club was designed first to comfortably fill an oval and then to be embroidered in gold thread on the club's blazers. In addition, it is used on their tournament flags, pro-shop items, napkins, matches, and menus. It is an upright formal script, with the cap *N* assuming the predominant role. When an upright script is used, I like to draw the letters with just a hint of an angle to keep them from appearing stiff and awkward. The initial downstroke of the *N* is predominantly vertical and helps to stabilize the leaning curves. A bit taller than the *C*, the normally descending loop of the *G* aligns with the *C*.

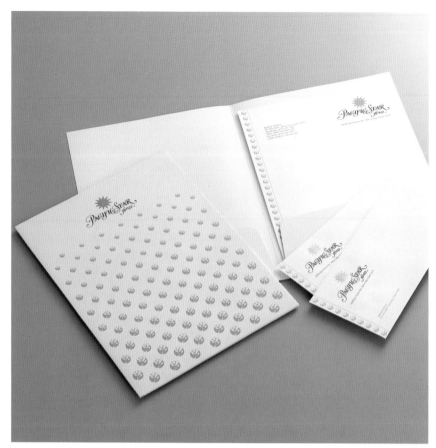

Pacific Star Hotel guest stationery folder.   (Menu designed by IDA)

Right, top—*As part of the client presentation, a one-line, equal-emphasis bold, ornate, formal script logotype.*

Right, bottom—*A two-line version of the same script style, with less emphasis on the word hotel, and drawn in a modified, extended Bodoni.*

Pacific Star Hotel

Pacific Star
HOTEL

The twelve-pointed star is the national emblem of the Republic of Nauru and was specially modified by IDA for use with this logotype.

International Design Associates

Tokyo, Japan

Mari Makinami, Executive Creative Director
Hideo Hosaka, Project Designer
Doyald Young, Designer/Artist
Pacific Star Hotel, Guam
Owned by The Republic of Nauru
Managed by ANA Enterprises, Ltd.
Corporate Signature

Four hours by jet from Tokyo, Pacific Star is a sparkling new addition to the beach at Tumon Bay, Guam, now a popular resort for the Japanese.

A Pacific island hotel seemed an apt place to use swash letters, which are reminiscent of the maps of Captain Cook's day. These were often elaborately drawn caps, widely spaced to fill the vastness of the oceans. Based on Caslon, a face popular in the captain's time, the proportions are even, the font is bolder, the swash strokes drawn more sedately, and the swelled pen endings are not as abrupt as the type. The ending shape follows Moorish arabesques used in printers' flowers for decorative ornaments on bookbindings and as typographical niceties for the printed page. The cap *A*s are embellished with a pen-flourish crossbar. The cap *S* swash overlaps the *C*, making a visually unified logo.

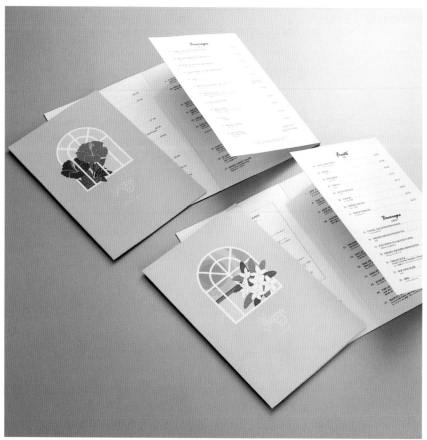

Sirena coffee shop breakfast and lunch menus. (Designed by IDA)

cafe sìrena

cafe Sirena

Right, top—*Thick/thin sans serif ink comprehensive, with softly curving stems, swash letters, and fine hairlines. Note the one-story* **a***.*

Right, bottom—*One-line script version, with a linear script word* **cafe** *and a bolder two-weight script, reminiscent of eighteenth- and nineteenth-century styles, with the greatest weight carried around the top and bottom curves.*

International Design Associates

Tokyo, Japan

Mari Makinami, Executive Creative Director
Hideo Hosaka, Project Designer
Doyald Young, Designer/Artist
Pacific Star Hotel, Guam
Owned by The Republic of Nauru
Managed by ANA Enterprises, Ltd.
Cafe Sirena Logotype

Homer relates that Odysseus plugged his crew's ears with beeswax to prevent them from hearing the Sirens' compelling and destructive song, but here the music is more apt to be rock.

This project was a great occasion for the use of romantic letterforms. The word *Sirena* is mythic—it demands style and departure from convention. This was fun. The letters seemed to be in the right place to do what was called for in this case—

swirl and beckon. It is a mix of sans serif, script, italic forms, and biform (same-size mixed caps and lowercase) to boot! The ogee-crossbar of the *A* is seen in many a Victorian decorative typeface.

A single-weight flowing script is a useful and deceptively simple form that often is not written but carefully drawn. In all linear forms, including sans serifs, the script's shape must be impeccable, for its beauty resides in this correctness.

Rendezvous

Rendezvous

RENDEZVOUS

Presentation ink comprehensives.
Top—*A condensed Bodoni with a swash cap* **R** *and* **z** *and an italic form* **s.**
Center—*Freely written single-weight pen script.*
Bottom—*Selected design.*

Actual-size detail of preliminary drawing for inked comprehensive.

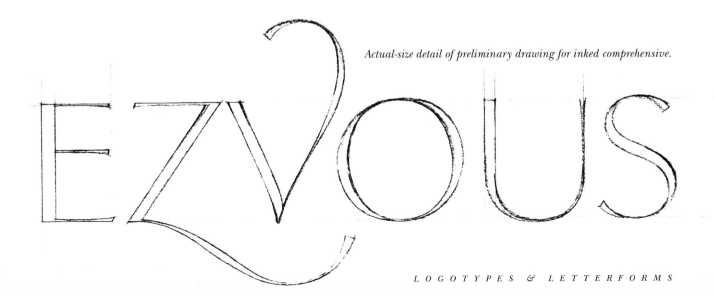

RENDEZVOUS

RENDEZVOUS

International Design Associates

Tokyo, Japan

Mari Makinami, Executive Creative Director
Hideo Hosaka, Project Designer
Doyald Young, Designer/Artist
Pacific Star Hotel, Guam
Owned by The Republic of Nauru
Managed by ANA Enterprises, Ltd.
Rendezvous Lounge Logotype

Adjacent to the hotel's main dining room, *Rendezvous* is a waiting lounge. The understated logotype is straightforward—letterforms drawn pristinely, relying on only two swash forms to establish its style.

The style is a marriage of Bodoni (without its serifs) and R. Hunter Middleton's Radiant, with greater contrast between the thick and thin strokes and a proportion that is generous and open. The *E*s are narrow, with horizontals widening to a definite ending that is on a slight diagonal. This widening is repeated on the vertical thins of the *N* and the terminals of the *S*. The vertical hairlines of the *N* clip the weighted diagonal for a more sturdy, structural joining.

Similar to Palatino, the lobe of the cap *R* is open, and its tail widens slightly at the baseline. The tail of the *Z* is an italic form found in many fonts: Arrighi, Times Roman, Cloister, and Baskerville.

International Design Associates

Tokyo, Japan

Mari Makinami, Executive Creative Director

Hideo Hosaka, Project Designer

Doyald Young, Designer/Artist

Pacific Star Hotel, Guam

Owned by The Republic of Nauru

Managed by ANA Enterprises, Ltd.

Le Patio Restaurant Logotype

This time, **le Patio** is a logotype for a restaurant with a relaxed atmosphere. (See page 98 for a very formal design approach to the same name.)

It was possible to show designs both with a capital and a lowercase *l* (see the opposite page) in an effort to create a more distinctive shape. The lowercase *l* projected an informal atmosphere and, drawn at the same size as *Patio*, maintained its relative importance. Instead of the usual partially curved upstroke of the *l*, a stroke with less curve is used and echoes the angle of the downstroke of the *P*. The exuberant beginning lobe stroke of the *P* serves also to underscore **le** and creates a tie-in to the important word. These short words—*le, The, A*, etc.—are always troublesome in a design because they often seem isolated. It is difficult, but important, to fashion them so that they are integral to the logotype design.

Preliminary comprehensive designs rendered in ink, then reproduced in color for client presentation.

International Design Associates

Tokyo, Japan

Mari Makinami, Executive Creative Director
Hideo Hosaka, Project Designer
Doyald Young, Designer/Artist
Pacific Star Hotel, Guam
Owned by The Republic of Nauru
Managed by ANA Enterprises, Ltd.
Food and Beverage Logotypes

One-half-dozen to a dozen very tight pencil designs for each logotype are usually presented to IDA for consideration. A diverse group is desirable. These are precisely drawn, with an F pencil on Clearprint vellum, with the design problems solved. From these, three or four inked comprehensives are made (above) for client presentation in an actual application, at actual size, in actual printer's colors. To accomplish this, the ink comprehensives are drawn at 300 to 400 percent with a sharp felt-tip pen on tracing paper, photostatted and retouched where necessary, and then reduced to actual size. A typical presentation might include a menu cover, napkin, coaster, matchbook, and swizzle stick—sometimes in two color schemes. A design is selected, minor modifications are suggested, and final art is drawn at a large size to accommodate the requirements of signage.

HOTEL *East 21* TOKYO

1.

Hotel EAST 21
TOKYO

2.

Hotel East 21
TOKYO

3.

Hotel East 21
TOKYO

4.

5.

6.

7.

8.

9.

Hotel East 21 *Tokyo*

10.

HOTEL
EAST/21
TOKYO

11.

EAST 21 HOTEL
TOKYO

12.

HOTEL
EAST
21
Tokyo

13.

To complement the hotel's Biedermeier-
style interior, designs 10, 13, 17, and 19
are interpretations of the typeface Walbaum,
a style designed by J. Walbaum in the
early nineteenth century.
To lessen the dominance of the number **21**,
a gravure style is used in 8. The figures
in 9 are lighter weight.
The distinctive pyramidal roofs of the
three major buildings were used as an identifying mark for the hotel (opposite, 21).

HOTEL **EAST 21** TOKYO

14.

18.

East 21 Hotel

22.

Hotel
EAST TWENTY·ONE
T O K Y O

15.

19.

H O T E L
East Twenty-One
T O K Y O

23.

Hotel EAST 21
T O K Y O

16.

20.

Hotel East 21 Tokyo

24.

H O T E L
East 21
T O K Y O

17.

21.

Hotel East 21
T O K Y O

25.

International Design Associates
Tokyo, Japan

Mari Makinami, Executive Creative Director
Hideo Hosaka, Project Designer
Doyald Young, Designer/Artist
Kajima Corporation
Hotel East 21, Tokyo
Logotype Comprehensives

East 21 is a multipurpose land project developed by Kajima Construction Company, one of Japan's major builders. Situated on the eastern part of Tokyo Bay, the large square block includes a major first-class hotel, office tower, plaza, underground shopping mall, and event hall.

A logotype design often faces many committees and officers of a company for approval. This was no exception. An extensive group of designs was submitted

to International Design Associates. From these preliminary pencil designs, inked comprehensives were drawn and shown to a number of committees that included the parent company, Kajima Corporation, Kajima Hotel Enterprises, and Kajima Tokyo Kaihatsu. When the choice was narrowed, color presentations were developed for several applications that included stationery and business cards. The final choice is on the following page.

Top—The standard logotype for general printing purposes.

Bottom—A weighted version for use in very small sizes, light color value, or when the logo is reversed from a solid color.

International Design Associates

Tokyo, Japan

Mari Makinami, Executive Creative Director
Hideo Hosaka, Project Designer
Doyald Young, Designer/Artist

Kajima Corporation
Hotel East 21, Tokyo
Corporate Logotype

After the many variations were tried—roman caps; script; roman with script; gravure style; script and sans serif; one-, two-, and three-line configurations; figures spelled out—and many tested in varying weights and arrangements, this is the final logotype.

Hotel East 21 Tokyo's interiors are Biedermeier, an aristocratic style popular in Germany and Austria from the 1820s to the 1840s, with influences of Empire. In France the concurrent typeface was the elegant Didot, and in Germany the corresponding style was Walbaum (see pages 118 and 119, designs 10, 13, 17, and 19, which are derived from this type style).

In Manhattan alone, Le Parker Meridien, St. Moritz on the Park, the Carlyle, the Pierre, and the Plaza, internationally renowned hotels of quality, share a common bond: formal script logotypes. While this is not a mandatory solution for a four-star hotel's signature, it is often prudent to include the style in a presentation as a point of reference. The modern styles—Bodoni, Torino, Didot, and Fenice—can also be used to suggest quality and elegance and to imply that a guest will be luxuriously pampered. They combine handsomely with the formal scripts.

The figure *2* of the logotype has a swelled reverse curve for its bottom finishing stroke; this is often found in script and italic styles, though seldom in the upright romans. It is similar to Monotype's ultra Bodoni and American Type Founder's Engraver's bold. Here it is a complement to the curves of the script.

To match the softness of the *2*, the figure *1* has bracketed serifs and the top serif is cupped. These figures overlap and create a snug unit with the word *East*. This is a typographic ploy that neatly ties disparate words and shapes together. Both the bottom volute of the *E* and the generous arc of the *t*'s ending stroke are carefully drawn to divide the terminal of the *2* and the top triangular shape of the *1*.

The style of the word *East* may be classified as a free-style or casual Spencerian script. While it retains the formal script weight distribution, the letter size and alignment are varied. The curved crossbar of the *t* is sometimes drawn as a straight line with sides of equal length; here it is drawn in sympathy with the curved texture of the word.

Hotel and *Tokyo* are a handlettered News Gothic condensed and were designed to fit both the light- and medium-weight uses. The *k*'s diagonals converge above center and barely touch the stem.

The logotype in a one-line configuration, used when a three-line version would be too small.
This is particularly important for computer bookkeeping forms and for the hotel's guest services.

1.

2.

3.

4.

5.

6.

MISTY RIDGE
HOTEL

MISTY RIDGE
HOTEL

International Design Associates

Tokyo, Japan

Mari Makinami, Executive Creative Director

Doyald Young, Designer/Artist

Hakone-Kokusai Mansion K.K.

Cypress Resort, Ltd.—Misty Ridge Hotel

With a view of the lake and mountains in Hakone, Kanagawa Prefecture, Misty Ridge is an evocative name which I tried to capture with the use of very romantic

swash caps (opposite). Many are drawn with beginning loops, evident in the *S, G*, and *E*, in example 1. Number 6 is a wider, more restrained drawing of the same style. Number 2 is a Bodoni that lets its cap *R* have all of the emphasis. Comprehensives 1, 5, and 6 pay homage to Jan van Krimpen's Cancelleresca Bastarda, the ultimate romantic letterform, which he based on script forms from fifteenth-century Italian writing masters.[1]

The chosen version (above), boldest and simplest, has some script forms, a lowercase *Y*, an *ST* ligature, and a swash *M.* The letters have vestigial serifs, the thick/thin ratio is slight, and some of the letters are similar to Ernst Friz's Friz Quadrata and Hermann Zapf's Optima.

1. *Three Classics of Italian Calligraphy: Writing Books of Arrighi, Tagliente and Palatino* (New York: Dover Publications, 1953), and Alfred Fairbank, *A Book of Scripts* (New York: Penguin Books, 1955).

café
patisserie

Café
PATISSERIE

CAFÉ
PATISSERIE

CAFÉ
Patisserie

CAFÉ
Patisserie

HILTON'S
Café
カフェ パティセリー
PATISSERIE

HILTON'S
Café
カフェ パティセリー
PATISSERIE

International Design Associates

Tokyo, Japan

Mari Makinami, Executive Creative Director

Doyald Young, Designer/Artist

Osaka Hilton Hotel

Café Patisserie Logotype

Originally an espresso bar, the Café Patisserie evolved into a shop selling pastries and bread (see page 126).

The above example demonstrates the frequent necessity of combining several elements. In the design of these logotypes, space had to be allotted for the phonetic Japanese script spelling—usually at the bottom left or right. Here it is sandwiched between the name *Hilton* (not the official logotype) and *Patisserie.*

The script is wide, with an *f* that is more italic than script. With serendipity, the descender of the script *f* bisects the crossbar of the *T* to form the *A*'s crossbar.

Patisserie is a lightweight sans serif letter style with slight references to Optima. It is condensed, and the swelled tips of the letters are pronounced. The waist of the *R* is open, with a tail that has a very subtle reverse curve on its left side. The *T*'s crossbars end obliquely and parallel.

espresso

ABCDEFGHIJKLMNOPQRSTUVWXYZ

BLOCK — H. HOFFMANN, BERTHOLD 1908

International Design Associates

Tokyo, Japan

Mari Makinami, Executive Creative Director

Doyald Young, Designer/Artist

Osaka Hilton Hotel

Espresso Coffee Bar Logotype

(now Hilton's Café Patisserie, see page 125)

Moda Italia seems to always suggest the ultra-modern, slim and trim. These sleek, stretched forms have been around for a long time; they are the familiar forms of art deco reinterpreted. They hark to another era, the brutal sans serifs developed in Germany around the turn of the century by H. Hoffmann, named Block, from the German for block or log, which the original surely resembles. Since that time sans serifs have been known generi-

cally as "block letters." The style lent great atmosphere to posters of its day. It was one of the first large x-height types which today we call "contemporary ad fonts." A few of its capital round forms are similar, with rather flat tops and bottoms.

The letters *e* and *s* are a boon to the logotype—both shapes lend distinctive repetition. The crossbar of the *e* that follows the *r* has been extended to fill the space. The descender of the *p* is short.

THE**IN**PLACE

THE**IN**PLACE

A B C D E F G H I J K L M N O P Q R S T U V W X Y Z &

PHENIX — MORRIS F. BENTON, ATF 1935

International Design Associates

Tokyo, Japan

Mari Makinami, Executive Creative Director

Doyald Young, Designer/Artist

Osaka Hilton Hotel

The In Place Lounge Logotype

A declaration of exclusivity, the lounge logotype is pure art deco, suggesting the brittle elegance of ladies gowned in marabou-trimmed satin, accompanied by moustachioed, monocled gentlemen in white tie and tails.

Reminiscent of ATF's Huxley Vertical, but closer in style to M. F. Benton's Phenix with its domed cap *A*, the logotype includes crossbars that extend beyond their boundaries, a device that creates a handy space filler beneath the *T*'s crossbar. The diagonal of the *N* is high and relates to early turn-of-the-century German letterforms. The weighting of *IN* is a not-so-subtle manner of emphasizing one word while allowing all three to be run together to create a single wordmark. The lobe of the *P* and the curves of the *A* and *C* are elliptical. The word is legible because, as in other short words that appear on open signs that can be read from both sides—dine, bar, eat, gas—all are familiar and easy to read, even with the distortion of perspective.

Palace Hotel

Mark designed by Mari Makinami

Mark designed by David Solon

International Design Associates

Tokyo, Japan

Mari Makinami, Executive Creative Director
Ken Nakata, Project Designer
Doyald Young, Designer/Artist
Palace Hotel, Tokyo,
Corporate Logotype

Formal scripts suggest quality and propriety and stem from times of courtly manners—George Bickham wrote his treatise

The Universal Penman on the elegant letter in 1743. Their style remaining very much unchanged, scripts reflect the vanished pomp of coronations and grand balls. Bets are that for years to come, they will still suggest refinement and elegance.

The Palace Hotel, located in one of the most enviable locations in all of Japan—across from the emperor's palace—recently opened a new resort hotel on Guam Island, only four hours from

Tokyo (see page 136). The same script is used for both hotels, though with a different weight and mark.

This is the bold version designed for exterior signage and for reductions. The *H* descends lower than the *P*. Its bold weight prevents hairlines from breaking in reduction and when reversed from solid colors. The regular logotype is used for stationery and the many printed items of collateral that luxury hotels require.

1.

3.

2.

4.

International Design Associates

Tokyo, Japan

Mari Makinami, Executive Creative Director

Ken Nakata, Project Designer

Doyald Young, Designer/Artist

Palace Hotel, Tokyo

The Palace Scotch Whisky Label

First-class hotels in Japan often feature a special brand of liquor especially blended by a distiller for the exclusive use of the hotel. Custom-designed labels complement this exclusivity. Because they are often in a cabinet by themselves, they do not face the rigors of shelf competition.

Scotch and bourbon, like wines, are frequently labeled with engraved formal script letterforms. The Seagrams VO whiskey label was formerly written en-tirely in script. Through tradition, formal scripts lend credibility and suggest a product of quality.

Shown above are script with inline caps after Jan van Krimpen (1); script and italic caps crowning bold condensed Bodoni caps (2); italic swash caps with the *A*'s crossbar decoratively filling the open space of the *LA* combination (3); and the client's selection, narrow classic caps enveloped in formal script volutes (4).

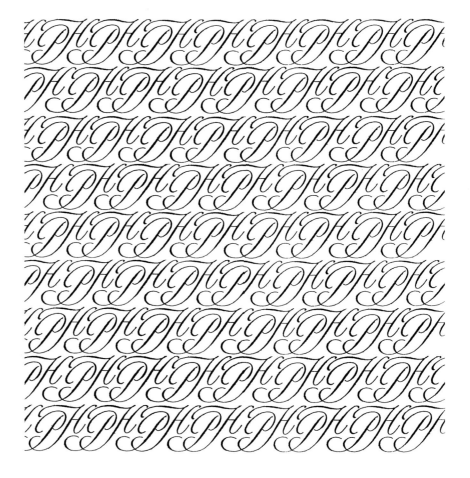

Top— *A study for a step-and-repeat pattern for the hotel gift wrapping and wallpaper.*

Center—*Caps from the Palace Hotel logotype redrawn and modified to meet the requirements of the step-and-repeat pattern.*

Bottom—*Alternate designs that departed from the basic logotype capitals.*

International Design Associates

Tokyo, Japan

Mari Makinami, Executive Creative Director

Ken Nakata, Project Designer

Doyald Young, Designer/Artist

Palace Hotel, Tokyo

Monogram (unpublished)

Many objects in a hotel—packaging labeling for soaps, towels, bathrobes, wrapping papers, menus, wallpapers, match-books—are frequently enhanced by the use of a monogram, singly or as a repetitive pattern.

Letterforms, particularly script ones, are useful shapes in creating step-and-repeat patterns. The soft curves and their swash extensions create graceful textures. This study used variations of the initials

from the logotype, plus the actual initials without modification. Because the design is often used in small scale, and frequently in reverse, the thin strokes are weighted to prevent filling. The tips are chopped and pointed. The version shown above overlaps, and the left-hand ogee curve of the *H* is extended to overlap the downstroke of the *P* at its thinnest area. The drop extension also creates a nest for the following overlapped double curves.

Humming

Humming

ABCDEFGHIJKLMNOPQRSTUVWXYZ
abcdefghijklmnopqrstuvwxyz

BODONI ITALIC — BAUER 1926

International Design Associates

Tokyo, Japan

Mari Makinami, Executive Creative Director
Ken Nakata, Project Designer
Doyald Young, Designer/Artist
Palace Hotel, Tokyo
Humming Coffee Shop Logotype

For a bustling coffee shop, the name Humming seemed to demand a light touch—and why not a lilting curved line?

These are Bodoni italic letterforms drawn in an upright orientation that is tangent to the curving baseline, thereby creating a mass of problems. The letters frequently must be distorted to fill spaces that are created when the letters roll away from each other at the top. The stems are drawn softly, by which I mean in a curved manner. The stems are ever so slightly concave, flaring minutely at the top and bottom of the x-height. The ending hairline curved strokes vary in width, again to enhance color spacing. Serifs are perpendicular to the curve and flare at their tips. The traditional two-story *g* is replaced with a lobed form found on the *b*, *d*, *p*, and *q*. The *H* and the tail of the *g* terminate with teardrop shapes that relate to sixteenth-century Italian penmanship.

ABCDEFGHIJKLMNOPQRSTUVWXYZ
abcdefghijklmnopqrstuvwxyz

SNELL ROUNDHAND — MATTHEW CARTER, LINOFILM 1966

International Design Associates

Tokyo, Japan

Mari Makinami, Executive Creative Director
Ken Nakata, Project Designer
Doyald Young, Designer/Artist
Palace Hotel, Tokyo
Royal Lounge Logotype

Designed to complement the script of the hotel's logotype (see page 128), ***Royal*** differs from the signature logotype in having a wider proportion and more open spacing. The *l* is unlooped in the style of writing exercises from the seventeenth century. Related to the downstroke of the cap ***R***, the descender of the ***y*** arcs generously under the ***R*** in a manner that only a special alternate character of a font could do. Connecting hairline curves are drawn parallel and join the following stroke or letter at the same height, which varies, depending on the style, weight, and proportion, from one-third to one-half the x-height. The top of the ***a*** is similar to Americana italic. A secondary weight is found on the right-hand side of the lowercase ***o*** in many formal scripts. Snell Roundhand, adapted from the handwriting of Charles Snell by Matthew Carter, is typical of this style.[1]

---

1. Joyce Irene Whalley, *English Handwriting 1540–1853* (London: Her Majesty's Stationery Office, 1969), plates 48–50.

ABCDEFGHIJKLMNOPQRSTUVWXYZ
abcdefghijklmnopqrstuvwxyz

TORINO ITALIC (ROMANO MODERNO) — NEBIOLO C. 1908

International Design Associates

Tokyo, Japan

Mari Makinami, Executive Creative Director
Ken Nakata, Project Designer
Doyald Young, Designer/Artist
Palace Hotel, Tokyo
Swan Restaurant Logotype

The cap *S* of the name, derived from the swans that swim in the emperor's moat across the boulevard, allowed for an illustrative treatment. The letterform is a modern style widely used in the nineteenth century and is almost identical to the connected letters of script. In reality, the type is a narrowed version of Bodoni, but with hairline beginning strokes called pothooks, instead of the horizontal hairline serifed stems of Bodoni. The curved stems of the *w* and *n* are the same, and the lobes of the *a, b, d, g, p,* and *q* are weighted below the center. A minimum of weight is carried around the center of the pothooks and the ending hairlines.

The modern type forms were much derided around the turn of the century because their hairlines were exceedingly fine and were difficult to read as text faces. Many were slightly condensed, further impairing the ease of reading them.

1.

2.

3.

4.

5.

CORAL *Palace*

CORAL *Palace*

International Design Associates

Tokyo, Japan

Mari Makinami, Executive Creative Director

Hideo Hosaka, Project Designer

Doyald Young, Designer/Artist

Palace Hotel, Guam

Coral Palace Main Dining Room Logotype

For the grand menu of the main dining room, the logotype borrows *Palace* from the hotel logotype, though the bowl of the cap *P* has been enlarged to comfortably wrap around the *RA* and do duty as a curved hairline crossbar for the *A*.

In keeping with the formality of the script, a classic roman is used for the word *Coral*. The letter style has slight contrast between its thick and thin strokes and is similar to Friz Quadrata, though lighter

weight. The *RA* is joined to help close up the space that the tail of the *R* creates.

The initial design brief did not specifically request the use of the parent logotype, though the three lower pencil comprehensive versions took advantage of the tie-in (opposite). With its staggered baseline, design number 3 offered a snug placement of *Coral* instead of a usual straight-line treatment that would result in a misspacing created by the *P* 's tail.

1.

2.

5.

3.

6.

7.

International Design Associates

Tokyo, Japan

Mari Makinami, Executive Creative Director

Hideo Hosaka, Project Designer

Doyald Young, Designer/Artist

Palace Hotel, Guam

KoKo Bar Logotype

In Chamorro, the native language of the Mariana Islands, koko is a bird and not the coco palms of the Pacific.

The ascenders of the word are a useful design element that imparts distinctiveness because, as shown opposite, they may be looped (1), or their convergence can be looped (2); the word may be staggered at its syllable break (3), or overbalanced with a reverse curved diagonal (4), or the diagonals may be de-signed like frigate birds (5 and 6). The elegant treatment in the seventh design relates to the parent logotype script. Number 3, the selected design, has a **K** whose diagonals are separated from the stem, producing a cleaner and more contemporary shape and reducing the mass of the letter. The diagonals taper as they meet for the same reason. The bowl of the **B** is overbalanced, and the **R** is open with a descending tail ending at a right angle.

Above—A 350 percent enlargement of the original pencil comprehensive and the final art reduced in size for its smallest application.
Below—Initial rough pencil sketches shown approximately same size.

International Design Associates

Tokyo, Japan

Mari Makinami, Executive Creative Director
Hideo Hosaka, Project Designer
Doyald Young, Designer/Artist
Palace Hotel, Guam
Sala Lounge Logotype

Sala is of Spanish, Italian, Hindi, and Sanskrit origin, meaning a large, important room; it is related to the French *salon.*

A short word, or a word containing a letter that is repeated, often lends a hand in the design of a logotype. The *A*, treated as a design element, forms a repetitive pattern that is the basis for a distinctive design or word-shape. More often than not, the shape of the word is more memorable than the type style, case, boldness, or orientation of the letters. The intrinsic shape suggests a carefree holiday mood, and any number of type styles can work.

The logotype is based on Caslon and uses a simplified swash italic cap in an upright roman orientation. It is not always necessary to use crossbars for the *A*s; the word is for an informal situation and reads easily without them.

This is a rather loosely rendered pencil sketch—it lacks finesse, the proportions and letterspacing vary, as do the stem weights, but I like the directness of the 350 percent pencil enlargement.

International Design Associates
Tokyo, Japan

Mari Makinami, Executive Creative Director
Doyald Young, Designer/Artist
Tokyo Hilton Hotel
Teppan Grill Restaurant Logotype

Teppan is a shortened name for *Teppan-yaki*—a popular method of cooking food at a high temperature on a large griddle. The informal logotype is composed of contrasting faces, roman and script. Its arced baseline and the nestling formal script *G* create a strong, identifiable image. *Teppan* is modeled after ATF's Century Schoolbook, with long, generously bracketed serifs and modified tips. The vertical thins on the *N* taper from the serif. The center arm of the *E* and the crossbar of the *A* are horizontal to prevent distortion and serve to stabilize the extreme arc of the baseline. Popular in Victorian designs, the arc is often identified with graphics of the Old West.

Formal scripts may be relaxed as this one is: instead of the tangent joinings of most script fonts, the *I*s are drawn as two large continuous loops with a slight carriage of weight across the bottom curves.

ROYAL 🌹 PARK
H O T E L

*The stylized rose, evocative
of English monarchy, was designed
by Mari Makinami.*

International Design Associates
Tokyo, Japan

Mari Makinami, Executive Creative Director
Hideo Hosaka, Project Designer
Doyald Young, Designer/Artist
Royal Park Hotel
Corporate Signature

This graphics program was first conceived as a contemporary statement—but evolved into a traditional image.

Ms. Makinami designed the stylized rose, a symbol of English monarchy. Preliminary drawings of the rose were presented to me before I began work on the initial logotype design.

The condensed proportions of the letters reflect the formal qualities of the name. The logotype style is an amalgam of the type families known as Scotch Roman, designed in the early nineteenth century. The logotype has some qualities of Bulmer, Caledonia, and Century Nova, a condensed Century designed by Charles Hughes for American Type Founders in 1966.

Serifs are generous, and there is more contrast between the thick and thin strokes than Century; the tail of the *R* is minimized and joined to the serif of the *K*. The weighted strokes of the *A*s are cupped. The diagonals of the *K* are isolated; the thin one is weighted for color.

L'AVENTURE

L'AVENTURE

ABCDEFGHIJKLMNOPQRSTUVWXYZ
abcdefghijklmnopqrstuvwxyz

SERIF GOTHIC REGULAR—HERB LUBALIN AND ANTONIO DISPIGNA, ITC 1972

International Design Associates

Tokyo, Japan

Mari Makinami, Executive Creative Director

Hideo Hosaka, Project Designer

Doyald Young, Designer

Royal Park Hotel

L'Aventure Restaurant Logotype

Designed to evoke the likes of mahouts, lumbering elephants, and Bengal tigers, ***L'Aventure*** is a slight two-weight sans serif with softened alternate forms. The *n* and *u* are true inverted forms with references to the romantic fancies of the Victorian age. Even the *R* has been sweetened with an ogival diagonal tail that extends well into the counter of the lobe. The *E* is a semi-uncial rounded form with opposing diagonal endings that are repeated on all horizontal strokes. The apostrophe, from the Greek *apostrophein,* to turn away, does not turn but is instead is a thin exaggerated sliver. The long thin swash of the *A* ends with a diagonal. The *A*'s apex is exaggerated with a taller peak than usual, and the crossbar of the *T* terminates in parallel diagonals.

The style is similar to Lubalin and DiSpigna's sophisticated Serif Gothic for ITC, though without its minuscule serifs.

Fontaine

Fontaine

FONTAINE *Lounge*

Top—*Reduced version of logotype.*
Bottom—*A more formal treatment using condensed roman caps and formal script.*

International Design Associates

Tokyo, Japan

Mari Makinami, Executive Creative Director
Hideo Hosaka, Project Designer
Doyald Young, Designer
Royal Park Hotel
Fontaine Lounge Logotype

The word *Fontaine* is a lucky combination of letters. Its two ascenders and forced descenders of the *F*, *t*, and *e* give the word its shape. The reverse curve of the top crossbar of the *F* is repeated on the cross-stroke of the *t*, while the *o* is not looped or connected to the following letter. The style is indefinite, with qualities of both brush and pen script, though the latter predominates. The letters bounce on the baseline but to a lesser degree than the tops of the letters, whose uneven alignment is created by an extreme change of letter size, evident in both the *i* and *n*.

Openly spaced, the letters are based on forms that I like—narrow ellipses, with deep joinings on the *n*s and high joinings on the lobed forms. There is a change of thickness on the upstrokes and an occasional break in the word to give the appearance of real handwriting.

International Design Associates

Tokyo, Japan

Mari Makinami, Executive Creative Director
Hideo Hosaka, Project Designer
Doyald Young, Designer
Royal Park Hotel
Palazzo Restaurant Logotype

Royal Park Hotel's elegant main dining room, with a name evoking imposing Italian buildings, and specifically palaces.

The formal script version was drawn first and approved, but a newly commissioned designer for the dining room preferred the classic roman letter.

The formal script is much more successful in its design resolution than the roman caps, for the loops of the *z*s overlap and nest gracefully, their endings balancing the initial loop of the cap *P*—all that is really needed to give the word shape and grace. The exercise is a prime example of personal preference, for it can be argued that while the classic roman letter is more appropriate to the Italian word, the script suggests more elegance, nuance, refinement, and epicurean cuisine than the roman caps.

The roman version is troublesome with its difficult **LA** combination. The **Z**s are italic shapes forced into script forms and lack the ease of the opulent script loops, which can be drawn to fit a need.

Royal
SCOTS

International Design Associates

Tokyo, Japan

Mari Makinami, Executive Creative Director

Hideo Hosaka, Project Designer

Doyald Young, Designer

Royal Park Hotel

Royal Scots Bar Logotype

To be geographically correct, the word *Scots* should be set in Scotch Roman, a style developed in Edinburgh in the early nineteenth century. It was used extensively in England, but like its cousin, Modern, its thins are rather brittle, and this logotype was to be reversed out of four-color process. Therefore I drew the more handsome Baskerville, with its sturdier thin strokes and heavier bracketed serifs. It belongs to an earlier period and

geographically a little farther south, to Birmingham. These proportions are modified: the *T* and *C* are more narrow, and the stem thickness has been lightened. The logotype is closer in style to Fry Baskerville, a font cut around 1768 and attributed to Isaac Moore.

An appropriate unadorned English roundhand upper- and lowercase formal script crowns the word, with its exaggerated looped cap *R* and an exuberant *l*.

TAKARAZUKA
Hotel

Takarazuka
H O T E L

TAKARAZUKA
Hotel

TAKARAZUKA
Hotel

TAKARAZUKA
HOTEL

Takarazuka
HOTEL

TAKARAZUKA HOTEL

TAKARAZUKA HOTEL

Takarazuka
H O T E L

Takarazuka Hotel

Takarazuka Hotel

International Design Associates

Tokyo, Japan

Mari Makinami, Executive Creative Director
Hideo Hosaka, Project Designer
Doyald Young, Designer/Artist
Hankyu Corporation
Takarazuka Hotel Logotype

Long names are difficult to work with and should generally be restrained in style. This logotype is for a famous sixty-five-year-old hotel located in a resort area developed by the Hankyu Railroad Company eighty-four years ago.

The word is normally spaced, and the lowercase forms are straightforward formal script of average proportions, weight, and angle. Only the caps and looped descender of the z have been exaggerated. With their straight stems, the caps are more italic than script in spirit. The ascenders are not looped and are taller than the caps but relate because of their rigidity. The descender of the z has a plump loop, and its repose is almost lateral. The reverse-curve finishing stroke is weighted and crosses the downstroke, violating a suspect rule: never cross a weight with a weight in formal script, because the juncture becomes a bulls-eye. But because both strokes are light, it is acceptable here. The crossbar of the t is high and wide, a personal preference.

THE Duke

THE DUKE

THE Duke

The DUKE

The Duke

The Duke

ABCDEFGHIJKLMNOPQRSTUVWXYZ

abcdefghijklmnopqrstuvwxyz

CASLON BOLD CONDENSED—ATF C. 1911[1]

International Design Associates

Tokyo, Japan

Mari Makinami, Executive Creative Director

Hideo Hosaka, Project Designer

Doyald Young, Designer/Artist

Hankyu Corporation, Takarazuka Hotel

The Duke Membership Bar Logotype

Caslon, a typeface designed in the 1720s by William Caslon, more than any other old style is quintessentially English. A book face, it has with some modification gained a solid reputation as a display face.

Similar to Caslon, *The Duke* is lighter, more condensed, the strokes softened, serifs widened and cupped, and the ascender is taller than the *D*. The down-and cross-stroke endings of the script *T* use the widening found in writings of English roundhand forms popularized in the 1743 *Universal Penman* by George Bickham, a copybook for bookkeepers. The word *The* is nestled between the *D* and the ascender of the *k*. The scale of the word, its weight, and angle are a foil for the main word *Duke*. The ends of the strokes of the script *T*'s crossbar result from pressure applied to a slotted pen.

1. Condensed Caslon, a modified New Caslon by Inland,1907, inherited by ATF, who named it bold condensed. Mac McGrew, *American Metal Typefaces of the Twentieth Century*, preliminary edition (New Rochelle, New York: The Myriade Press, 1986), page 73.

Renaissance

Renaissance

RENAISSANCE

Top—*Reduced version of logotype.*
Bottom—*A submitted design that employs
descending swash forms only.*

ABCDEFGHIJKLMNOPQRSTUVWXYZ&
abcdefghijklmnopqrstuvwxyz

ARRIGHI ITALIC — FREDERIC WARDE, MONOTYPE 1929

International Design Associates
Tokyo, Japan

Mari Makinami, Executive Creative Director
Hideo Hosaka, Project Designer
Doyald Young, Designer/Artist
*Hankyu Corporation, Takarazuka Hotel
Renaissance Restaurant Logotype*

A chancery italic, so named for the office where a diocese's business is recorded. The Arrighi italic is the wellspring of the style. In the sixteenth century, Arrighi worked as a scribe writing papal briefs, and these italics descend from his marvelous pen script. The original letters were written with an angled-edge quill or reed held roughly 30 degrees from the horizontal, creating a heaviness around the top and bottom turns. Trajanus, Palatino, and Cancelleresca Bastarda owe much to the style. The chancery italic forms are even in proportion, and the structure of the letters is carefully related; when written by masters, their color is even. Note the absence of an ear on the **g**.

Initial caps may relate to the following letters or, more often than not, contrast in style. Usually they are larger, and many are ornamented; some are classified as gravure, hand tooled, open, or shaded. This initial **R** is drawn with a separated shadow to the left on only two of its strokes, to suggest quality and richness.

ABCDEFGHIJKLMNOPQRSTUVWXYZ
abcdefghijklmnopqrstuvwxyz

TIMES ROMAN SEMI-BOLD — STANLEY MORISON, MONOTYPE 1936

International Design Associates

Tokyo, Japan

Mari Makinami, Executive Creative Director
Hideo Hosaka, Project Designer
Doyald Young, Designer/Artist
Dentsu Inc. and Orbis Corporation
Yugashima Club Resort Logotype

Located in the resort area of Izu peninsula two hours from downtown Tokyo, Yugashima Club Resort is a Georgian-style complex surrounded by lush greenery and groves of rhododendron.

Georgian architecture suggested formal and baroque styles of the period, but the script and the bolder roman capital-and-lowercase was favored, in part because script is a popular style and suggests a resort atmosphere. *Yugashima* is related to Times Roman, though its thins are much heavier. It uses a footed *a* instead of the normal tail, and its beginning stroke repeats that of the *s*. The x-height is large, and the stem tops are horizontal instead of angled as in Times Roman. The serifs are short and bracket generously into the stems. The bowl of the *g* lacks an ear, an anomaly found also in Frederic Warde's Arrighi italic (opposite).

The casual single-weight script was carefully sized and judiciously drawn over the letters without creating fussy spaces.

1.

2.

3.

4.

Alpine Rose

Alpine Rose

International Design Associates

Tokyo, Japan

Mari Makinami, Executive Creative Director

Hideo Hosaka, Project Designer

Doyald Young, Designer/Artist

Dentsu Inc. and Orbis Corporation

Yugashima Club Resort

Alpine Rose Coffee Shop Logotype

Occasionally, a job is fun, whether because an ebullient mood is the driving force, or the particular assignment offers more than the usual possibilities. Here there was much to chose from, for the name is a European and Asiatic flower: Alpine rhododendron, cousin of the *edelweiss*.

The sketches opposite use the black letter (1); very romantic swash caps (2); a decorative sans (3); and an Optima neatly aligned with a looped swash *A* (the novel spelling *Alpin* was changed to the traditional *Alpine*). The one-line free-style script version was preferred and chosen for its informality, appropriate for a coffee shop/luncheon dining room. It employs some of my favorite treatments: a strong upstroke for the *A* and a wide beginning stroke for the *R*. As usual the *p* is not joined to the following letter to avoid massing at the bottom of the lobe.

1.

2.

3.

4.

The Black Bar

International Design Associates

Tokyo, Japan

Mari Makinami, Executive Creative Director
Hideo Hosaka, Project Designer
Doyald Young, Designer/Artist
Dentsu Inc. and Orbis Corporation
Yugashima Club Resort
The Black Bar Logotype

Monochromatic color schemes have intrigued many designers. Elsie de Wolfe and Syrie Maugham, wife of the famous novelist, both popularized all-white rooms in the twenties. Yugashima Club Resort's The Black Bar follows this tradition in a room sheathed all in black of different textures and materials.

The word *black* suggests a design direction. In the twenties, the French graphic designer A. M. Cassandre de-

signed a minimalist block letter that he used on posters. A version of that is shown opposite (1). Hand-tooled fonts were popular then. Known as gravure, they were originated by the eighteenth-century French founder Pierre Fournier. Chicago and Bodoni open are examples. A condensed variation is shown in number 4. The accepted version is an ultra-black, ultra-extended italic/script, with serifs bracketed like the original Bodoni.

La Marguerite

La MARGUERITE

La Marguerite

La Marguerite

La Marguerite

Preliminary pencil comprehensives.
Logotypes designed for a select, captive resort audience need not be bold and aggressive
and can be tailored to the esthetic needs of a specific amenity.

LA MARGUERITE

LA MARGUERITE

International Design Associates

Tokyo, Japan

Mari Makinami, Executive Creative Director

Hideo Hosaka, Project Designer

Doyald Young, Designer/Artist

Dentsu Inc. and Orbis Corporation

Yugashima Club Resort

La Marguerite Coffee Shop Logotype

Logotypes that are designed for a captive audience and that are not competitively advertised in the marketplace need not meet the rigorous demands for commercial attention. They can be designed with a lighter touch and still satisfy esthetic and printing requirements.

These particular letters offer an abundance of design possibilities: *L, M, T, e, g*. The horizontal strokes of the *L* and *T* and the diagonal of the *R* are easily transformed into restrained or ebullient swash shapes. These are often drawn with ogee curves. Without the design flexibility of two-weight letters, only the skeletons of the letters can be modified.

Lobes of the *R*s are held high, and they establish a visual grid line-up for the *E*'s center bar. The *M* and *A* are wide; the *G*'s straight stem is tall. The high center point of the *M*, the narrow *R* and *E*, and the *L, R,* and *T* add style to the word.

LE ROSAGE

1.

2.

3.

4.

International Design Associates

Tokyo, Japan

Mari Makinami, Executive Creative Director

Hideo Hosaka, Project Designer

Doyald Young, Designer/Artist

Dentsu Inc. and Orbis Corporation

Yugashima Club Resort

Le Rosage Restaurant Logotype

Le Rosage is the French word for azalea and rhododendrons. The choice for the main dining room's logotype borrows its style from the resort's signature logotype (page 153), and it is married to the same overlapping linear script (4).

There is a tradition of formal script for matters epicurean. The magazine *Gourmet,* an arbiter of taste, employs a formal script for its masthead and some

features, and many an over-scaled menu, whether it is luncheon or dinner, makes use of formal script.

In design 2 the script is baroque, overly fancy, ornate, encrusted with swirls and loops that are carefully designed to fill spaces and that optically align with the script's angle. The caps' alignment is jogged and tailored for a desired shape; their sizes are different— all acceptable within the confines of a logotype design. A more reserved approach, a hand-drawn version of Hermann Zapf's Palatino swash caps, is used in the first design. A small cap *E* is used in *Le,* aligning at cap height instead of the baseline. The arm of the *L* underscores the *E,* and the swash of the *R* lends importance to its beginning. I like to use a swash on a letter at the syllable break

because it often aids legibility. In this case the *S* falls in the center of the word, emphasizing its formality.

Design 3 is a classic roman, familiar on Georgian buildings, with the traditional narrow letters of the *E* and *S* exaggerated. The round forms *O* and *G* follow proportions of the Trajan roman.[1] It is thought that the Romans based their alphabet on a square (hence the name *quadrata*); the *N* is drawn to fill a square, and the *O* is almost a circle. The *A* is also wider than normal. The Trajan *R* is divided in half, but here the lobe is higher and its open waist is joined by the diagonal tail that descends below the baseline. The *R* follows Hermann Zapf's Palatino.

1. See Frederick W. Goudy, *The Capitals From the Trajan Column at Rome* (New York: Oxford University Press, 1936).

International Design Associates

Tokyo, Japan

Mari Makinami, Executive Creative Director
Hideo Hosaka, Project Designer
Doyald Young, Designer/Artist
Orbis Corporation Corporate Logotype

Yugashima Club Resort is one of many properties owned by Orbis Corporation. Their major thrust continues to be projects where ecology is of prime concern. The leaf symbol was chosen to reflect this interest and became an integral part of the logotype.

The final design, shown at the top, is a classic roman form, openly spaced with sturdy thin strokes. Lobes of both the *R* and *B* diminish to a hairline at the juncture of the diagonal and lower lobe respectively. The lower lobe of the *B* is slightly wider than normal. With parallel rigid stems that gently flare into a softened bracketed serif, the style is reminescent of Friz Quadrata.

Comprehensive number 1 is a semi-stencil sans serif with an overbalanced *S*; number 2 is a high-contrast thick/thin Optima with a romanized italic *b* and a decidedly old-style weight distribution along its lobe. Number 3 is a mixture of Avant Garde and Handel Gothic; number 4 is a light classic italic with a swash *S*. Number 5 mixes a widened Garamond *S* with flattened spurs, an *R* referenced to Palatino, and the general color and proportion of Richard Isbell's Americana for ATF. Number 6 has an overbalanced *S*, a high-waisted *R* and *B*, and qualities of Egon Weiss's Weiss roman.

1.

2.

3.

4.

5.

6.

Cosmetics

Cosmetics

JO-ANN STABILE
Creative Director, Max Factor & Co.
Los Angeles, California

IT SHOULD BE EMPHASIZED that a buyer makes a purchase based on the mood of a package. The success of a fragrance, cosmetic, or skin or hair care product is dependent on the marriage of design, logotype, color, shape, material, *and* advertising. "Two-thirds of the initial success of a perfume lies in its name, its design and promotion. Only one-third is actual fragrance."[1]

If the product is mass market (unkindly known as low-end), the name must be strong and legible to carry its message effectively to a hurried supermarket or drugstore shopper. Such products are usually displayed in racks in supermarket and drugstore aisles and must sell themselves. Their product names are usually generous in size and boldness—they must shout, for some customers have poor vision, yet they must project quality and elegance in a crowded environment, where as many as four-dozen products demand shelf space.

A logotype design may begin with twenty to thirty sketches, often establishing the package design direction; alternatively, the design and logotype are developed together. For a greater size advantage, a long logotype or product name can run uphill. Script logotypes are popular and are usually spirited and free-styled, particularly those products that are targeted to a youthful market.

Small products for eye makeup are the greatest challenge for the designer, for the logotype must be reduced and reproduced on difficult materials to dimensions as small as one-eighth inch in height. It must be legible, even if the name is extravagant in length, and in one line— "Splish Splash Water-Proof Mascara." This same minuscule logotype must also be attractive and seductive at a three-inch height for full-color counter placards.

Printing techniques burden a logotype's design. The limitations of silkscreening and foil stamping make it difficult to reproduce a fine hairline letter at one-eighth inch in height. These same restrictions apply to glass and plastic containers whose registration limitations of one sixty-fourth of an inch often influence the logotype's shape and style. Finer artwork is required for foil stamping to prevent clogging in small areas on plastic materials that tend to spread with heat.

Expensive high-end products—fragrances and special skin-care products that are sold in department stores—are traditionally low-key in design, subtle, conservative, and are often embellished with elegant graphics. In this *haute couture* environment, the formal scripts, the light condensed romans, and the lithe sans serifs are *de rigueur.* These products are heavily advertised in print media and television and rely on quick recognition for their purchase. Always displayed behind a counter, they must be shown by a salesperson. Rarely avant-garde design, these packages and their logotypes reflect a timeless understated elegance.

---

1. Maurice Roger, president of Christian Dior Perfumes, in a *New York Times* story (November 9, 1991) reporting on the splashy introduction of Dior's *Dune* fragrance at Nicolas Fouquet's seventeenth-century Château de Vaux-le-Vicomte.

Opposite—
Detail of unpublished
Max Factor monogram
(see page 182).

Aquarius

ABCDEFGHIJKLMNOPQRSTUVWXYZ
abcdefghijklmnopqrstuvwxyz

MODERN NO. 216 BOLD ITALIC — ED BENGUIAT, ITC 1982

Max Factor & Co.

Hollywood, California

James Engelmann, Creative Director
Carolyn Morrow, Art Director
Doyald Young, Designer/Artist
Aquarius Bath Product Line Logotype
(introduced in the late 1960s)

This line of cosmetic bath products was introduced in response to the romantic movement of the 1960s. The logotype was always used in combination with a highly stylized drawing of Hebe, the water carrier of Greek mythology.

A design of soft, flowing letterforms, though not necessarily script ones, was requested. While the strokes at the top of the cap *A* are very rigid, its incipient volutes help soften the shape. It is part script, part italic. The medium-bold image was printed in a light blue color that required strongly weighted strokes with substantial thins to be easily read, and especially to hold in very small reductions. The *Q* is a capital aligning with the lowercase. Pothook beginnings of the *u*s and *r* are from nineteenth-century moderns; Modern No. 216 is a redrawing. For even color spacing, the pothook of the *i* has been deleted. The normally circular shape of the *r*'s terminal employs a calligraphic pen shape. This shape is repeated on the top and bottom curves of the *s*.

ABCDEFGHIJKLMNOPQRSTUVWXYZ

abcdefghijklmnopqrstuvwxyz

CORONET — R. HUNTER MIDDLETON, LUDLOW 1937

Max Factor & Co.

Hollywood, California

James Engelmann, Creative Director
Ray Perez, Art Director
Doyald Young, Designer/Artist
Born Rich Logotype
(market-tested in the early 1980s)

A terrific name for a fragrance, one that satisfies any number of fantasies. The script style is pure twenties and thirties—a bleached-blonde Constance Bennett sheathed in white satin.

Coronet is one of the "social faces" that is still used extensively for announcements and invitations. In the 1930s it was in the type case of every small-town printer throughout the land. Lucky Strike cigarettes used similar scripts in advertisements as a lure for the sophisticated.

Coronet's x-height is small and its caps are wide; it is called script but in actuality is a disconnected italic (not all italics possess a roman). This version is different, though its basic design is similar. The connected thins are weighted for small-scale reproduction. The caps are wide. It is lighter in weight, more condensed, and more like handwriting than the typeface. The ascender of the *h* is rigid and relates to the cap's stems. The dot of the *i* floats to avoid the cap *R*. For variation, the stem of the *R* is short.

California Blonde

California Blonde

Max Factor & Co.
Hollywood, California

James Engelmann, Creative Director
Ray Perez, Art Director
Doyald Young, Designer/Artist
California Blonde Logotype
(introduced in the late 1970s)

Light, casual scripts usually suggest fashion and are conversational in tone. They are often used for quotations; in that context they are usually stylized versions of handwriting. Mostly they strive to convey style and flair.

This treatment for a hair-tinting product is casual but drawn with a rather formal weight distribution. It aligns visually but has a very slight bounce. Some of the letters change size—for instance, the first *a* lobe is enclosed and the second drawn smaller, with an opening. The logotype employs some italic forms: *o, r,*

and *e.* The pothook of the first *n* tucks under the *r.* The stem beginnings have rounded tips for a soft and more feminine quality. Both caps and the *f* have beginning and ending pen strokes. The descender of the *f* is brutally shortened to avoid the graphics directly beneath it. As in many hand-drawn forms, the dots of the *i* s are low so as not to become lost. Many faces, both text and display, align the dots of the *i* s with ascenders.

california bronze

california bronze

ABCDEFGHIJKLMNOPQRSTUVWXYZ
abcdefghijklmnopqrstuvwxyz

RADIANT BOLD EXTRA CONDENSED — R.HUNTER MIDDLETON, LUDLOW C.1940

Max Factor & Co.

Hollywood, California

James Engelmann, Creative Director
Nelson Davis, Art Director/Designer
Doyald Young, Artist
California Bronze Logotype
(introduced in the late 1960s)

It has been suggested that the decorative arts mimic architectural fashions. Typography follows the pack, for the 1930s fell in love with skyscrapers and shared their enthusiasm with typeface proportions to match. There were many: Tower, Corvinus Skyline, Eden, Huxley Vertical, Radiant bold condensed, and ATF's Empire, which commemorated the May 1, 1931, opening of the Empire State Building.

California Bronze tanning cream touts California sunshine. The letter style suggests elegance, with its sleek narrow proportion that allows for a much larger image. While more condensed and less bold than Radiant, the lobed forms maintain a taut elliptical shape. The top of the *f* swings freely, unencumbered by the restrictions of font design, wherein a following ascender must be considered to prevent a misspacing. The lobe of the *a* flows smoothly into the stem, while the ascender of the *b* forms the *i* and makes a vertical ligature. Short strokes are added to the *z* for more even color.

Collagen Care

Collagen Care

Collagen Care

Collagen Care

**Vidal Sassoon and
Don Sullivan**

Beverly Hills, California

Lawrance Taylor, Director

Jo-Ann Stabile, Art Director

Doyald Young, Designer/Artist

Collagen Care Logotype

Two comprehensive designs to be used for market research for a line of skin-care products now owned by Don Sullivan.

The product name at top (opposite) is a casual script that has traces of the action of a rigger brush—one that is long and very flexible with a flat tip. Held at a normal writing angle it will produce a generous amount of weight around the top and bottom curves of the letter. By contrast, a pointed brush held at the same angle will produce a thinner stroke at the center of the curve's turn, depending on the amount of paint in the brush and whether the brush has spread from usage. These letters align somewhat regularly at their base, but the heights change radically, creating in effect a bouncing look. The lobes of the *o, a,* and *g* are open and taper sharply. Hurried handwriting produces much the same effect, though not as extreme.

The lower example is composed of brush letters — ones that are not usually connected and are not as cursive (connected and flowing). Here it seems natural to join the *en.* While the bottom curves of the *C*s and *o* thin somewhat, the rigger-brush quality is evident in the bottom turns of the *es* and *n.* The cap *C*s descend.

Many compromises must be made in the design of casual script types. Murray Hill,[1] designed by Emil Klumpp for American Type Founders in 1956, was a successful and popular font, but in the strictest sense it is not a true script because its letters do not connect.[2] The letters are upright script forms, and no attempt has been made to connect them. Some dry-transfer and photolettering faces have done this but with more restrained letterforms. In order for the script to appear spontaneous, the letters must change size, and there must be subtle variations in the spacing, or it will look monotonous and mechanical. The easiest way to effect a casual quality is to enlarge the round forms. There must be variations in these sizes and ultimately multiple or alternate forms. Once these beasts are tamed, a typographer who is sensitive to the nuances of script must be found to create words that are well balanced, without groups of large and small letters.

It is more practical to handletter script forms because the letterforms can be tailored for weight and designed to fit. It is a general rule that capitals must be exuberant, both in expression and in scale, for in effect they carry the memorable shape and image of the logotype.

---

1. Reputedly named after a New York telephone exchange before numeric dialing. Mac McGrew, *American Metal Typefaces of the Twentieth Century,* preliminary edition (New Rochelle, New York: The Myriade Press, 1986), page 243.

2. There is much disagreement about the definition of script forms. Jaspert, Berry, and Johnson in their superb *Encyclopaedia of Type Faces* define script as imitative of cursive writing, page xv.

MURRAY HILL — EMIL KLUMPP, ATF C. 1956

*ABCDEFGHIJKLMNOPQRSTUV
WXYZ& abcdefghijklmnopqrstuvwxyz 1234567890*

Colorific

Colorific

ABCDEFGHIJKLMNOPQRSTUVWXYZ
abcdefghijklmnopqrstuvwxyz

(FIRMIN) DIDOT — DEBERNY & PEIGNOT 1784

Vidal Sassoon

Beverly Hills, California

Lawrance Taylor, Director
Jo-Ann Stabile, Art Director
Doyald Young, Designer/Artist
Colorific Logotype
(introduced in the early 1980s)

A mass-market product—a mousse packaged in a slender aerosol can with a minimum amount of space in which to wrap

a longish logotype. The x-height is large in an effort to gain maximum size for attention in supermarket aisles. It is a style reminiscent of the *Vogue* magazine masthead (see page 42).

Colorific is Bodoni bold condensed with elongated bracketed Didot terminals occurring on the cap *C*, the *r, f,* and *c.* To even the color spacing, the *r*'s terminal has been slimmed and canted. The *C* is a lowercase form, and the *f* is an

italic form. Because the letterspacing is tight, an *fi* ligature is used, and the serif of the first *i* has been deleted.

The logotype is a blended word, called a "portmanteau" (traveling bag) by Lewis Carroll, creator of *Alice in Wonderland,* who wrote, "You see, it's like a *portmanteau*...there are two meanings packed up in one word." To illustrate typographically, the logotype is "Didoni"—a combination of the styles Didot and Bodoni.

CORDAY

CORDAY

ABCDEFGHIJKLMNOPQRSTUVWXY&Z

TRAJAN REGULAR — CAROL TWOMBLY, ADOBE ORIGINAL 1989

Max Factor & Co.

Hollywood, California

James Engelmann, Creative Director
Ray Perez, Art Director/Designer
Doyald Young, Designer/Artist
Corday Logotype
(introduced in the early 1980s)

A redrawn logotype for Corday, creators of a famous French fragrance, *Toujours Moi*. A classical form with condensed pro- portions, the logo is related to that group of classical faces that includes Centaur (see page 211). Centaur was designed by Bruce Rogers as a titling font for the Metropolitan Museum of Art.[1] Based on Nicolas Jenson's classic roman, it was is- sued by Monotype in 1929 accompanied by Frederic Warde's Arrighi italic. Carol Twombly's Trajan follows this classical tradition. The logotype's serifs are heavily bracketed and blend deeply into the stem. The spur of the *C* has been soft- ened. The *R* and *Y* are exuberant swash forms. Claude Garamond is thought to have first used them for his italic types in the sixteenth century to fill the space created by italics on a rectangular piece of metal. Many old-style fonts have in- corporated the swash caps as alternates.

1. Joseph Blumenthal, *Bruce Rogers, A Life in Letters,* (Austin: W. Thomas Taylor, 1989), pages 32–33.

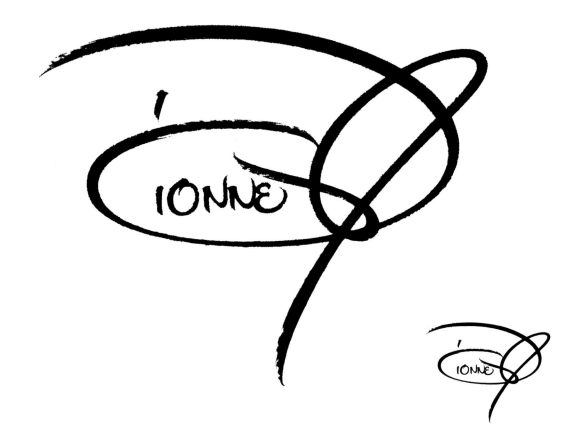

Dionne Warwick

Dionne Warwick, President
Beverly Hills, California

George Brown, Art Director
Doyald Young, Artist
Dionne Signature Logotype

A signature logotype designed for one of
pop music's legends. It is for a fragrance
first introduced by the bastion of chic—
Neiman Marcus, Beverly Hills. Fragrances

that employ a personal signature for a
logotype—bijan, Giorgio, and Cher are
recent ones—require skillful packaging
and even more skillful marketing to be
successful, for the signature is a very personal statement and in many cases difficult to read, relying only on word shape
for recognition. Many gain identification
only by extensive and repetitive advertising with the full name spelled out in the
ad. This exuberant example was modi-

fied from a ballpoint pen signature of
Dionne Warwick. The single-weight qualities produced by the ballpoint have been
transformed into a brush letter with dry-
brush texture.

This highly personal signature is unusual in that the *D* and *N* are capitals and
the *i*, lowercase; the *O* and *E* are ambiguous and can be read as cap or lowercase.
The effect is of a monogram where letters
vary in size, and the spacing is disparate.

ABCDEFGHIJKLMNOPQRSTUVXYWZ

MICROGRAMMA BOLD EXTENDED — A. BUTTI AND ALDO NOVARESE, NEBIOLO 1952

Don Sullivan, Inc. (Vidal Sassoon)
Beverly Hills, California

Lawrance Taylor, Director
Jo-Ann Stabile, Art Director
Doyald Young, Artist
Corporate Signature

Vidal Sassoon's professional-line products are marketed in beauty-care salons in Canada and the United States under the name Don Sullivan, Inc. The original Vidal Sassoon salon products were developed by Mr. Sullivan.

This is a redrawn and modified version of the original logo. For greater legibility the *D* was drawn more roundly, and a slightly heavier weight was used. Its design heritage is Microgramma bold extended. The broken curved lobe of the *D* creates a ligature with the *S* and is reminiscent of a Möbius strip. The center stroke of the *S*, as in most traditional alphabets, is placed above center for optical balance, as well as to clear the connecting stroke from the *D*.

The stylish script with large capitals is based on Mr. Sullivan's hurriedly written signature, redrawn for greater legibility. This is a favorite ploy, especially in the fashion industry, where a signature implies a one-of-a-kind original—that which is custom and special.

Eldona

ELDONA

1.

4.

eldona

Eldona

2.

5.

Eldona

Eldona

3.

6.

*Comprehensives
reduced to the same horizontal
width for a size comparison.
The client and Dentsu Advertising
selected numbers 1, 3, and 4
for market-testing
on packages.*

ELDONA

7.

Eldona

Eldona

ABCDEFGHIJKLMNOPQRSTUVWXYZ
abcdefghijklmnopqrstuvwxyz

(FIRMIN) DIDOT — DEBERNY & PEIGNOT 1784

International Design Associates

Tokyo, Japan

Mari Makinami, Executive Creative Director
Hideo Hosaka, Project Director
Doyald Young, Designer/Artist
Mikimoto Pharmaceutical Co., Ltd.
Eldona Skin-Care Product Line Logotype

Prestigious lines of cosmetics are sold to very affluent Japanese women in their homes by appointment only.

Eldona is based on modern letterforms and is another combination of Bodoni and Didot. Firmin Didot popularized his modern letter in France around 1800, and Bodoni's specimens predate Didot by thirty years. The Didot influence is evident here in the teardrop terminal of the **a** (Bodoni's is circular). The initial pencil sketches were drawn much the same weight. With the exception of the cap in number 3 (opposite), the letters are very simple and restrained shapes, relying mainly on taller-than-cap ascenders and nuances of letterform design for the quiet elegance that was requested. The word has a special balance between its weight, its proportion, and its letterspacing. These negative spaces (inside and between the letters) appear optically equal and create an even color, enhanced by straight-to-curve spacing repetitions that make for easy reading.

1.

4.

7.

2.

5.

8.

3.

6.

9.

*Comprehensive logotype sketches
for a full cosmetic line.
Reduced approximately 50 percent.
Numbers 1, 2, and 7 were inked
for package market testing.*

10.

11.

14.

17.

12.

15.

18.

13.

16.

19.

International Design Associates

Tokyo, Japan

Mari Makinami, Executive Creative Director

Doyald Young, Designer/Artist

Shu Uemura Cosmetics, Inc.

iks Logotype

First presentation pencil sketches to the client for a full cosmetic line targeted to a youthful, affluent market. "iks" is a working name for the proposed line of products. The assignment allowed for trial of an enjoyably wide variety of directions, from simple austere sans serif shapes (10), to bold romantic art nouveau letters (15), overlapping ligatures (7, 9, and 14), decorative pen-striped sans serifs (1, 2, and 5), and the fashionable revival of

gravure, or hand-tooled, letters (8). The lowercase *k* with its normally straight diagonals has been changed into the lobed forms of the italic (3, 9, 14, 16, and 19). Number 3 uses the sixteenth-century calligraphic terminal of the ascender drawn with a slight ogee curve.

The short three-letter word consists of the basic building blocks of the alphabet: verticals, diagonals, and curves, all variable in weight, proportion, and style.

Intrinsica

Intrinsica

ABCDEFGHIJKLMNOPQRSTUVWXYZ
abcdefghijklmnopqrstuvwxyz

TORINO (ROMANO MODERNO) — NEBIOLO C. 1908

Max Factor & Co.

Beverly Hills, California

Jo-Ann Stabile Creative Director
Doyald Young, Designer/Artist
Intrinsica Logotype
(introduced in 1985)

An elegant play on the word *intrinsic,* coined for a line of skin-care products, this type style borrows much from Nebiolo's elegant and enduring Torino, a re-drawing of condensed nineteenth-century moderns. In this instance the italic form has been drawn upright in a roman orientation. Despite their often austere, brittle appearance, Torino, Didot, and Bodoni have long been popular in graphics and advertising for cosmetics.

For a softer appearance, the stem weights have been blended more gradually into the hairlines than in the types. The word is rather snugly spaced—as al-ways in an effort to get as much mileage from the size as possible within a very small area. Most letters connect, yet the style does not give the impression of a script face, because the *n*, *i*, and *r* have hairline serifs. Both *s* and *c* have the bracketed teardrop terminals of Didot.

The slightly weighted ornamental hairline flourish attached to the *i* is an embellishment used to happily fill the space created by the terminal of the *r*.

Max Factor & Co.

Hollywood, California

James Engelmann, Creative Director
Bert Pearse, Art Director
Doyald Young, Designer/Artist
It's My Affair (market-tested in the early 1980s)

The name chosen to market-test a fragrance for the liberated woman, introduced to compete with Revlon's enormously successful *Charlie. It's My Affair*

was tested by Max Factor's marketing department, who first considered *Just Call Me Maxi,* and finally *Maxi,* as the product name.

Written with a number three Winsor & Newton series seven brush many times, combinations of letters were then selected for size, weight, angle, and consistent style, cut out, assembled, and retouched. As in most free-style scripts, the letter angles vary slightly, the letters

change size, and there is an unpremeditated bounce. The spacing, too, has a subtle random quality that helps create a feeling of spontaneity. Generally, in a normally spaced script, whether formal or casual, the letters will contain more counter, or interior, space than the space between letters. This rule does not apply to very bold or extremely condensed scripts or to the greatly extended styles that attempt to mirror the fashionable.

*Below—The original script cartouche
designed in the late 1950s.*

Max Factor & Co.

Hollywood, California

James Engelmann, Creative Director
Bert Pearse, Art Director
Doyald Young, Designer/Artist
*MF Monogram and Monogram Cartouche
Market-tested in the late 1960s*

In addition to container shape and color,
many lines of cosmetics packaging rely
on type or letterforms for their image.

Often a subordinate decorative element
is used to convey elegance and quality.
Abstract, monogram, or cartouche, the
embellishment is used to strengthen and
enrich the over-all design.

This cartouche was the result of over
sixty-odd sketches. No firm parameters
were given for letter style, but there was a
general agreement that script was probably the best direction. An attempt was
made to reference the original design,

hoping for acceptance based on slight
familiarity. It was necessary to make both
letters read equally. The design is a simplified extra-bold formal script with beefy
hairlines to hold in reductions. Careful attention was given to the balance of white
space to prevent very small areas from filling in reductions as small as the end of a
lipstick applicator. The greatly explored
project was never resolved, and the original script cartouche is still used today.

MONSIEUR

MONSIEUR

ABCDEFGHIJKLMNOPQRSTUVWXYZ

BASKERVILLE BOLD — C. H. GRIFFITH, LINOTYPE 1939

Max Factor & Co.

Hollywood, California

James Engelmann, Creative Director
Ray Perez, Art Director/Designer
Doyald Young, Artist
Monsieur (introduced in the late 1970s)

One of the few lines of men's toiletries that Max Factor produced, this is dressed up with a French name, revealing the common perception that French im-ports are special. The choice of type is almost right, for John Baskerville's work originally found little admiration in his native England. After his death, his punches were sold to the French, who had long admired his work. In 1953 the punches were presented to Cambridge University Press by Deberny & Peignot.

This redrawing of the illustrious letter adjusts the proportion to a more even set and then weights the thin strokes generously. The serifs are shortened and pointed and blend deeply into the stems, much like Times Roman. The overbal-anced aspect of the *S* and *R* has been exaggerated, the *M* splayed and nar-rowed. It is tightly spaced for greater impact, but because of this it does not color well—the counters of *O* and *U* dominate and seem misproportioned. This is acceptable for style, and wide letters often bolster a logotype's image.

OVELAN

OVELAN

ABCDEFGHIJKLMNOPQRSTUVWXYZ

UNIVERS 63 — ADRIAN FRUTIGER, DEBERNY & PEIGNOT   1957

ABCDEFGHIJKLMNOPQRSTUVWXYZ

FRANKLIN GOTHIC WIDE — JOHN L. RENSHAW, ATF   C. 1952

OVELAN

OVELAN

International Design Associates

Tokyo, Japan

Mari Makinami, Executive Creative Director

Hideo Hosaka, Art Director

Doyald Young, Designer/Artist

Shu Uemura Cosmetics, Inc.

Ovelan Skin-Care Products and

Makeup Products Logotype

For the constantly expanding affluent, youthful market, the client requested a pristine sans serif design. Two versions were finally considered: a slightly extended single-weight sans serif (top) and a two-weight, light sans with overtones of Franklin Gothic wide (bottom).

The letters that make up the logotype are shapes that seldom change form from sans to sans. The differences here are changes of weight within the letter, proportion, and stroke overlap. In the top version, the crossbar of the *E* is considerably shorter than in Univers. The total word is more monotone than Frutiger's face, and it does not possess the clefts of white space at stroke conver-

gence that prevent ink from clogging in the smaller sizes. The same proportions have been used in the two-weight version. It is a troublesome word to space because *LA* is a spacing nemesis. This is difficult to overcome. The *A* can sometimes be narrowed, and the horizontal stroke of the *L* can be shortened, but for purists, a ligature is too often a bull's-eye. (I once had the honor of an audience with Jan van Krimpen at Joh. Enschedé & Zonen, and asked him what rules of proportion he used. "There are none," he replied.)

From 1903 to 1912 Morris Benton drew the family of Franklin Gothics for American Type Founders, where he was type director. Despite the types' nineteenth-century heritage, his vision was so complete that they have been the workhorse sans serifs of the twentieth century. He drew News Gothic, a lighter face, in 1908 (Adrian Frutiger has recently drawn a version of the News Gothic). Subsequently other designers and foundries introduced a succession of sans serifs: Erbar, 1922; Futura,1927; Venus, 1927; Gill

Sans, 1928; Metro, 1929; Tempo, 1930; Spartan, 1951; Helvetica, 1957; Univers, 1957; and Standard, 1960. All of them found a receptive market and, like all new good faces, were used in an exploding, saturating, numbing manner. Doggedly, Franklin Gothic survived the fashions—and in a sense it has never been equaled, despite its rather idiosyncratic branch and lobe joinings. I confess to an inordinate fondness for both the condensed and wide versions.

Benton designed the condensed and extra-condensed versions in 1906; the wide was drawn by John L. Renshaw in 1952, and the condensed italic by Whedon Davis in 1967.[1] In 1980 the International Typeface Corporation commissioned Victor Caruso to adapt the original 1903 Benton version to four new weights and, in 1991, David Berlow to create twelve new condensed weights.

---

1. Mac McGrew, *American Metal Typefaces of the Twentieth Century*, preliminary edition. (New Rochelle, New York: The Myriade Press, 1986), page 151.

FRANKLIN GOTHIC DEMI — VICTOR CARUSO, ITC 1980

ABCDEFGHIJKLMNOPQRSTUVWXYZ

PERLETEAR

PERLETEAR

PERLETEAR

PERLETEAR

PERLETEAR

PERLETEAR

PERLETEAR

Very tight pencil tissues, 80 percent of actual size.
International Design Associates requested three approaches:
a light sans serif, an ornate script, and a serifed letter. The sans was
to be "sharp and minimal." The logotype really designs itself
*because of the repetition of the **E**s and the **R**s.*

PERLETEAR

PERLETEAR

ABCDEFGHIJKLMNOPQRSTUVWXYZ

EMPIRE — ATF 1937

International Design Associates
Tokyo, Japan

Mari Makinami, Executive Creative Director
Hideo Hosaka, Project Director
Doyald Young, Designer/Artist
Mikimoto Pharmaceutical Co., Ltd.
Perletear Skin-Care Product Line Logotype

Perletear is a luxurious line of skin-care products for the fashionable, affluent Japanese woman. Restrained, formal, and elegant, the logotype is comfortably spaced and is similar to Empire but, for the sake of legibility and restraint, not as narrow or bold as Empire. (For my sensibilities, restraint is the essence of elegance and style.)

The lobe of the cap *P* is drawn more deeply than that of the *R* to help fill the negative space that it creates. The endings of the *L* and *E*'s horizontals widen subtly, creating minute serifs, and termi-nate with a slight diagonal. The crossbar of the *T* repeats the design finesse. To create an even color, the thin diagonal of the *A* is weighted. The lobes of the *R*s are not closed, and their curved stems diminish into hairlines where they join with the diagonal stroke. The tail has been changed from the vertical stem of the type to a traditional and more legible diagonal stroke. The *E*'s horizontals differ in length: medium, short, and long.

SASSOON

SASSOON

ABCDEFGHIJKLMNOPQRSTUVWXYZ

FRUTIGER 45 — ADRIAN FRUTIGER, STEMPEL 1976

Vidal Sassoon

Beverly Hills, California

Lawrance Taylor, Director

Jo-Ann Stabile, Art Director

Doyald Young, Designer/Artist

Sassoon D (introduced in the early 1980s)

Vidal Sassoon's entry into the mass market of dandruff shampoo, packaged in a vibrant blue bottle. This is a redrawing of Adrian Frutiger's eponymous face, de-signed in 1968 for the Charles de Gaulle Airport signage in Paris. Its system of numbered weights is also used for his Univers family: 45, 55, 65, 75, and 85. The logotype is lighter in weight than the original face, with a slight thick and thin quality to the letters; the horizontal stems, top and bottom curves, and the diagonal of the *N* are thinner than the vertical stems. (Many sans serifs are drawn this way to appear monotone.) The *N* and *O*s are wider than the type. The crossbar of the *A* is high, and its stems have a slight taper, thinning as they converge to avoid a mass of weight. Curved endings are vertical.

The concentric *D*s are based on R. H. Middleton's 1940s typeface, Radiant, for the Ludlow Typograph Company, manufacturers of handset type cast on multiple-slug-producing machines, once widely used in newspaper typesetting.

Vidal Sassoon

Vidal Sassoon

Vidal Sassoon

Vidal Sassoon

Vidal Sassoon

Beverly Hills, California

Lawrance Taylor, Director
Jo-Ann Stabile, Art Director
Doyald Young, Designer/Artist
Vidal Sassoon Script Signature
(market-tested in the 1980s)

Two test versions of a stylized Vidal Sassoon signature, used sometimes on products but mostly on collateral folders and information sheets that are enclosed with hair-care products. No attempt was made to follow the unique style of the original personal signature.

Instead of a rapid spontaneous execution, the script is premeditated. It has an irregular baseline and varying letter heights. Its weight is almost monotone, suggesting writing with a pointed brush held in an almost vertical position. The bolder version has a lowercase double-*s* that echoes the capital *S*. To avoid a rigid look, all stems must curve slightly. Because scripts follow the circular motion of overlapping loops, all downstrokes will have curves that are the left side of a circle and all upstrokes will follow the right-hand curve. The shape will vary depending on the width of the individual letters.

1.

2.

3.

4.

5.

6.

7.

Comprehensives for a personal logotype.
1. A redrawn, stylized signature.
2. Single-weight script with a sans serif cap **S**.
3. A variation of number 2, but as ultra-bold
thick and thin, and the selected logotype.
4. Another variation of number 2,
this time drawn as all lowercase.
5–7. Separate studies, with a more
formal approach that explores thick and
thin upright scripts, in a range of
weights and proportions.

Shu Uemura

Shu Uemura

ABCDEFGHIJKLMNOPQRSTUVWWXYYZ&
abcdefghijklmnopqrstuvwxyz fff fi fl g g j k p r r s y z æ ø ß

ÉCLAT SCRIPT — DOYALD YOUNG, LETRASET PREMIER SERIES 1984

International Design Associates

Tokyo, Japan

Mari Makinami, Executive Creative Director
Hideo Hosaka, Art Director
Doyald Young, Designer/Artist
Shu Uemura Cosmetics, Inc.
Personal Logotype

Shu Uemura is Japan's counterpart to Max Factor. Both became famous for cinematic makeup and then even more famous for their salons and cosmetics. There are now ultra-contemporary Shu Uemura Beauty Boutiques in Paris, New York, Tokyo, Hong Kong, and Century City, adjacent to Beverly Hills.

Shu Uemura wanted a personal logotype designed expressly for engraved stationery and calling cards and for an occasional informal business letter. The opposite page shows the development from his highly stylized personal signature to a stronger and simplified logotype. This was accomplished with the use of sans serif capitals with a bold extended script. The small capitals are an old-style idea and are not as tall as the *h*. The logotype is drawn freehand, with a slight flaring of the straight strokes.

Éclat, a bolder and more crisp version with very heavy secondary strokes and simple scriptorial capitals, was developed for Esselte Letraset (see page 252).

UltraLucent

Pencil comprehensive for initial presentation.

UltraLucent

ABCDEFGHIJKLMNOPQRSTUVWXYZ
abcdefghijklmnopqrstuvwxyz

RADIANT MEDIUM — R. HUNTER MIDDLETON, LUDLOW C. 1938

Max Factor & Co.
Hollywood, California

James Engelmann, Creative Director
Bert Pearse, Art Director
Doyald Young, Designer/Artist
UltraLucent (introduced in the late 1960s)

Another portmanteau logotype, from *ultra*, beyond, and *lucent*, glowing or clear, for a line of skin-treatment products for the domestic and international market.

By definition, the word demanded a clean, contemporary approach. A serifed letter with spindly thins was lacking in punch for application on very small packages. A two-word logotype was first considered. To gain more punch, the words were combined, which allowed the word to increase in size on the small packages and containers. For an emphatic beginning, the cap *U* was weighted on both sides, and to increase legibility, a cap *L* used. In place of curves, the tails of the *t*s and **a** are footed. The top of the **a** and the endings of the *c* and *e* finish with a widened horizontal and carry the same optical weight as the straight stems. Branches of the *u, r,* and *n* join deeply, and the vertical stem is narrowed at that joining point. The style is similar to Middleton's Radiant and Zapf's Optima, and the logotype's x-height is generous. (See page 218 for a showing of Optima.)

The Brand Name

The Brand Name

RAY ENGLE

President and Creative Director
Ray Engle & Associates, Designers
Los Angeles, California

THE DESIGN of logotypes for products offers the quintessential challenge to the graphic designer. The number of applications required for a manufacturer of a wide variety of consumer products presents a set of complex issues in itself. But these issues, coupled with the multitude of constraints established by marketing objectives, competition, product positioning, market research, focus groups, reproduction limitations, manufacturing restrictions, and the realities of the costs of production, add an even more formidable set of conditions. Then, factor in the personal tastes of the client. What remains is the ultimate design challenge to the designer.

I gaze with awe and admiration upon those few "successful" design programs that can integrate these constraints and limitations and still remain memorable and esthetically correct, as well as stand up to the many requirements necessary to survive in today's marketplace.

The role of the designer today is more a marketeer than an artist, and in the area of product design and product graphics this is indisputably the case. To gain preeminence in the supermarket is the real objective, and not the beautification of the shopping cart. Moving product is what pays the rent, not creating art for the marketplace.

This is all well and good except that the problem that arises for most design professionals is that these are not the reasons they became designers in the first place. Most designers pursued their careers because of a love for design, form, art, craft, and a desire to express this love to an audience. In other words, to give life to their creative talents.

There is an incipient danger in the designer becoming successful. The designer becomes the mass-market maven, the purveyor-of-product, and frequently ignores the esthetic sensibilites that initially attracted him or her to this profession. The design becomes trendy at best but more often banal. It lacks the integrity that allows it to endure the test of time—to be regarded as classic.

The designer must walk the fine line between meeting the expectations of the client—that of making a contribution to the bottom line—and maintaining and perpetuating the finely tuned sense of craft, demonstrating the desire to make this a more visually pleasing world and at the same time expressing oneself artistically.

I believe that the most successful examples of logotype design embody these attributes at the highest level—the competent execution of the task we were retained to perform with the sensitivity to people's needs, and the keen sense of craft coupled with creative drive.

Some of the examples that I regard as exemplary are the IBM logotype and design program, Westinghouse logotype and design program, Mobil logotype and design program, Canadian National Railways logotype and design program, *Avant Garde* magazine logotype, CBS logotype and design program, and Esprit logotype and design program.

Opposite—
Detail of Almonds Royale for Morinaga & Co. Ltd.
(see page 196).

Almonds Royale

Almonds Royale

Peanuts Royale

Peanuts Royale

ABCDEFGHIJKLMNOPQRSTUVWXYZ&

abcdefghijklmnopqrstuvwxyz 1234567890

GRAYDA — FRANK H. RILEY, ATF 1939

International Design Associates
Tokyo, Japan

Mari Makinami, Executive Creative Director
Doyald Young, Designer/Artist
Morinaga & Co., Ltd.
Nobuhiko Tashiro,
Corporate Director, A.K. Project
Almonds Royale, Peanuts Royale
Product Logotype

Logotypes for brand and product names stand the severest test when applied to small packages that are sold in supermarkets. Not only must they command attention and reflect the qualities of the product: their first obligation is to legibility.

Because the package size was small and the name must be large, it was necessary to force the logotype into a very condensed proportion. The ascenders of *Almonds* are taller than the cap for greater legibility; the *o* is unconnected to open up the word—this is repeated in *Royale*. When script forms are bold, there is usually too much weight carried around the bottom of the joining curves. Instead of trying to minimize this, which would create tiny radii, I chose instead to increase the carriage of weight as a design feature.

To create order, the joining strokes are all made at the same height, and they flow tangently into the following letter.

CHOC·O·CRISP

Choc·O·crisp

Choc·O·crisp

*A typical theater-lobby showcard poster from
the early 1930s that uses casual, relaxed letter styles
rendered with a flat-tipped rigger brush.*

International Design Associates

Tokyo, Japan

Mari Makinami, Executive Creative Director

Doyald Young, Designer/Artist

Morinaga & Co., Ltd.

Nobuhiko Tashiro,

Corporate Director, A.K. Project

Choc·O·Crisp Logotype

Choc·O·Crisp is a coined name, breezy, memorable, and aimed at a youthful market. These casual styles (and there are many) are important for a variety of products that demand a friendly image: toys, games, fast food, theme parks.

The top version owes much to showcard lettering (quick lettering for placards and signs) with its bold single-weight strokes and its relaxed stance.[1] Often showcard artists used a wide rigger brush

to double-stroke each stem, thereby exercising greater control of the letter, and then neatly squaring off the corners with the brush turned almost ninety degrees.

---

1. See, for example, *Martin's Complete Ideas for Signmen, Artists, Displaymen* (Galesburg, Illinois: Dick Blick Co., [IDEA-BOOK], 1960). It contains inventive letterforms for point-of-purchase display, theater-lobby posters, and a wealth of vigorous brush styles that were popular for more than fifty years. Many were based on quickly rendered art deco forms, for economy was paramount in the 1930s.

1.

2.

3.

4.

5.

International Design Associates

Tokyo, Japan

Mari Makinami, Executive Creative Director
Hideo Hosaka, Project Director
Doyald Young, Designer/Artist
Lumière S.A. (Kosuen Company, Ltd.) Logotype

Chateau Lumière, or House of Lights, is the oldest winery in Japan.

Designs 3, 4, and 5 (opposite) play on what is perceived to be a French typographic style to complement the name. The roman caps are modeled after Didot, a pristine style popular in France during the Empire period. Designed to be classical, the face originally was supported by typographic ornaments that are pure classic Greek.[1] These narrow French faces became very popular, and their popularity lasted well into the nineteenth century. When they are used with formal script the marriage is complete, because both rely on very thin hairlines and a modern stress for their curved stems. Thin hairlines are a drawback in packaging or advertising, because they fade with distance viewing (but note that stencil letters, which lack a portion of their thins, are easily read at a distance when seen on railroad cars). If the stems of a formal script are weighted sufficiently, the word will still be legible depending on its size, proportion, and spacing, because we tend to read these strokes first.

In the bottom sketch (opposite), the grave accent is used as a design element, particularly where it bisects the hairline rule that is designed to wrap around a bottle. The word *Lumière* is embellished by *Chateau,* which is drawn with sixteenth-century swash caps. The other designs impart a "wine look" with the use of formal script that in each case begins with extravagant capitals. The top design is underscored with the extended reverse curve of the *L*. The second design gains its distinction from the *L*'s initial voluminous loop that frames *Chateau*. Design number 3 is distinguished by its generous beginning hairline and an arching uphill finishing stroke.

The chosen design (below) is the boldest weight of all, and *Lumière* is larger than *Chateau* for emphasis. Its letterforms are simply drawn, with an absolute absence of fussiness, and rely only on weight, angle, proportion, spacing, and relative size to impart classic distinction and quality. *Chateau* is hand-drawn in a light condensed roman, with a double-serifed *C* and angled beaks for *T* and *E*.

1. D. B. Updike, *Printing Types, Their History, Forms & Use,* vol. 2 (Cambridge: Harvard University Press, 1937), pages 181–184.

introducing RCA's

Dimensia

Dimensia® is a registered trademark of Thomson Consumer Electronics, Inc. Reprinted with permission.

Design West, Inc.

Mission Viejo, California

Arthur Ellsworth, President and CEO
George Gaw, Vice-President and
Creative Director
Doyald Young, Artist
RCA/Consumer Electronics Division
David D. Tompkins,
Vice-President, Industrial Relations
Sound Systems Logotype

Felt-tip markers have provided an expressive medium for people who draw and design letters. George Gaw, creative director, once headed the Graphics/Packaging department at Art Center College of Design in Pasadena, and this product name is quintessentially his handwriting. He wrote it several times with a blunted felt-tip pen and then gave it to me to finesse, to even its color without destroying the spontaneous quality

of the writing. The original is not to be found, but the differences are very slight.

Its style suggests flair, drama, and the contemporary. Linear script is fused with fashion, whether it is for state-of-the-art sound systems, high-tech lighting fixtures, or *haute couture*. The rules of brush script apply to the felt-tip style: letters that bounce and change size; slight changes of angle and letterspacing; and forms that suggest a hurried execution.

Harmony

Harmony

ABCDEFGHIJKLMNOPQRSTUVWXYZ
abcdefghijklmnopqrstuvwxyz

RADIANT BOLD — R. HUNTER MIDDLETON, LUDLOW 1938

Leach, Cleveland & Associates
Architecture, Engineering and Planning
Los Angeles, California

Ron Cleveland, AIA
Sterling Leach, President/Art Director
Doyald Young, Designer/Artist
Harmony Logotype (unpublished)

Sterling Leach and his partners were architects for many different commissions: elegant department stores, shopping malls, museum exhibits; they were even consultants to the *Queen Mary* project for the city of Long Beach. A number of food-market chains found their talents indispensable, wanting them to design not only their buildings, but advertising and packaging as well. *Harmony* was designed for a food product. The let-

ter style is reminiscent of Radiant but with decidedly more thick/thin contrast. The logotype's x-height is extra large for prominent display on narrow cartons. With the exception of the *y*, all of the straight stems are angled away from the connecting branch to allow a deep joining without a massing of weight. The *m, n,* and *y* have symmetrical counters. In place of the standard thick and thin diagonals, the *y* has two vertical stems.

HENRY

HENRY

HENRY

HENRY

HENRY

HENRY

HENRY

HENRY
HENRY
HENRY
HENRY
HENRY
HENRY
HENRY

*A presentation that retains much of the original
logotype design (top), conceived to convince the client of the need
for a more contemporary and appropriate logotype for a
line of products for the building trades.*

HENRY

HENRY

ABCDEFGHIJKLMNOPQRSTUVWXYZ

EUROSTILE BOLD CONDENSED — ALDO NOVARESE, NEBIOLO 1962

Sheridan/Solon & Associates

Los Angeles, California

Mary Sheridan and David Solon,
Executive Creative Directors
Doyald Young, Artist
The Henry Company Product Logotype

Manufacturers of quality adhesives for the building trades and retail consumers, The Henry Company was reluctant to change its logotype when its product line was redesigned by Sheridan/Solon & Associates. This presentation cinched the deal. From a very weak art deco style, the shapes were gradually weighted, simplified, and drawn more structurally.

The *E* is semi-uncial, a transitional lowercase form dating from the tenth century, while the *R* has a lobe that is similar to Microgramma bold condensed, though its diagonal tail is reminiscent of Eric Gill's Gill Sans bold. The *Y* is essentially a lowercase form occupying the full cap height. The diagonal of the *N* does not completely overlap the verticals. The horizontal crossbar of the *E*, as in many bold faces, is thinner than the top and bottom horizontals to prevent the letter from assuming too much mass.

Microgramma, a titling face (caps only) was so successful that Novarese drew Eurostile, a corresponding cap-and-lower-case, in several proportions and weights.

WHITE KING

WHITE KING

Sheridan/Solon & Associates
Los Angeles, California

Mary Sheridan and David Solon,
Executive Creative Directors
Doyald Young, Artist
White King Corporation
(now Huish Detergents, Salt Lake City, Utah)
White King Soap® Logotype

Laundry soaps and detergents have a history of bold, shouting, aggressive product names, as if the bellowing would make dirt skedaddle. This design from Sheridan/Solon is more restrained than most, though its letters are still muscular, strong, squarish shapes that promise diligent thoroughness. Mary Sheridan has a penchant for shapes that are organized, relate to each other, line up, and in toto become a word shape, easily remembered. These were printed in bright ultramarine blue on a white background for maximum attention. The squarish letter style is biform, with a lowercase *t, e,* and *n* as an aid to legibility, character, and color. A cap *T* would admit space unlike the other spacing, while the lowercase *t* with its ascender is a stronger shape. The *N* maintains the repetitive pattern of the vertical stems, which allows adjustments of its proportion for the line-up.

Academia

Academia

EDWARD HUTCHINGS, JR.

Director of Publications 1952–1979
California Institute of Technology
Pasadena, California

I WORKED for a number of years as a writer and editor on general-circulation magazines in New York City before I got the chance to run a magazine of my own at the California Institute of Technology in Pasadena. In the beginning, this was a one-man operation, and it was a new and very heady experience to be responsible to nobody but myself. But there were new responsibilities too. I had to be my own editor, proofreader, ad salesman, photographer, layout man, and—something that had never before concerned me in the least—designer.

It is still painful to stumble upon my first attempts at magazine design. After some nights in the library and many visits to many print shops, I began to put out a respectable-looking—not great, not even very good, but respectable—publication.

In time I set up an office to produce all of Caltech's publications, and when I did that I knew I needed help. Which was how I met Doyald Young.

Our first assignment was to produce a new seal for Caltech. The original seal, the work of a Belgian designer, dated back to the twenties—and looked it. It showed two young men, wearing winged helmets and little else, racing through the clouds, while one youth (apparently, though not visibly, older than the other one) is passing the torch of knowledge to his fellow runner.

By the sixties, this seal was beginning to show its age. The Caltech students, in particular, were beginning to find it slightly risible—to put it politely. Eventually, the Caltech Board of Trustees appointed one of their number—the industrial designer Henry Dreyfuss—to work with Doyald and me to produce a new seal. Mr. Dreyfuss turned out to be very hard to please. Was that supposed to be a torch? It looked like a tulip to him.

The design was reworked until Mr. Dreyfuss could come up with no more objections. Not that he actually *approved* of it; he simply couldn't think of any more reasons to *dis*approve. The finished seal can be seen on page 210.

Doyald has gone on to work on many more Caltech assignments—besides the magazine (*Engineering and Science*), there have been bulletins, a pictorial history of the Institute, and stationery. One of the more interesting assignments was the design of a quarterly publication to be sent to donors during a Caltech fundraising campaign.

This was no vanity publication, listing prominent contributors to the Institute, but was instead a magazine about research and interesting people at Caltech. The material, more often than not, was adapted from *Engineering and Science*—simplified, broadened, and dressed up with more color and illustrative material.

The seal and mastheads for both the *Quarterly* and *Engineering and Science* established a graphic continuity for the Institute's publications—essential in the design of development brochures reflecting that Caltech is small, select, distinguished—in every way a special institution.

Opposite—
Detail of the
California Institute of Technology's
Quarterly *magazine masthead*
(see page 211).

Art Center College of Design

Art Center College of Design
Pasadena, California

E. A. Adams and Don Kubly,
Art Directors
Doyald Young, Designer/Artist
Diploma Lettering

In designing a logotype for this school's diploma, to be blind-embossed and used in a large size, emphasis was given to the traditional, historical, and even sentimental elements of the graduation ceremony, in deliberate contrast to the highly contemporary orientation of the school's curriculum.

"Tink" Adams, the founder of Art Center, had a fondness for the elegant formal scripts drawn for the *Ladies' Home Journal* magazine. The script was extremely condensed, with florid capitals, and was used for articles and story titles. This was modeled after that style, and though not as condensed, it is drawn with more restrained capitals.

The counters of the letters are only slightly wider than the space between the letters, yet appear optically alike, thus ensuring even color and legibility. The crossbars of the *f* and *t*s are drawn at the x-height. The descender of the *g* has been kicked out with a subtle ogee curve to allow for the high hairline joining. The *s* does not join the following letter.

A roman cap shown in Bodoni's 1818 Manuale Tipografico *illustrating his use of bracketed serifs.*

B

ABCDEFGHIJKLMNOPQRSTUVWXYZ

BODONI BOLD CONDENSED — MORRIS F. BENTON, MERGENTHALER LINOTYPE C. 1939

Alumni Association
Art Center College of Design
Pasadena, California

Jean Parry, Director
Project Coordinators:
Christopher Carr
Ramone Muñoz
Monica Predazzi-Florian
Doyald Young, Designer/Artist
Event Logotypes

The gala nature of the two events as well as the elegance and importance of the black-tie occasion suggested the combination of a formal typeface and a more carefree script.

The event names are drawn in a bold condensed Bodoni similar to Monotype's Bodoni bold condensed, though not as narrow. It is a formal, black-tie letter. The top of the *A* has been chopped to help fill the space. The bowl of the *R* is a bit smaller and higher. Unlike Monotype's version, the serifs have been bracketed in the same manner as the original showing in Bodoni's 1818 *Manuale Tipografico*.

The swanky script is freely written—handwriting in a sense, but weighted like a formal script—all very light. And like hurriedly written script styles, the letters change size, the spacing is bit irregular, there is a pronounced bounce, and the angles of the letters are purposely tilted.

1.

California Institute of Technology

Pasadena, California
Tom Branigan, Director of Public Relations
Paula Di Conti, Director of Public Relations

Edward Hutchings, Jr.,
Director of Publications 1952–1979
The Board of Trustees
Doyald Young, Designer
Midge Quenell, Artist
Final art (1960) inked by Donald Pepper
Centennial logotype:
Doyald Young and David Solon
Official Logotype

The official logo of a long-established and internationally renowned institute, its design has been slightly modified over more than twenty-five years, but cannot support major change.

The lettering of the 1960s logotype is a condensed Optima (1). Because the credo is long, it posed problems of legibility when smaller than one inch. By necessity it was tightly spaced and required a slight widening of the tops of the letters to create a more even color around the edge of the circle. The words at the top and bottom of the circle are drawn smaller in height to optically match the size of the words on the vertical portions of the circle. The present version, with a simplified torch (2, 3, 4, and 5), is set in Friz Quadrata, a beautiful classic roman face designed by Ernst Friz, winner of a Visual Graphics Corporation competition.

The type style is also used for stationery, business cards, and collateral as part of the Institute's identity program.

2.

3.

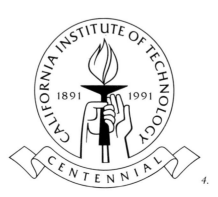

4.

1. The Institute's seal/logo designed in the early 1960s.
2. The official logo.
3. The official logo for reverse applications.
4. The official centennial logo.
5. Minimum size for reproduction. The logo at the right is used on the Institute's business cards.

5.

QUARTERLY

ABCDEFGHIJKLMNOPQRSTUVWXY&Z
abcdefghijklmnopqrstuvwxyz
1234567890

CENTAUR — BRUCE ROGERS, MONOTYPE 1929 (FIRST CUT 1914)

California Institute of Technology

Pasadena, California

Edward Hutchings, Jr., Editor
and Director of Publications (1952–1979)
Doyald Young, Designer/Artist
Quarterly Magazine

A magazine's name as it appears on the cover is called a masthead. This actual-size example was designed for a publication created for the Friends and Associates of the Institute, and complemented the Institute's official and more technical research magazine *Engineering & Science*.

The capitals are drawn freely from Bruce Rogers's Centaur, one of the most famous types of the twentieth century. It was designed in 1914 and first shown in a book of the same name published by the Montague Press (see page 173).

The proportions of **Quarterly** are more even than classical and are a bit narrow, with long cupped serifs. The tail of the **R** is drawn with a soft ogee curve similar to Baskerville. The crossbar of the **A** is higher than the Centaur and the **E**'s angled horizontal bar serifs parallel the angle of the crossbar of the **T**. Both are reminiscent of Hermann Zapf's Michelangelo, as is the **Y**. The tail of the **Q** is separated and drawn with exuberance. The cap letters are very light with a stem width:height ratio of 1:16.

OTIS|PARSONS
OTIS ART INSTITUTE OF PARSONS SCHOOL OF DESIGN

Above—*Camera-ready art for building sign (reduced).*
Below—*Actual-size gouache comprehensive, rendered on the presentation drawing of the façade.*

OTIS|PARSONS
THE OTIS ART INSTITUTE OF PARSONS SCHOOL OF DESIGN

ABCDEFGHIJKLMNOPQRSTUVWXYZ
abcdefghijklmnopqrstuvwxyz

VENUS EXTRA BOLD EXTENDED — BAUER 1907–27

The Otis Art Institute of Parsons School of Design
Los Angeles, California

Neil Hoffman, Dean
Doyald Young, Designer/Artist
Exterior Building Sign

When Parsons School of Design and The Otis Art Institute of Los Angeles became affiliated in 1978, it was necessary to establish a graphic representation of the combined institutions without sacrificing entirely the individual entities. For this building sign we chose the handsome face Venus extra bold extended, a grotesque introduced around the turn of the century. Its proportions are even and the lobes and crossbars are held high; the *K* in lighter versions appears to be on stilts. In this extra-bold version, there is a pronounced thick/thin quality. The crossbar of the *A*, because of the stem boldness, is by necessity very low. It was used extensively in the 1950s because of its variety of weights and proportions and because the public had grown weary of a twenty-year stint with Futura. The Standard series is similar but drawn with less flavor. Venus helped popularize the extended type fashion of the 1950s.

Helvetica was introduced in 1957 and was an immediate success. Venus then fell victim to the whim of fashion.

UCLA

UCLA

ABCDEFGHIJKKLMNOPQQRRSSTUVWXYZ

MICHELANGELO TITLING — HERMANN ZAPF, STEMPEL 1950

Morava & Oliver Design Office

Santa Monica, California

Morava & Oliver Design Office: Design
Art Direction: Douglas Oliver
Doyald Young, Artist
UCLA Logotype Design

The key element of a graphics identity program designed by the Morava & Oliver Design Office for the University of California at Los Angeles. The let-ters are derived from Hermann Zapf's unequaled Michelangelo titling face (in metal types, capitals that occupy the full face of the metal sort, which are often lighter in weight than their text face complement). Drawn in 1950 and modeled on Renaissance letterforms found in the Vatican and Laurentian libraries, it is a very light face with classic proportions, with a stem thickness to height ratio of 1:12 (Palatino is 1:9).

The logo was designed to repro-duce clearly in small sizes as a reversed image in a variety of printing methods. The letters are bolder than the typeface, so that it can be reduced easily without clogging. The *A*'s graceful crossbar is extended to overcome the most difficult spacing combination in all of the capital letters: *LA*. The serifs are longer than the original Michelangelo and end in a crisp diagonal for sharp reproduction.

THE FRIENDS OF THE GRAPHIC ARTS AT UCLA

Above—
Original colophon drawing.
Left—*Same-size pencil drawing*
used to test letter weight, spacing, and
proportion for small-size art.
Below—*Camera-ready art.*

ABCDEFGHIJKLMNOPQRSTUVWXYZ
abcdefghijklmnopqrstuvwxyz

BOOKMAN OLD STYLE — C. H. GRIFFITH, LINOTYPE 1936

The Friends of the Graphic Arts, UCLA
Suzanne Labiner, President

Dickson Art Center
Grunwald Center for the Graphic Arts
University of California at Los Angeles
Doyald Young, Designer/Artist
Colophon

Suzanne Labiner, president of the "Friends," defines the organization as "composed of persons who admire and collect prints and drawings and who support the Grunwald Center at UCLA out of sheer appreciation for the extremely high standards of scholarship and education that such a department provides for the community.

"The publications which the Friends make possible are sent to academic institutions throughout the world. They carry their message of high standards and scholarship in the graphic arts."

This is a cabochon shape and is reminiscent of a printer's mark or colophon (literally, finishing touch or summit). The letterforms are based on a combination of two typefaces: Morris Fuller Benton's Century Schoolbook, for the American Type Founders, and Bookman (from Miller & Richards), which was drawn as a bold face for Antique Oldstyle, an early name for the Egyptians. Swash capitals are used to fill the shape.

*Actual-size stamp for use
on rare prints and drawings,
with a registered isotope ink from
the Library of Congress to
guarantee ownership.*

ABCDEFGHIJKLMNOPQRSTUVWXYZ
abcdefghijklmnopqrstuvwxyz
1234567890

LUTETIA — JAN VAN KRIMPEN, ENSCHEDÉ 1923–24

University of California at Los Angeles
Dickson Art Center

Grunwald Center for the Graphic Arts
James Cuno, Director
Cynthia Burlingham, Curator
Doyald Young, Designer/Artist
Grunwald Center Colophon

The principal criterion in the design of this colophon was legibility in small sizes: its primary application was for a stamp less than half an inch wide on the backs of drawings and prints for the Grunwald Center's extensive print collection. The typeface is Jan van Krimpen's beautiful and seldom used Lutetia[1] (the classical name for Paris). The type design was modified for Porter Garnett for use in his 1926 Frick Museum catalog. A favorite typeface, it has the master's imprint of his other remarkable faces: Romanée, Romulus, Spectrum, Open Roman Capitals, and Cancelleresca Bastarda (see "Entertainment," page 53). The type was weighted for extreme reduction, and an ink with a numbered isotope issued from the Library of Congress is used with the stamp to guarantee ownership of the art.

---

1. The type was designed for Enschedé, and introduced at *L'Exposition Internationale des Arts Décoratifs et Industriels Modernes,* Paris, 1925. John Dreyfus, *The Work of Jan van Krimpen* (Haarlem: Joh. Enschedé en Zonen, 1952), pages 7–8, 23–28.

THE FRIENDS OF THE GRAPHIC ARTS AT UCLA

ANNUAL LECTURES

Delivered on the occasion of **Reading Hogarth**

An exhibition emphasizing the printing history, narrative changes, and narrative techniques in the prints of William Hogarth

MURRAY ROSTON

RONALD PAULSON

MAXIMILLIAN NOVAK

January 10 — March 13, 1988

GRUNWALD CENTER FOR THE GRAPHIC ARTS, UCLA

Hogarth's Aesthetics

RONALD PAULSON

The Johns Hopkins University

Above—One of the three same-size essay
headings with the mix of Baskerville lowercase
and Caslon italic swash capitals.

University of California at Los Angeles

Dickson Art Center

Grunwald Center for the Graphic Arts

James Cuno, Director

The Friends of the Graphic Arts, UCLA

Doyald Young, Designer/Artist

Typecraft Printers, Pasadena, California

Reading Hogarth

This small book records three lectures given on the occasion of an exhibition of Hogarth prints drawn entirely from the extensive collection of Suzanne and Gerald Labiner, curated by the late Professor Richard Vogler.

The headings are set in lowercase Baskerville italic, with Caslon swash capitals. I chose the ornate capitals to reflect the opulence of eighteenth-century typography. The mix does not match ex-actly, for the Caslon is bolder and has a greater lean (above). This is acceptable because even Baskerville caps are bolder than its lowercase. This design feature became even more pronounced in the Scotch Romans of the early 1800s.

The difference in angles reflects the design of many an italic face. Garamond, one of the greatest of all typefaces, has italic caps with many different angles, caused by trying to fit a leaning letter on a rectangular shape without creating an excessive amount of space on its right side (this has been solved with kerning programs in computer composition). This disparity of weight and angle becomes exaggerated when the type is set at a large size. So, I handlettered the title to match the angle and weight of the capitals to the lowercase (opposite). I drew the thins more finely than the small-er sizes of type (as all good display types should be) and rounded the pothook beginnings and endings slightly, carried more weight around the curves, and ta-pered the strokes for more sparkle. The small leaning ear of the original *g* was retained, the caps condensed and drawn with larger swash extensions. The tip of the top swash of the *H* was drawn to cor-respond to the *R*.

The fleuron is Monotype Corpora-tion's number 482—a beautiful geo-metric design from the original number 9 in the broadside dated 1776 by Isaac Moore & Co. Letter-Founders, Bristol.[1]

---

1. D. B. Updike, *Printing Types: Their History, Forms and Use*, vol. 2 (Cambridge, Massachusetts: Harvard University Press, 1937), fig. 276.

Opposite—The title page
from a publication by the
Friends of the Graphic Arts at UCLA,
recording three lectures that celebrated the
Grunwald Center's exhibition of
Suzanne and Gerald Labiner's collection
of Hogarth prints. The title,
a combination of two typefaces—
Baskerville and Caslon—has been hand-
lettered to match both the weight and the
angle of the ATF Baskerville.

The original setting of ATF Baskerville italic
married to Caslon's swash italic capitals with
divergent angles and weight.

ABCDEFGHIJKLMNOPQRSTUVWXYZ
abcdefghijklmnopqrstuvwxyz

OPTIMA — HERMANN ZAPF, STEMPEL 1958

International Design Associates

Tokyo, Japan

Mari Makinami, Executive Creative Director

Doyald Young, Designer/Artist

Tokyo Communication Arts

Corporate Logotype

This logotype, designed for a privately owned school in Tokyo, strives to convey contemporary functionalism within a traditional esthetic. It is based on Her-

mann Zapf's pristine Optima, issued in 1958 after a seven-year labor. It belongs to a group of two-weight sans serifs: Radiant (1940) and Stellar (1929), both designed by R. H. Middleton for Ludlow; Pascal (1960) designed by José Almeida for Amsterdam; and an earlier face, Globe Gothic, from Lanston Monotype, issued in 1918. Optima is based on classical proportions and is drawn less mechanically than the other typefaces,

with slightly flaring concave strokes. The logotype uses large capitals only slightly taller than the small capitals. The thins are finer than Optima. An uncial *U* has been introduced, and the *C* has been shortened at the bottom to allow the *A* to be drawn closer to the *C*. The *T*s have opposing angled terminations, and the diagonals of the *K* are separated from the stem. Its rather open letterspacing makes for easy reading in small sizes.

Scripts

Scripts

ALLAN HALEY

Vice-President, International Typeface Corporation

SCRIPTS are more than just simple letters on a page. Most letterforms—however beautiful or well designed—only communicate information. It is in combination with other graphic elements that they gain a personality or voice. Scripts, however, are emotional, passionate, even lyrical communicators. Words in script are a classic example of that special something in which the total is equal to more than the sum of its parts.

Scripts are among our most ancient communication tools. Before there were typefaces or fonts or printing presses, there were scripts. Introduced to most of Europe through the waging of war by the Romans, scripts were spread even farther by missionaries.

More than any other alphabets, scripts are tied to our daily lives. They certify our date of birth, they document our education, they express our love and proclaim our marriages. Promissory notes, deeds of trust, and certificates of accomplishment are all written in script. And finally, the announcement of our passing from this life is often displayed in script type.

Our freedoms, the Constitution and the Bill of Rights, are written in the finest of penmanships. At the seats of power the skills of the scribe are constantly on call: the White House and Buckingham Palace benefit from such masters of the written form.

Perhaps the most expressive of all letter styles, scripts reflect the mood of their writer, the sense of the time in which they are written, and the tools that create them. The rotund strength of the Gaelic minuscule is very different from the verve and passion found in sixteenth-century Spanish writing manuals, and both of these are distinct from the strong lateral flow of eighteenth-century Italian writing masters. The Papal Chancery influenced writing and lent its name to this enduring style. The copperplate scripts of England, so named because they were engraved in copper plates for printing stationery and calling cards, set a style still in use today.

Only within the last hundred years, however, have scripts been replicated as fonts of type. As the nineteenth century came to a close, type foundries began to release numerous script types based on free-flowing letters with strong contrasts of stroke weight, flourished capitals, and severely inclined angles. Many became widely successful advertising designs, others became the mainstay of social printing, while still others became the foundation of formal and legal documents.

Phototype gave scripts a new vitality. The myriad of technical difficulties present in rendering connecting letterforms in fonts of metal were eliminated with the simpler, less expensive method of setting type photographically.

Today, there are more script typefaces to choose from than ever before. From the exquisite revivals of past masters to electronically created forms by new-wave artists, the palette of scripts has never been as great or more diverse.

Opposite—
Detail of cartouche,
The Art of Steel Die Engraving
(see page 223).

Top—*The steel die for
embossed monarch letterhead.*
Bottom—*Monarch envelope die identified
and wrapped to prevent corrosion.*
Photo: Chris Fifthian

Virginia Legakes Adams
(Mrs. E. A. Adams)
Pasadena, California

Vice-Chairman, Board of Trustees
Art Center College of Design
Doyald Young, Designer/Artist

Virginia Legakes, the wife of "Tink" Adams, founder of Art Center College of Design, instructor of both color and illustration, program director, and now vice-chairman of the Board of Trustees, has been continuously involved in the school's activities since its founding in 1936. Formal script is a favorite, and this was designed for her personal monarch stationery (7¼ by 10½ inches), beautifully engraved, hand-finished, and embossed on Crane's kid-finish paper.

The caps are tall and descend deeply but do not align at their base. Uneven alignments are a personal choice; many type script caps align with the lowercase. The lower loop of the *L* finishes with an ogee diagonal curve that serves as a generous underscore. By choice, neither the ascenders or descenders are looped; instead they end with small teardrop shapes reminiscent of sixteenth-century forms. All of the lowercase is drawn as traditional forms, and only the caps with their elaborate, generous beginning and ending lines establish the logotype design.

The Art of Steel Die Engraving

Doyald Young, Designer/Artist

Cartouche (unpublished)

A cartouche is an ornate border found in baroque or rococo architecture as a bas-relief frame to contain a name, number, or street address. It was this device, a ring around Ptolemy's and Cleopatra's names,

that enabled Jean-François Champollion to decipher the Rosetta stone.

Conceived as the frontispiece for a facilities brochure for an engraver, this elaborate Spencerian cartouche (after Platt Rogers Spencer, a nineteenth-century American writing master) was formed by extensions of the letterforms only. It was designed to be showy and ornate, to set off the engraver's skill, with very condensed letters and caps that change size

to fill the circular design. There are no rules for this, for every design is a different problem, though the densities of the surrounding loops are best kept optically equal. I like to draw the major axes of the open looped curves parallel to the slope of the words, so that they are in harmony. This is personal preference. Less important words may be drawn smaller to emphasize the key words, and to further the design of the cartouche.

Margretta Melvin

Los Angeles, California

Margretta Melvin, Art Director
Doyald Young, Designer/Artist
Mark Bevan, MBA Monogram

A monogram designed to be engraved on silverware and stationery and embroidered on fine linens. Traditionally, monograms are vertically oriented, with one letter dominating. Almost circular, this shape is formed by extensions of the letters. The overall design is simplified for primary use in small sizes, and bound with a separate nuptial swash.

Composed of formal script capital letters that are often seen on Tiffany gold monogram rings, all of the strokes terminate with a slightly flared line. Boldest in weight, the lobes of the *B* are joined with a filled, minuscule loop. With the exception of the beginning stroke of the left loop of the *B*, all of the letter extensions that define the shape of the monogram are swelled with a third weight. Parallel to the nuptial swash, the large left volute of the *A* begins in a related ogee curve, which creates a visual base for the design.

Robert McKim and Company

Los Angeles, California

R. C. McKim, President and CEO
Doyald Young, Designer/Artist
The Brock Collection, Brochure Title

A custom home builder, Brock has left its elegant imprint on the sprawling hills surrounding Los Angeles.

Lettered for a sales brochure, the name is a casual, friendly brush script to match southern California's lifestyle. The spontaneous two-weight writing is a dry-brushed technique, aided and abetted by judicious retouching. To maintain the spontaneous quality, there are variations in letter size, very apparent in the caps, with the greatest emphasis on the *B*, with its expansive beginning lobe stroke. The name is emphasized further with an exuberant reverse ending stroke on the *k* that carries more weight than the rest of the lowercase. There is considerable variation in the bounce of the letters at the baseline. This can be planned with an up/down, up/down bounce relieved by an occasional interruption of the pattern. A long word like *Collection* may be broken intermittently, for it is difficult to load a brush with sufficient paint to write the word in one-inch letters in a continuous line. Many of the beginning strokes are spread, the effects of a loaded brush.

Carnation Company

Los Angeles, California

Quito Trujillo, Creative Art Director,
Corporate Merchandising

Quito Trujillo, Designer

Doyald Young, Artist

Point-of-Purchase Display Lettering

Supermarket aisles are filled with point-of-purchase display easels and signs that add to the staggering welter of images that confront a shopper. Designed by Quito Trujillo, this streamer script is for a point-of-purchase display easel for the introduction of a new product.

Actually more illustration than lettering, **Celebrate** is saddled with complex problems. Not only must it appear as a flowing streamer; it presents perspective problems that include diminished letter widths, streamer width, spacing, *and* a curving baseline! To read properly, it must appear to unfurl. This is accomplished by drawing large radii at the bottom of the turns. The rest is by eye—draw it till it looks right, or gradually angle the centerline of each letter as the word unfurls toward the viewer.

The large reproduction size was drawn with french curves for sharpness.

ABCDEFGHIJKLMNOP2RISTUVWXYZ
abcdefghijklmnopqrstuvwxyz

COMMERCIAL SCRIPT — MORRIS F. BENTON, ATF 1908

Rothstein & Memsic
Design for Corporate Communications
Los Angeles, California

Jerry Rothstein and Rick Memsic,
CEOs and Creative Directors
Rick Memsic, Designer
Doyald Young, Artist
Security Pacific Corporation,
Common Trust Fund
Brochure Lettering

Stocks and bonds, bank notes, and matters fiduciary connote money when lettered in script. Until recently, bank names and the information on checks were invariably set in script—there is even a well-known typeface called Bank Script. This title was for one of a trio of brochures, and it is bolder than usual to accommodate a reverse printed image.

The bold caps are elaborate and are centered on the lowercase x-height. The volutes of *T* and *F* are drawn to bisect the weighted stems of the *m* and *u* to avoid creating small areas of trapped negative space—unavoidable though, with the *Co* ligature. The *r* and *u* are enveloped with beginning strokes that start well below the baseline. The even color of the line is produced by the repetition of similar letters. Type designs were once tested using Latin phrases because of the preponderance of the letters *h,n,m*, and *u.*

Maddocks & Co.

West Los Angeles, California

Mary Scott, Creative Director
Carson Pritchard, Art Director
Doyald Young, Designer/Artist
Hitachi
Product Brochure Lettering

The age, size, and shape of the brush (pointed, flat, or angled), the density of the medium (gouache, ink, or watercolor), the amount of medium in the brush, the texture of the writing surface, the speed of execution, the angle at which the brush is held, and your particular self-possession at the moment—all these factors influence the shape, substance, and style of words written with a brush. This word is defined by

hurried writing, a semi-thick gouache, a number three Winsor & Newton brush, and a piece of textured writing paper.

Designed to enliven a brochure cover for the introduction of a new television model, *Digital* is formed of five separate breaks: D-i-g-it-al. These breaks were determined by how many times the brush had to be filled to produce the word, in turn determined by the length, height, and weight of the word.

Dailey & Associates, Advertising

Los Angeles, California

Bill Parsons, Art Director/Designer
Doyald Young, Designer/Artist
Advertising and Souvenir Products Logotype

The extreme boldness and angle of this condensed script/cartouche has been used primarily for magazine advertising and for printing on souvenir items sold at the racetrack gift shop.

The trick with a cartouche is to surround the words naturally, to make it appear as though it is an integral part of the design. It can be accomplished two ways: by using an independent shape of flowing lines and loops, usually greater in negative volume than the letters themselves, or with lines that are natural extensions of the letters, or with a combination of both. The extensions and additions may be drawn as a line of constant thickness, or they may assume the swelling, either slight or moderate, that occurs in formal script, particularly in the secondary weights found on the extensions of capital letters. Small loops should be avoided: they tend to be undesirable bull's-eyes.

L'Épicure

Robina Begoumian

Los Angeles, California

Steven R. Moore, Art Director

Doyald Young, Designer/Artist

L' Epicure Restaurant

Corporate Logotype

Belle époque, style of the halcyon days before World War I, was suggested as a design theme by Steven Moore for the logotype of this restaurant on La Cien-ega Boulevard's restaurant row, only blocks from Beverly Hills.

The chosen design (above) is not *belle époque* but of the Empire period and is based on the roman popularized by Fimin Didot in France, used extensively in the late nineteenth century.

The example is a classic admixture of styles, a leaning script form against a formal two-weight serifed roman with condensed proportions. The letters are drawn simply, with no idiosyncrasies, relying only on contrast of fonts and an overlapping traditional formal script *L* for distinction.

The top version (opposite) is more accurately of the *belle époque* period, which was gradually relaxing after the firm grip of Victoria, in manners and morals. The style relies on exaggerated shapes with swash endings and a cap *E* embellished with an intertwining loop.

Faces
about town

Victoria Creations

Warwick, Rhode Island

Robert Andreoli, President and CEO
Robert Keene, Art Director
Doyald Young, Designer/Artist

Faces about town, Restaurant
Corporate Logotype

The lowercase letters *a, c, e* of *Faces* are italic forms that are joined to become script. An italic swash form, the *s* descends to create a frame for the lower line of italics. Because the x-height is unusually large for scripts, the name can be used successfully as a display face. The lower line of italics, ***about town***, is a hand-lettered version of Baskerville italic, slightly extended, with an angle parallel to the angle of *Faces* with heavier thin strokes for reduction. Additionally, the boldness accommodates reverse images and the demands of foil stamping.

Script typefaces and italics are rarely drawn at the same angle, the italics being the steeper of the two, with an average 12-degree list from the vertical. Traditional metal script types, leaning more, required more space between the letters to accommodate the right-hand edge of the metal. Most were evenly spaced, with a vestigial hairline on the left side of the letter that connects to the preceding letter. When these metal types were used for a long period of time, small telltale white spaces appeared between the connections. Experiments with angled script fonts were cast (actually a parallelogram of metal to allow tighter spacing) and were mortised to interlock, but these notches often became worn, and they were short-lived. With the advent of photocomposition all of these barriers were removed. Scripts could be more tightly spaced, but because connecting turns near the baseline are normally drawn with the same width and angle, the joinings will be lower on the lobed forms within the x-height of the letter. Once again compromise was required—tighter letterspacing at the expense of beautiful, tangent joinings.

ABCDEFGHIJKLMNOPQRSTUVWXYZ
abcdefghijklmnopqrstuvwxyz

COMMERCIAL SCRIPT — MORRIS F. BENTON, ATF 1908

ABCDEFGHIJKLMNOPQRSTUVWXYZ
abcdefghijklmnopqrstuvwxyz
1234567890

BASKERVILLE BOLD ITALIC — GEORGE W. JONES, LINOTYPE 1931

The Quiet Season

Dailey & Associates, Advertising

Los Angeles, California

Bill Parsons, Art Director/Designer
Doyald Young, Designer/Artist
Air New Zealand
The Quiet Season
Advertising and Brochure Lettering

Designers of metal type often indulged in exuberant bursts of drawing for the tail of a *Q* because in the English language the *q* is almost always followed by a *u*, permitting the two to be drawn together, and cast as one piece of metal, called a *logotype* (!), not to be confused with a *ligature*, where two letters are physically connected: fl, fi, Œ, æ, Æ. By casting two letters on one body, difficult spacing combinations, particularly caps, could be avoided: AW, WA, TA, AT, VA, AV, etc. If a font did not have these niceties, the troublesome sorts could be painstakingly notched with a mortising machine to allow them a more friendly proximity. The technology of computer composition has alleviated all of this tedium with super-smart kerning programs.

While there are approximately a couple of hundred examples of scripts in the 1983 edition of Jaspert, Berry, and Johnson's *Encyclopaedia of Type Faces,* there are few that are conservative, bold, formal script styles. Perhaps the most handsome is Matthew Carter's redrawing of Snell Roundhand that is now available in a series of weights. Before that, American Type Founders' Commercial Script and Typo Script were the most popular. *The Quiet Season* example is an ad-weight somewhat related to Commercial Script, though the letters are not as extended. Many script types are drawn with cap *S*s that read more like *L*s. This drawing is the traditional italic shape, though embellished with top and bottom loops. The word *The* is drawn smaller than *Quiet Season*. It is not a straight photographic reduction, but instead the weight of the word has been increased ever so slightly so as to appear optically the same weight as the larger-sized words. The hairlines are generously weighted to allow the image to be reversed out of a solid color without the hairlines filling. Because the logotype is tightly spaced and a bold weight, the hairline joinings are lower than lighter-weight versions (compare *The Art of Steel Die Engraving,* page 223). The word spacing has been omitted, so the hairline tail of the *t* joins smoothly into the cap *S*.

In this handlettered logotype the generous ogee curve of the *Q*'s tail does double duty as an underscore and cradle for the name. This strong graphic element, including the generous size of both the cap *Q* and the cap *S*, create a distinctive shape—often a vital element in the design of a logo or headline.

COMMERCIAL SCRIPT—MORRIS F. BENTON, ATF 1908

ABCDEFGHIJKLMNOPQRSTUVWXYZ
abcdefghijklmnopqrstuvwxyz

Resultful

The Enright Company

Los Angeles, California

Timothy Enright, President and CEO
David Parry, Consultant
Doyald Young, Designer/Artist
Billboard and Brochure Lettering

In *Born Yesterday*, the classic play and film, Judy Holliday knew the value of advertising when she bought space on billboards proclaiming her name.

This script lettering first appeared on a forty-eight-foot-wide billboard on the Sunset Strip with Beverly Hills as a backdrop. The assertion *Resultful*, chosen by a word maven, David Parry, and substantiated by Mr. Enright, was painted in bright red, seventeen feet wide, on a black background. Used subsequently for the front of a special brochure for select prospective clients, the script serves two functions. It supports the logotype, yet allows it to stand by itself. It also suggests a friendly, efficient attitude and contrasts with the company's formal logotype, as shown.

Written quickly several times at a small size—in fact handwriting size—on tracing paper, from which the most successful version was picked, the word was carefully traced, the spacing modified, relative sizes changed, and a slight bounce at the baseline created. It was then enlarged 300 percent, and with a soft HB pencil, weight was added to the linear writing. Still on tracing paper, the forms were inked with a felt-tip pen. The design was then photostatted and presented to the client in comprehensive form.

The adjective is not common, and the trick was to make it read easily. Its large scale helped—it reads easily from three-quarters of a block away. Increasing the space between the *t* and *f* (*Result-ful*) improved the reading of the bunched ascenders, *l t f*. The letters change size radically, and the resulting slight irregularity of the baseline aids legibility. Most of the upstrokes are thinned to simulate quick writing and to prevent the word from appearing monotonous. Because the turns at the baseline are not the thinnest part of the letters, they appear to be written with a round-tipped brush.

*Reduced version of finished art for 14- by 48-foot-wide
handpainted billboard.*

Mary B. Sheridan & Associates
Los Angeles, California

Mary Sheridan, Executive Creative Director
Doyald Young, Designer/Artist
George Hunt Associates,
Philadelphia, Pennsylvania
Frank Glisson, Art Director
Paul Mellon (unpublished)

This name is drawn in the spirit of English roundhand forms popularized by George Bickham in the late seventeenth century, but with letters less wide and less openly spaced than his specimens.

These lightweight letterforms vary greatly from the typical script type, with large caps that are taller than the ascending *l*s. When compared to the ascenders, the x-height is large. The hairlines join tangently at half the x-height (my preferred way of drawing script). The high joining is possible because the line is not bold nor is it tightly spaced, both of which would prevent this elegant ploy. The looped *l*s bend softly to prevent a rigid appearance, and there is a subtle widening at the top right of the loop's hairline, reflecting the pressure of a flexible pen-point. This is repeated on the *e*. Three swelling strokes form a gently undulating ogival curve: the downstroke of the cap *P*, the first downstroke of the *M*, and the second stroke of the *n*.

Typefaces and Alphabets

Typefaces and Alphabets

COLIN BRIGNALL

Type Director, Esselte Letraset Ltd
Letraset and Letragraphica Premier
London, England

TODAY there is a typographic awareness made possible by sophisticated desktop publishing programs and extensive font libraries. The choice is so wide that once selected, the style appears to have been expressly designed for the layout. The graphic designer, the typographer, and the lettering designer should be acutely aware of this wealth of styles.

Typography is composed of two major divisions: text faces for normal reading, and unique display types conceived to convey different moods and effects and to reflect different periods of time. Each requires a different design concept. It is more important to develop eye-catching styles for display; whereas a text face may be scaled to large sizes, readability and legibility are its prime considerations. I have been involved in both areas, but I prefer designing display typefaces—it is more fun and, for me, more rewarding in the creative sense. Headline typography also has a history that gives it substance and credibility.

In the late 1800s when the poster became a means of commercial advertising, Mucha, Toulouse-Lautrec, Bonnard, and Eugène Grasset were influenced by the designs of Jules Chéret, who attempted to harmonize form, color, and typography.

The art nouveau period produced many fine examples of headline typography which, like the movement itself, broke many established rules. Influenced by eccentric lettering styles, designers like Peter Behrens and Otto Eckmann produced designs for metal types that have been recently revived through phototypesetting. (The originals can be seen in Ludwig Petzendorfer's *A Treasury of Authentic Art Nouveau Alphabets*.)

By contrast, the linear typefaces of the 1920s and 1930s were opposed to the organic styles of the late nineteenth century. The work of A. M. Cassandre reflects this art deco period, when elegance and simplicity of line were the order and influenced the overall design. In 1929 Paul Renner designed Futura for the Bauer typefoundry, while in England a design that seemed to encapsulate this elegance was Stephenson Blake's Vogue.

The dry-transfer and phototypesetting technologies in the early 1960s provided an inexpensive method of bringing new typefaces to the marketplace. These new typesetting technologies provided graphic and lettering designers an opportunity to have their ideas easily and inexpensively produced for widespread use in display typography.

With the mood of the 1960s, brash experimentations in lettering were prevalent. Many were designed with a compass and ruler, with little consideration for legibility or esthetics, though some had substance and have endured.

During the last thirty years we have seen the demise of metal typesetting and witnessed the birth of dry-transfer and photo-digital typesetting. All of this has provided more flexibility for the designer. It is not by chance that designers are more aware typographically—they must be, to cope and survive.

Opposite—
Detail of preliminary drawings
for Jeune Roman
(see page 258).

1234567890

1234567890

Great Primer (18-point) arabic figures and enlargement, from the Deberny & Peignot John Baskerville matrices recast by Walter Fruttiger Ltd., Münchenstein, and handset by Charles Whitehouse, Die Handpresse, Zurich, Switzerland.

1234567890

George W. Jones's version of John Baskerville's 1762 type (Mergenthaler Linotype, 1931).

1234567890

1234567890

Old-style figures based on John Baskerville's 1747 Grand Primer Type.

The Grunwald Center for the Graphic Arts, Dickson Art Center
University of California at Los Angeles
James Cuno, Director
Cynthia Burlingham, Curator
Doyald Young, Designer/Artist
The Rudolf L. Baumfeld Collection
of Landscape Drawings & Prints,
Exhibition Catalog
Baskerville Old-style Figures

These figures were drawn expressly for the Baumfeld exhibition catalog (opposite) because old-style figures were not available in PostScript fonts offered for the Macintosh when the project began. Old-style figures seemed a necessary requirement for a text laden with figures—cap-high figures would have dominated the page (some pages contained more than fifty). From an18-point showing of Baskerville's Grand Primer type I drew a set of figures to match the x-height and color of ITC's Mergenthaler font whose x-height is far more generous than Baskerville's original typeface. The font's "hints" were encoded, requiring trial-and-error drawings. The carefully drawn outline tissues were then pasted into the background of the Fontographer program and spline fonts were drawn and tested repeatedly. Each figure was then selected and changed into the new font.

[Dutch & Flemish]

JOSUA DE GRAVE

71

The Town of Grave (1674)

JOSUA DE GRAVE
(Amsterdam 1643–1712 The Hague)
Pen and brown ink with gray wash
102 x 156 mm
Inscribed *J de Grave fecit* lower right; dated and
titled on mount
Provenance: Zeitlin and Ver Brugge, Los Angeles
Bibliography: van Hasselt 1967, no. 123a

The date assigned to this drawing assumes added significance as the town of Grave was liberated by William III in October 1674 after having been besieged for two years by the French under the Marquis de Chavigny (Breitbarth-van der Stok 1969, p. 104). While de Grave depicts the town in a traditional cityscape, the presence of the Dutch army is duly indicated by the boat in the center filled with several small figures and two cannons as well as two additional cannons standing on the shore. De Grave usually drew the everyday activities of the army rather than its battles.

De Grave made another drawing of this subject (Amsterdam, Rijksmuseum inv. no. A4549), which is dated by the artist on the image November 15, 1674, just as the Grunwald Center drawing is dated by another hand on the mount.[1] While the two drawings are almost identical, the Amsterdam version displays slightly looser handling of details such as the boats on the left and the small church on the right.[2] It is possible that this drawing was made by de Grave after the one in Amsterdam, but the purpose of the drawings that he made on his travels with the army or of copies of these drawings is still unclear.

1. Both drawings are accepted by van Hasselt as by de Grave (van Hasselt 1965, no. 12e, and van Hasselt 1967, no. 123a).
2. The Grunwald Center version extends slightly further on the right and upper edges; it is possible, however, that the Amsterdam drawing was cut down.

A portion of a typical page from the UCLA *exhibition catalog,*
The Rudolf L. Baumfeld Collection of Landscape Drawings and Prints,
*with the specially redesigned font of Baskerville old-style figures. The style was individually
selected as a separate font apart from the book's Adobe/ITC Baskerville font.*

Old-style figures are designed to complement the lowercase alphabet, possessing an x-height, ascenders, and descenders. The style has been used in Europe since the twelfth century, and the *Encyclopaedia Britannica* suggests a Hindu/Persian origin, though several cultures take credit for them. The 1, 4, and 6 have been found in Hindi manuscripts dating from the third century B.C., and the 2, 4, 6, 7, and 9, from the second century A.D. The Persians added the cipher (zero) in the ninth or tenth century, and as old style it is drawn at x-height. The industrial revolution created a need for bookkeeping, and columns of figures were of paramount importance in a ledger. "Modern" cap-high figures were developed in the late eighteenth century to fill this need.[1]

Old-style figures are disruptive when used with large caps (*i.e.*, ZENITH CO. 1347 WEST 19TH). They are more compatible with small caps because their x-height is the same (ZENITH CO. 1347 WEST 19TH). Advertising has favored modern style for greater impact. Therefore, font manufacturers now offer old-style figures only as typographic luxuries—a separate font within the type family—to a more sophisticated PostScript public.

1. Walter Tracy, *Letters of Credit: A View of Type Design*. (Boston: David R. Godine, 1986), page 68.

LORI PS — HIROJI INAZUKA / DOYALD YOUNG, BROTHER IMPACT PRINTER FONT 1984

ABCDEFGHIJKLM
NOPQRSTUVWXYZ
abcdefghijklmnopqr
stuvwxyz ij'nßªº
ÄÅÆÍÌÖØÜÇÑ
àäåæéèóòöøúùüçñ

ABCDEFGHIJKLM
NOPQRSTUVWXYZ
abcdefghijklmnopqr
stuvwxyz ij'nßªº
ÄÅÆÍÌÖØÜÇÑ
àäåæéèóòöøúùüçñ

Left—*Of special note
in the fourth line is the character* **'n,**
*offered in South Africa where it is used
by itself for the word* and.

HELVETICA LIGHT — M. MIEDINGER, HAAS 1957

ABCDEFGHIJKLMNOPQRSTUVWXYZ
abcdefghijklmnopqrstuvwxyz
1234567890

Design West, Inc.

Mission Viejo, California

Arthur Ellsworth, President and CEO
George Gaw, Vice-President,
Creative Director
Donald Bartels, Art Director
Doyald Young, Artist

Brother Industries, Ltd.
Nagoya, Japan
Kenichi Kita, Manager,
Product Design Group
Hiroji Inazuka, Senior Designer
Date of development: March 9, 1984
LORI PS — Brother Impact Printer Font

Typeface designs or alphabets are products, and as such they are subject to the public's insatiable hunger for the new. Typefoundries and producers of types (and all good businessmen) need a well-rounded inventory. These makers of type must have a pantheon of classic romans, sans serifs, and scripts, and a smörgåsbord of display faces. Some license fonts from other producers, as many have done with ITC fonts, or they may develop their own version, style, or redrawing of a popular face, often creating a distinct and highly marketable font.

Lori is Brother's interpretation of a traditional sans serif and is drawn in the same spirit as the evenly proportioned grotesques of the late nineteenth century. Lori was drawn in Brother's design department under the leadership of typeface director H. Inazuka. Many decisions regarding proportion and fit had been made before Design West was commissioned to evaluate the preliminary font

for final drawing and production. Working with George Gaw and Don Bartels, drawings were made from the original premise, and these were submitted to Brother for comments. These were modified, and outline pencil drawings on tracing paper were given to Brother to produce the final art for the daisy wheel.

A daisy wheel is an impact (strike-on) method of producing full-formed, nondigitized characters. The wheel has long, flexible spokes and moves at great speed, thus contributing a whole new set of forces that bear on the basic problems that have been the scourge of type makers for centuries.

Of great consideration in type design, especially for text faces, is the desirability of even color, for no one letter should stand out from the rest. Ideally, the letters should not be divided in a manner that creates small clotted areas, which become dark spots on a page of type. If a roman *a* is two-storied (a), it colors more darkly than the *n*. In the same vein, the *g*, *k*, *s*, *w*, and *x* are troublemakers too. Points of convergence optically mass. To compensate the designer must either thin or angle the stroke. This is particularly true in bold fonts. The branches and lobes of Franklin Gothic are examples. These problems pale in comparison to the difficulties that the sides (called beard or draft) of a bas-relief letter create. Where these sides converge, *i.e.*, where a lobe or branch joins a stem, the space is diminished, and the areas become traps for ink or carbon ribbon residue that creates a darker letter.

Photo: Chris Fifthian

Top—Enlarged photograph (600 percent) of Brother Lori PS daisy wheel spokes showing reverse bas-relief letter with beard (or draft).

Bottom—Brother daisy wheel (reduced).

CALABASAS PARK ALPHABET — DOYALD YOUNG, 1968

ABCDEFG

HIJKLMNOPQ

RSTUVWXYZ

abcdefghijklmno

pqrstuvwxyz

1234567890

Bechtel Corporation, San Francisco
Southern California Edison, Los Angeles

Robert Follett, Project Manager
Stuart Ripley, Marketing Director
Young & Dodge Graphic Design
Doyald Young, Designer
Doris Krause, Finished Art
Calabasas Park Project Alphabet

Calabasas Park is a sumptuous development on the old Warner Ranch. Large elegant homes march up ridges of the Santa Monica Mountains with spectacular views of the San Fernando Valley and, on clear days, the Pacific Ocean. The three-thousand acres have an illustrious Hollywood heritage, for many movies were filmed there (one of the most famous, *National Velvet,* starred an ingenuous and very young Elizabeth Taylor).

The logotype is modeled on a Victorian face named Latin Antique. The *New York Times* has used a condensed version of it for some of their article heads for many years. The original type has triangular pointed serifs—these were softened, using instead a serif modeled on William Caslon's forms.

After trading with the Venetians in the fifteenth century, the Moors swept in from the Levant, conquered Spain, and enriched the Spanish culture with many of their design motifs. One of their arabesques is repeated here on the lowercase letters with their pen-script beginning stroke. The quadruple repetition of the *a* and the twice repeated *s* lends a basic distinction to the word, for the pen shape is repeated eleven times in the two words. The alphabet contains the italic lowercase letters *e, k, g,* and *s,* drawn in an upright position. Mostly the caps are drawn with a modern weight distribution, while most of the lowercase is predominantly old style. It is even-proportioned with cap-high modern-style figures. No punctuation was drawn. Because the two words form a long shape, the letters were condensed to gain a size advantage in advertising.

Many of the capitals and lowercase forms are roman (vertical) swash letters, drawn to give the alphabet a less rigid look and to impart a style with Spanish/Mediterranean influences. The font was designed primarily for use as capital with lowercase. Traditionally, swash letters are drawn as alternate letters for an italic font. The spacing of the logotype was slightly increased for use on large signage using individually cast bronze letters.

Additionally the alphabet was used for occasional signage and collateral for the park's various amenities: Californian Restaurant, Riding Club, Golf Course, Tennis Club, and Skeet and Trap Club.

Calabasas Park

ERASMUS LIGHT— DOYALD YOUNG, COMPUGRAPHIC 1980

ABCDEFGHIJK
LMNOPQRST
UVWXYZ&⬚⬚m
abcdefghi
jklmnopqr
stuvwxyzß
f …

. .

1234567890$¢£/%#ᵃºO
− ± = × ÷
½ ¼ ¾ ⅛ ⅜ ⅝ ⅞ ⅓ ⅔
1234567890$¢ . / 1234567890

.,:;¿?¡!——/()
’'·⬚«‹.›»*†‡§
ÅÆæÇç2ıÑñØøCcSsð

REGULAR STORY (charcomp 01)

PERHAPS THE BIGGEST ”SURPRISE“ OF
THE $23.95(£14.67 IN THE U.K.) COMPU-
TERIZED STUDY WAS THAT IT SHOWED THE
ENORMOUS VOCABULARY THAT QUEENSLAND‘S
CHILDREN ARE ASKED TO TAKE IN! THE
SURVEY SHOWED THAT «CHILDREN ARE
ASKED TO READ NEARLY TWICE AS
MANY TEXTBOOKS* IN THE SEVENTH
GRADE AS THEY ARE IN THE SIXTH OR
EIGHTH GRADES.» THE WORD FRE-
QUENCY BOOK LISTS ALL 86,74⅔ WORDS
(GIVE[OR TAKE?]A FEW) ALPHABETICALLY
WITH REFERENCE TO THEIR FREQUENCY
OR OCCURENCE—AND DISTRIBUTION
BY GRADE AND/OR SUBJECT. THE
MOST-USED WORD IS ’THE.‘ ’OF, AND,
A, TO, IN, IS, YOU, THAT‘ & ’IT‘
COMPLETE THE TOP TEN.

Perhaps the biggest ”surprise“ of the
$23.95 (£14.67 in the U.K.) computerized
study was that it showed the enormous
vocabulary that Queensland‘s children
are asked to take in! The survey showed
that «Children are asked to read
nearly TWICE as many textbooks in
the seventh grade* as they are in the
sixth or eighth grades.» The Word
Frequency Book lists all 86,471 ⅔ words
(give[or take?]a few) alphabetically with
reference to their frequency of occur-
rence—and distribution by grade and/or
subject. The most-used word is ’the.‘
’Of, and, a, to, in, is, you, that‘ & ’it‘
complete the Top Ten.

Compugraphic Corporation

Wilmington, Massachusetts
(Now Agfa Division, Miles Inc.)

Allan Haley, Typographic Consultant
Doyald Young, Artist
Erasmus Font

This typeface is from the talented hand of S. H. de Roos, who also designed Egmont, Ella, Hollandse Mediaeval, Libra, Meidorn, Simplex, Zilver, and the face that he chose to name after himself. De Roos and Jan van Krimpen were contemporaries and their work was widely received. Of van Krimpen's types Spectrum is perhaps the most familiar; Cancelleresca Bastarda, Lutetia and Romanée, the most beautiful; and Haarlemmer, one of the most obscure. A revival of his work would be welcome.

Allan Haley, the typographic consultant at Compugraphic Corporation, requested that I redraw Erasmus (after the definitive Renaissance man) to their technical specifications. The request was to improve on the design where possible but to leave its essential flavor intact. It is an interesting face—romantic, with idiosyncrasies that border on the quaint, with fussy spurs on the *C, G, S,* and *t* and proportions that are more modern than classical.

Precise 4 H pencil tissues were evaluated at various stages in preparation for spline fonts created with the Icarus program. The system requires two drawings from which it develops multiple weights and proportions. Only basic elements were drawn—a single serif for caps, and one for the lowercase—that could be pasted and flopped on both sides of a

stem by the program. Only minor adjustments were made to the proportions: the *E* and *F* narrowed, the *U* widened, and the round lobes gently made more oval—but ever so slightly—for a fuller, more open shape. The cupped serifs on the top and bottom of the *B* and *D* were flattened, because the original forms turned too quickly at one o'clock and created corners. More than anything, I smoothed the shapes so that they curved more gracefully. The small tight serif at the top of the *A* was left because it is a distinguishing feature of the face. The *S* was subtly redrawn.

From the meticulously drawn (with french curves and a needle-sharp 9H pencil) pencil tissues, trial drawings of the test word *champion* were cut from Rubylith in the art department and reduced to different sizes for evaluation.

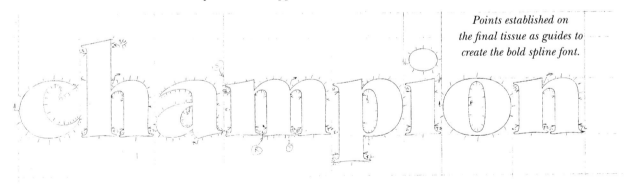

Points established on the final tissue as guides to create the bold spline font.

ABCDEFGHIJKLMNOPQRSTUVWXYZ

abcdefghijklmnopqrstuvwxyz

ERASMUS LIGHT — S.H. DE ROOS, AMSTERDAM 1923

DILLINGHAM CORPORATE ALPHABET — DOYALD YOUNG, 1970

ABCDEF
GHIJKLMNO
PQRSTU
VWXYZ
1234567890
&.,:;!?''/()- —

abcdefghij
klmnopqrst
uvwxyz

Dillingham

Ulf Helgesson Industrial Design
Woodland Hills, California

Ulf Helgesson, Design Director/Consultant
Dillingham Corporate Identity Program
Young & Dodge, Graphic Design
Doyald Young, Designer/Artist
Dillingham Corporation
Honolulu, Hawaii
(Now Dillingham Construction Corporation,
Pleasanton, California.)
Corporate Alphabet

The original Dillingham Company was made up of divisions and subsidiaries sprinkled on the Pacific Rim, with construction their major activity—the shape of Honolulu's skyline is part of their signature. With construction projects in the far east, oceanographic equipment, natural gas, tugboat fleets, land development and construction in northern California, their interests were far ranging, and their logotype and alphabet were designed to suggest these hearty endeavors.

When the logotype was commissioned, it came with the request that it was to be legible on heavy equipment viewed from a distance. Of particular importance were construction site signs. With its preponderance of vertical stems, the logotype is a difficult word to make legible. The extended letters and open spacing work to this end.

Corporate identity programs for large corporations are always faced with the problem of bringing divisions, departments, services, products, subsidiaries, partially owned companies, affiliates, and independent entities under the typographic umbrella of the logo. Often a bold compatible typeface is used. While it is expedient for ease of handling and cost effectiveness, it is often a weak solution, for it lacks the special distinction that stems from the parent logotype's unique letterforms. The corporation might then consider a corporate alphabet that uses the exact logotype forms or, as in this case, the same style but lighter stem weight. There are ardent supporters of both solutions. The font style should support and reinforce the corporate affiliation in an identifiable and memo-

rable manner. It is a burdensome choice, for as a corporation expands, great care is required to ensure that each new division is treated in a consistent manner. Departments are often created to police these mandates. When this program was initiated, Dillingham was the parent of seventeen divisions and subsidiaries. These names were created as part of the first phase of the design program.

The style has qualities of Venus extended, though its design structure is closer to Futura and Frutiger (see page 21 for a discussion of the logotype). This vertical manner of ending curved stems was known as "handlettered Futura," because its endings matched some of the endings of the condensed font.

The alphabet is composed of conservative shapes; only the *K* and *G* depart from generic forms. The x-height is generous, and the *L* and *T* have shortened horizontals for more even color.

The letters are subtly two-weight. Note that the lobe of the *g* is smaller than the other lobes to prevent its tail from descending too far below the baseline.

Dillingham Bros., Limited

Oceanographic Engineering

Hydro Products

Subsidiaries and divisions of the original Dillingham Corporation based in
Honolulu, Hawaii, set in the specially designed corporate alphabet.

ÉCLAT SCRIPT — DOYALD YOUNG, LETRASET PREMIER SERIES 1984

ABCDEFGHIJ

KLMNOPQRST

UVWWXYYZ

abcdefghijklmnopq

rstuvwxyz

ffffflggjkprrsy3

æøß&E?!£$%()

o•• ˘ ˄ ⁕
ˌ ~ .,;: ‹‹ ›› - —

1234456789o

Esselte Letraset Ltd

London, England

Colin Brignall, Type Director
Doyald Young, Designer/Artist
Vince Whitlock, Letraset, Finished Art
Éclat Script, Premier Series

Vigor, spirit, assurance, dash, verve, ardor, zest—the definition of *élan,* my original name for this gutsy script. The name had been used by the Stempel typefoundry in 1937 for a script face designed by Hans Möhring, so Letraset preferred to rename the face.

The style has been around for a long time: many showcard artists who specialize in point-of-purchase display have lettered variations of it for years. Sign shops still draw versions of it for exterior signs because its bold weight handily accommodates canned lighting. Edged in shiny brass and illuminated, its sturdy mass is easy to fabricate and install. Often used by sports clubs, it is friendly, assertive, and at ease where strength and grace are required. Its most important feature, chunky thin strokes, allows it to be reversed easily out of a solid printed background without the thin strokes clogging, also an asset for reverses in the four-color process. Many scripts are too fragile to meet this requirement and often require photographic weighting to prevent filling.

In the best of all possible worlds, a letter should be drawn for viewing at a specific size. This is a luxury that few faces offer. Machine faces were sometimes drawn individually for each point size, and many display faces were cast in their ranges of sizes from three separate drawings. Our computers are only now beginning to offer programs to supply this elegant finesse.

When type is reduced, many optical phenomena occur: the overall mass appears lighter than in original size; proportions appear more narrow; the spacing looks optically tighter; some letter combinations meld together to form an unwanted letter (**rn** can become **m**); small

Word sets from Letraset's final dry-transfer production sheets that demonstrate the sturdiness of Éclat's thin strokes in a reverse print reduction.

areas tend to clog; and the letters attract each other more than is desired. Spacing at a large size may be ideal, but difficult combinations often appear tighter in reduction; where lobes and branches join the stem, the area appears darker, and an overall refinement is lost.

Éclat was designed with an extremely large x-height, with a proportion and fit that allow more space within the letter than between the letters—the **ab** establishes this relationship. The straight to straight stems are designed to join tangently, and the straight to curved stem couplings to join obliquely. In a narrow definition, script letters are designed to connect, to flow into the next letter. Their spacing is then determined by the fixed width of the connecting stroke that does not differentiate between a straight or curve. Hence, many metal script types are equally spaced.

To avoid massing, the thin joining strokes here have been slightly tapered to allow a higher joining within the x-height. The ascenders are severe and unlooped, while the descenders are dressed with oval terminals that repeat the terminal of the **c**. The capitals are pared down to essential forms, and the swashes are as restrained as I could draw them as scriptorial shapes. The **M** and **N** are an obeisance to Hermann Zapf's Palatino italic.

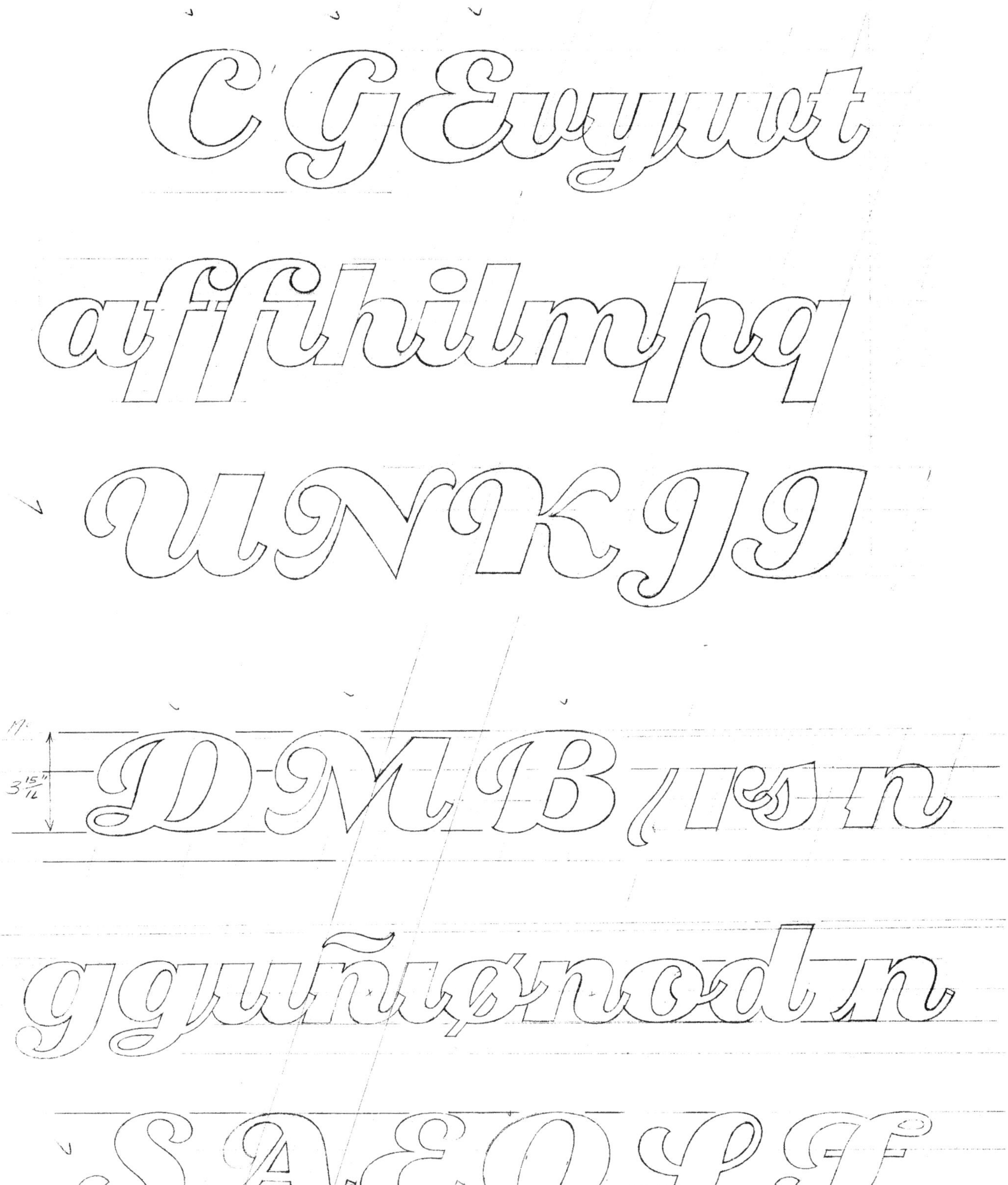

Élan

Same-size 2H pencil drawing on vellum, drawn to test proportion and fit.

Élan Script (Éclat Script)

Preliminary pencil sketch
submitted to Letraset
Doyald Young, Designer/Artist

This is a same-size reproduction of the original pencil drawing submitted to Letraset, drawn with a 2H pencil on Clearprint vellum (above). Colin Brignall, the type director, considered the hairlines too thin and wanted them bolder. The opposite page shows preliminary drawings of the thin strokes weighted considerably, which are drawn to join at approximately one-half of the x-height. These joinings establish the spacing and the amount of weight that must be carried around the curve at the baseline and taper required of the thin stroke to insure a high join. Check marks indicate that the letter needs to be wider. The third line from the bottom (preceding the *r*) shows a stem attachment used as a filler of space, though not submitted as a final character, as well as a coupling of the *rs*, an alternate looped *g*, and an *n* (second line from bottom) that illustrates an unsuccessful joining method.

Modern (cap high) and old-style (based on the x-height) figures were presented, but old style was preferred. Both favor the swash strokes of the caps, instead of the oval lowercase terminals.

GUTS — DOYALD YOUNG, VGC 1970

ABCDEFGH
IJKLMNOPQR
STUVWXYZ
ÆŒØ
abcdefghijk
lmnopqrstu
vwxyz
cæœøß
.,:;""'' &!¡?¿ --- ()/ »«*
1234567890
$$£¢¢%

JANA—RICHARD D. JUENGER, VGC 1966

ABCDEFGHIJKLMNOPQRSTUVWXYZ
abcdefghijklmnopqrstuvwxyz

Visual Graphics Corporation

Tamarac, Florida

Young & Dodge, Graphic Design

Doyald Young, Designer/Artist

Guts Typositor Font

If you decide to design a display type-face, chances are that it should be bold, though this is no guarantee for a fast buck, despite the American advertiser's love of the strident headline.

My initial name for this Typositor font was a very conservative *Anvil*, but the times dictated a jocular name for fonts, and Guts met with great approval from even my harshest critics.

The font began with a simple idea: a lowercase branch that makes an angled departure from the stem. (There have been other faces that do this—Jana is one, designed by Richard Juenger.) But after that, what shape does the letter assume? Should it be a sans serif in an already overcrowded library, or a serif letter to allow for more design flexibility? I finally settled on a squat, square, and chunky Egyptian with stubby serifs, the top side drawn with a slight diagonal. From this emerged an ultra-black font with a very large display x-height. The angled serifs—the ones that top the ascenders and end the *h, m, n,* and *u*—are an old-style idea. Jenson (c. 1690) has serifs with similar angles. The design ploy lends itself to a third of the caps—*A, K, R, V, W, X,* and *Y.*

When letters become this bold, the compromises become greater—the *f* and *t* must have an economical width to allow the tight fit that is *de rigueur* for these faces. The diagonal caps need steeper angles to prevent large surrounding chunks of white space. Laterally divided, or angled, letters must often be trimmed and drawn with thinner strokes: *B, E, F, H, R, S, a, e,* and *s.* The punctuation is often drawn thinner to prevent it from overpowering the words.

The font mingles in the company of other Egyptians that were popular in the 1930s: Cairo, Memphis, Obelisk, Beton, Stymie, City, Rockwell, and more recently ITC's Graph, a joint effort of Herb Lubalin, Antonio DiSpigna, Joe Sundwall, and Ed Benguiat. The style developed early in the nineteenth century after Napoleon had make his forays into Egypt, and the word mavens of the day labeled the black forms to match his campaign.[1]

---

1. For a discourse on these "barbarous" forms, see D. B. Updike, *Printing Types: Their History, Forms, and Use* (Cambridge, Massachusetts: Harvard University Press, 1937), vol. 2, page 195. For a more thoughtful discussion, see Alexander Lawson, *Anatomy of a Typeface* (Boston: David R. Godine, 1990), pages 308–23.

HAMBURGERFONS
hamburgerfons

Above—*A test word set in Guts that contains 12 letters, or one-half of the alphabet, used by International Typeface Corporation to evaluate proportion, fit, and general color of a font.*

JEUNE — DOYALD YOUNG, 1965

ABCDEFGHIJKLM
NQPRSTUVWXYZ
abcdefghijklmn
opqrstuvwxyz
– &?!().,:;“”’/*[] ¢$£%
1234567890

ABCDEFGHIJ
KKLMNOPQR
STUVWXYZ&&
abcdefghijklmnop
qrstuvwxyz

ABCDEFGHIJKLMNOPQRSTUVWXY&Z
abcdefghijklmonopqrstuvwxyz 1234567890

ABCDEFGHIJKLMNOPQRSTUVWXY&Z
ABCDEFGHIJKLMNOPQRSTUVWXY&Z
abcdefghijklmonopqrstuvwxyz 1234567890

GARAMOND — ROBERT SLIMBACH, ADOBE ORIGINAL 1989

Compugraphic Corporation

Wilmington, Massachusetts
(Now Agfa Division, Miles Inc.)

Allan Haley, Typographic Consultant
Young & Dodge, Graphic Design
Doyald Young, Designer/Artist
Jeune Font (study)

Garamond was a popular display face—ATF's in the 1920s, and Ludlow's in the 1930s. Linotype's version, based on Morris F. Benton's and T. M. Cleland's design for ATF, was used extensively for text and headlines by almost every printer in the land. The ITC Garamond by Tony Stan has enjoyed great popularity, and recently Adobe Fonts introduced Robert Slimbach's splendid drawing, shown above.

Mortimer Leach, great teacher, letterer, and my friend, once handlettered some Garamond italic for Hallmark greeting cards. It was a classy job, and it says, "When you care enough to send the very best." At the time, he griped about the rude forms of the particular Garamond font that he had to refer to, and saved his most vitriolic comments for the disparate angles of the type. Leach threatened to redesign the font but never found the time, so I took his cue and started work on this drawing in the early 1960s. The angle conflict was a hangover from Claude Garamond's original type, when

Garamond confronted a problem of topology: how to draw a leaning letter on a square or rectangular piece of metal in such a manner as to create even color spacing (see page 233 for a discussion of script spacing).

Jeune was conceived as a display face, despite its light color. I worked on it at odd moments, between jobs, and sometimes in the early hours of the morning before work began. After several years, I thought it was in good enough shape to peddle, so I put together a presentation, took the red-eye to Detroit, and tried to sell it to Cadillac's ad agency at that time. They liked it, but—*maybe it should be a little bolder.* I did make it bolder, but something mysterious happens to letterforms when you start fussing with their weight. The agency thought it was better but still too light for their taste. So, disheartened, I put it away in my vellum file.

Fifteen years later, Allan Haley, consultant for the Compugraphic Corporation, was scouting around for some new faces, saw it, and liked it. I began exploratory work on it anew. The italic had never been inked; it was just a tight pencil tissue, and I took it only to the stage at which it appears on the following pages.

Mort Leach showed me that there were no points in Garamond. All converging stems possessed a radius at their point

of joining. I thought of bracketing these a bit more against the danger of a spotty appearance in those areas. So that the face would be friendly and graceful all of the letters were drawn freehand, with every line a subtle curve. The width is a bit extended—because I favor letters with generous counters, but probably the reason is because I learned to draw letters in the 1950s when extended letters were the absolute cutting edge of fashion. Jeune is transitional in design, and its weight is distinctly light. The original drawing opposite shows my efforts. The italic reflects my admiration for Hermann Zapf's Palatino and Georg Trump's ampersand.

I never felt that the compromises for the final drawing retained the spirit of the original. Jan van Krimpen was concerned with similar problems. He discussed this (groused is a better word) in a letter to Philip Hofer.[1] It is a problem that many confront in translating a sketch into a finished piece of art. Invariably the sketch is better: it has more life, more surprise, and more artistry. The cold, rigid, unforgiving medium of solid black never quite equals the artistic spontaneity of letters that are drawn freehand in pencil.

1. Jan van Krimpen, *A Letter to Philip Hofer on Certain Problems Connected with the Mechanical Cutting of Punches* (Cambridge, Massachusetts: Harvard College Library; Boston: David R. Godine, 1972), pages 27–37.

Concourse d'elegance

Jeune—Preliminary word tests from cut-out photoprints.

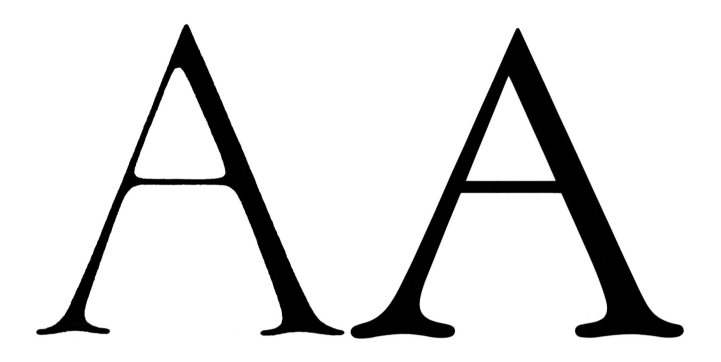

Compugraphic Corporation

Wilmington, Massachusetts

(Now Agfa Division, Miles Inc.)

Allan Haley, Typographic Consultant
Young & Dodge Graphic Design
Doyald Young, Designer/Artist
Jeune Font (study)

The letter *A* at top left is a blow-up of the original inch-and-a-half-high pencil drawing. It demonstrates the full bracketing at the juncture of thins with weighted stems and shows how very light the letter is. The drawing at the right is the final drawing, reduced in size. There was some objection to the idea of the brackets; it was thought they would clog and be spotty. The final drawing is almost double the thickness of the pencil drawing and has lost the gentleness of the original shape. The two lower-left illustrations are from the original Rubylith cuttings of the drawings done by the art department at Compugraphic to evaluate the sizes of 6-, 8-, 10-, and 12-point. The two right-hand illustrations are the actual early output from the Icarus-generated spline fonts, used to make further adjustments.

Opposite is a pencil drawing blow-up of the *B*, shown because I like big letters, and this one fills the page nicely. It demonstrates how scale so often visually changes our perception of an object.

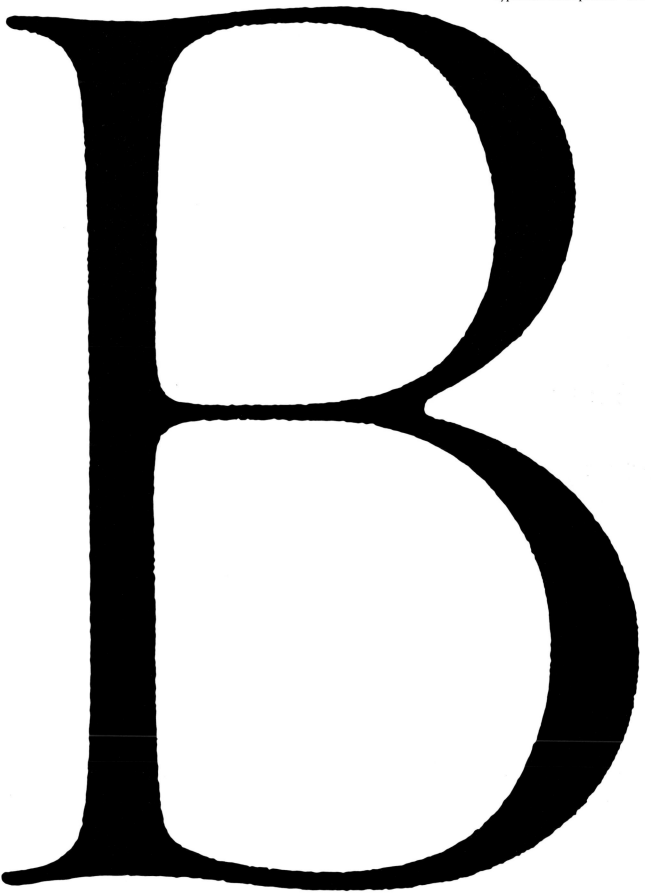

PURE MAGIC ALPHABET — DOYALD YOUNG, 1975

ABCDE
FGHIJK
LMNOP
QRSTU
VWXY
Z & . , -

MAX FACTOR

PURE MAGIC

ABCDEFGHIJKLMNOPQRSTUVWXYZ
abcdefghijklmnopqrstuvwxyz

STANDARD EXTRA LIGHT EXTENDED — BERTHOLD 1896

Max Factor & Co.
Hollywood, California

James Englemann, Creative Director
Ray Perez, Art Director/Designer
Young & Dodge, Graphic Design
Doyald Young, Designer/Artist
Pure Magic Product Line Alphabet

After a logotype for a product name has been designed, the product line is often extended and requires additional logo-types or product names. It was less expensive to do a cap alphabet than draw a series of handlettered product names.

These products hang on revolving racks in drugstores across the land. The name is large to catch the eye and to compensate for its rather light weight. It was first and foremost designed to be legible, and to possess that pristine look that is so prevalent in cosmetics packaging. It is a mixture of different styles: the *G* is based on an extended book weight Futura, with its lack of a vertical stem. The center crossbar of the *E* is short, in contrast to the equal-length strokes of Futura. It is evenly proportioned, and the lobe of the *P* has been lowered to help fill the gaping hole created by the triangular space of the *M* in the logotype.

The sans serif font has very rounded shapes, with curves of the lobes gradually extending well into a horizontal stroke.

SIGNFONT — EMERSON & STERN 1988

SignFont hand-shapes illustrations © Emerson & Stern Associates, Inc.

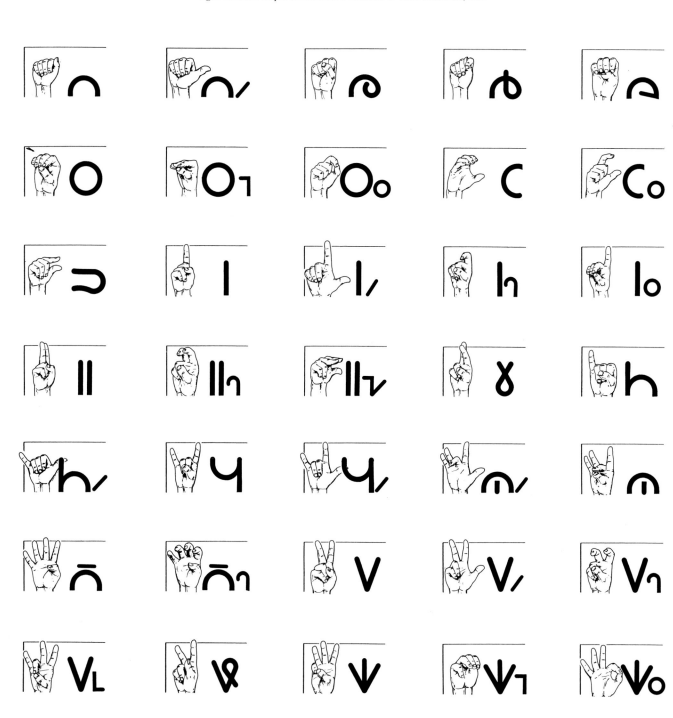

Emerson & Stern Associates
San Diego, California
Dr. Sandra Hutchins, President
Jan Zimmerman, CEO

Design Group:
Brenda Castillo
Dr. Sandra Hutchins
Don Newkirk
Don Nothdurft
Frank Allen Paul
Dr. Judy Reilly
Doyald Young

**The Salk Institute
for Biological Studies**
San Diego, California
Dr. Howard Poizner
Dr. Marina McIntire

I was asked to help out with this enormously interesting and vitally important project only *after* the major symbols were drawn and tested. I did the final drawings and devised some designs for the non-manual symbols that indicate position.

It is a written alphabet for the American Sign Language (ASL), developed jointly by The Salk Institute for Biological Studies and by the linguistic experts Emerson & Stern Associates, with a grant from the National Institutes of Health. It is designed to be easily handwritten and translates a complex three-dimensional language of hand-shapes, contact, movements, and locations into five separate groups with a total of ninety-four distinct symbols. One of the most difficult problems was to identify graphically (with a simple shape), the location of each sign, since a hand-shape assumes a different meaning when signed in different locations. One solution placed a sign on one of five horizontal lines. This proved too difficult to reproduce either by hand or on a 5- by 8-dot matrix printer. A different symbol was developed for each position in the plane of the body, and these are written after the hand-shape and action symbol.

The drawn symbols were then developed in 12-point using the FONTastic program and digitized into a 5- by 8-dot matrix form for an Apple IIe computer.

SIGNFONT — EMERSON & STERN 1988

Hand-shape

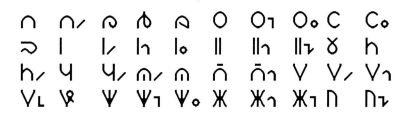

Action area

Location

Movement

Nonmanuals

Body locations

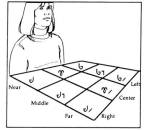

Ⅴ ｡ ⊕ ⊕ ✕ ⼋ ⅵ ＝
UNITY

Ⅰσ〰ⅹ⟨ⅵⅡⓞ℞ⅹＣ◌Ｊⅹ‑Ｃ⊕⊕ⅹ
(For My Wife)

ⅡⅣ✓ ℞｡Ⓞ Ⅱ⋔ⓐⅤⅤ⋔ⅹⅤ
by Don Newkirk

Don Newkirk was one of the major contributors to the development of Sign-Font. Sandra Hutchins, president of Emerson & Stern, comments about a poem written by him to his wife, "This literal translation does not begin to convey the form of the ASL original, with its alliteration of handshapes and rhyme of movements, both of which are apparent in the SignFont spelling."

The main body of the poem is set in 14-point SignFont regular and the title in 18-point. There is a condensed font and a boldface named Signfont Formal.

Right—*Poem set in 14-point PostScript SignFont.*

ⓤ Ⅰ◌◌℞ⅹ Ⅰσ℞ⅹ Ⅰ◌◌℞✓ⅹ, Ⅰ◌◌℞ⅹ.
When did I meet you?

⽊◌Ｊⅵ Ⅴ ⋔ ∩✓◌℞⟨ ℞◌Ⅱ◌℞ⅹ,
Long ago in another time,

Ⅰσⅵↅ⅄ ∩✓◌℞⟨ Ⅴ◌◌℞ⅹ.
Far away in another world.

Ⅴ◌◌℞ⅹ Ⅴ◌℞ⅹ Ⅴ◌⅃ⅹ‑Ⅴ◌◌ⅵⅤ, Ⅴ◌◌℞ⅹ.
Perfectly I perceived

Ⅰ◌ⅰ ◌｡⊕Ⅰσⅹ∧＝ Ⅰ◌Ⅱ◌℞ⅹ,
One special hour,

Ⅰ◌ⅰ ◌｡⊕Ⅰσⅹ∧＝ Ⅴ◌◌℞ⅹ
One special kind

Ⅴ｡⊕⊕ⅹ⼋ⅵ＝.
of Unity.

⋔✓◌Ⅴ＝ Ⅴ◌⼋ⅵ Ⅴ◌Ｃ⊕⊼Ⅴ Ⅰ◌ⅰ ∩◌℞⅄ⅹ,
Now we both have one attitude,

℞◌Ⅴ＝ Ⅴ◌⼋ⅵ Ⅴ◌Ｃ⊕⊼Ⅴ Ⅰ◌ⅰ Ⅰ✓◌℞⽊∧＝,
We both can live one life,

⋔✓◌Ⅴ＝″ Ⅴ◌⼋ⅵ Ⅴ◌Ｃ⊕⊼Ⅴ Ⅰ◌ⅰ Ⅰσ〰ⅹ‑ⅠσσⅵⅤⅵ,
We both have the same goal,

⅄✓σ〰ⅹ‑⋔✓σⅵ Ⅴ◌⼋ⅵ Ⅴ◌Ｃ⊕⊼Ⅴ Ⅰ◌ⅰ ∩✓◌℞⅄ⅹ.
Forever we both have one heart.

Ⅰ◌◌℞ⅹ Ⅰσ℞ⅹ Ⅰ◌◌℞✓ⅵⅹ
When I met you

Ⅴ｡◌◌℞ⅹ Ⅴ◌◌℞ⅹ‑Ⅴ｡⊕⊕ↄ✓ⅵⅹ
Perfectly I joined you

Ⅴ｡⊕⊕ⅹ⼋ⅵ＝.
in Unity.

Emerson & Stern Associates

San Diego, California

The following excerpt is reprinted from a Workshop Presentation to the American Sign Language Research and Teaching Conference in Newark, California, April 1986.

For further information, write to:
Emerson & Stern Associates
10150 Sorrento Valley Road
San Diego, California 92121

Abstract

From 1984–1988 Emerson & Stern Associates and the Salk Institute were engaged in a joint project to construct a computerized written form of Sign Language that would incorporate the structural principles of Sign Language and would be congruent with the needs of the deaf community. Such a system implies the capacity to create printed mass media, including textbooks, in Sign for the first time. It may also have dramatic implications on the ability of Signers to learn written English, since it is already well-known that those who are literate in their native language find it easier to master the written form of a second language. The impact of a computerized written form of Sign may be as great for the deaf community as the Gutenberg press was for Western Europe.

Why Write Sign?

American Sign Language (ASL), the fourth most used language in the United States after English, does not now have a commonly accepted written form. As a result, the deaf community does not have a way to use its native language to create written literature or communicate in print, formally or informally.

Researchers would also find their tasks easier if a straightforward notational system existed for daily communication. And, it is probable that hearing people learning Sign would find Sign easier to master (as a foreign language) if it had a written form.

Several notational schemes were previously devised by Sign Language researchers, but they have been cumbersome and difficult for "ordinary" people to learn because they were created for a purpose other than daily communication. Currently, the most common method of representing Sign Language, aside from the use of English glosses, is by laboriously illustrating a person producing each sign; other systems try to represent such movements as stick figures. However, it is possible to define semi-arbitrary graphic symbols that represent the actual positions and motions of Sign.

The existing approach uses a software-defined character set that (1) removes the constraints of Roman alphabetic characters to allow the creation of symbols that bear resemblance to the physiology of Sign; and (2) generates a typeface with the capability of evolving as Sign Language changes.

Ease of Learning Versus Long-term Utility?

The system had to provide a reasonable amount of information on an 8½- by 11-inch-page. Our goal was to develop a system "usable" by those fluent in Sign. The challenge, however, was to create a system that provides all the information needed for clear communication while remaining "easy to learn." A system may be immediately obvious to a native Signer but be inadequate to communicate complex thoughts. Alternately, it may preserve so much information that it takes too long to learn and would create a separate class of "literate" Signers. Our intent, then, was to balance these two somewhat conflicting objectives to produce a system that would be simultaneously easy to type with a computer system, easy to write by hand, easy to read, and easy to learn.

Why Use Computers?

Representing these images in a computer proves that Sign type-setting is possible, paving the way for printed mass media, including textbooks, written in Sign.

Why Linguistic Analysis?

The better the match between orthography and linguistic structure, the more efficient and effective a writing system will be. Given that we can't write every physical detail of every frame unfolding over time, decisions had to be made about what to include and what to leave out: those decisions were primarily based on the linguistic structure of Sign.

The Approach

In making decisions regarding what should be represented in this system and how it should be represented, there were two primary concerns:

- the system must be readily teachable and learnable;
- it must, as much as possible, agree with deaf users' intuition.

We began by divorcing ourselves from the standard English alphabet. Several things led to this decision: a desire to avoid the typical confusion of ASL and English; a wish to approach the task with a clean slate; and an interest in tapping into the tremendous potential of the computer. At the same time, of course, there was a real desire to avoid anything that looked like "cartoons" or that required artistic abilities.

We were also concerned that the process of writing Sign not require cognitive skills radically different from those required to sign competently and not require full consciousness of the deep structure of sign.

Work on this project was supported in part by Grant NS21409 from the National Institutes of Health/National Institute of Neurological and Communicative Disorders. The opinions expressed herein are solely those of the authors and do not reflect those of the Federal Government or NIH/NINCDS, or NSF.

TELETYPE MONOCASE — HENRY DREYFUSS AND DOYALD YOUNG, TELETYPE 1965

these paragraphs are set in monocase. we were requested to design this special typeface for the teletypewriter to satisfy the needs of upper and lower case without sacrificing the legibility of either. like all things that replace the traditional, it takes getting used to. space is left around the letters, which makes for comfortable reading.

these paragraphs are set in monocase. we were requested to design this special typeface for the teletypewriter to satisfy the needs of upper and lower case without sacrificing the legibility of either. like all things that replace the traditional, it takes getting used to.

aBCDefGhijklmnopqRstuvwxyz

LIBRA — S.H. DE ROOS, AMSTERDAM 1938

aBCDefGhijklmnopqRstuvwxyz

SIMPLEX — S.H. DE ROOS, AMSTERDAM 1939

Henry Dreyfuss & Associates

Pasadena, California

Design/Art Direction:

Henry Dreyfuss

Niels Diffrient

Donald M. Genaro

Young & Dodge, Graphic Design

Doyald Young, Designer/Artist

Teletype Corporation,

Monocase Font

Used by permission of AT&T Bell Laboratories

Teletype Corporation required a font for a high-speed impact printer that did not require shifting from caps to lowercase, which slows transmission. The legibility of lowercase was desired (caps were found to be 15 percent less legible), but proper names appeared too informal in all lowercase—the word *God* was used as an example. A semi-uncial form that retained ascenders and descenders was chosen because of its distinguishing characteristics. S. H. de Roos had designed two fonts in this style for Amsterdam Typefoundry: Libra in 1938 and Simplex in 1939. Libra is a calligraphic letter with liturgical qualities, and Simplex is a single-weight sans serif.

Teletype approved the cutting of the design in metal as shown but considered its monocase style too radical for commercial release. Instead, the traditional font of caps and lowercase was issued.

TELETYPE IMPACT PRINTER FONT — HENRY DREYFUSS AND DOYALD YOUNG, TELETYPE 1965

ABCDEFGHIJ
KLMNOPQRST
UVWXYZ&%¢$
1234567890
abcdefghij
klmnopqrst
uvwxyz

.,:;!?/-¨`
^{}()=+*#

ABCDEFGHIJKLMNOPQRSTUVXYZW
abcdefghijklmnopqrstuvxyzw

EUROSTILE CONDENSED — ALDO NOVARESE, NEBIOLO 1962

Henry Dreyfuss & Associates

Pasadena, California

Design/Art Direction:

Henry Dreyfuss

Niels Diffrient

Donald M. Genaro

Young & Dodge, Graphic Design

Doyald Young, Designer/Artist

Teletype Corporation

Impact Printer Fonts, 12 fixed pitch

Used by permission of AT&T Bell Laboratories

Impact printer fonts whose letters are drawn on equal-width shapes are known as fixed pitch and are troublesome esthetic compromises. Their homeliness is exacerbated by design features that force the letter to remain visually open to facilitate a sharp impression through carbon ribbons that clog areas of joining stems.

A rectangular letter captures the greatest amount of negative area. The large counters produced by a generous x-height are helpful in overcoming less than ideal printing conditions. The descenders are shorter than the ascenders. The bowl of the g is small to gain more descender space. The i, j, and l are serifed to ease and fill the erratic spacing of fixed pitch. Dots for the i, j, and punctuation are large to prevent punched holes. Figures have high frequency of use; these were italicized a few degrees for faster recognition. A 10-pitch was presented also.

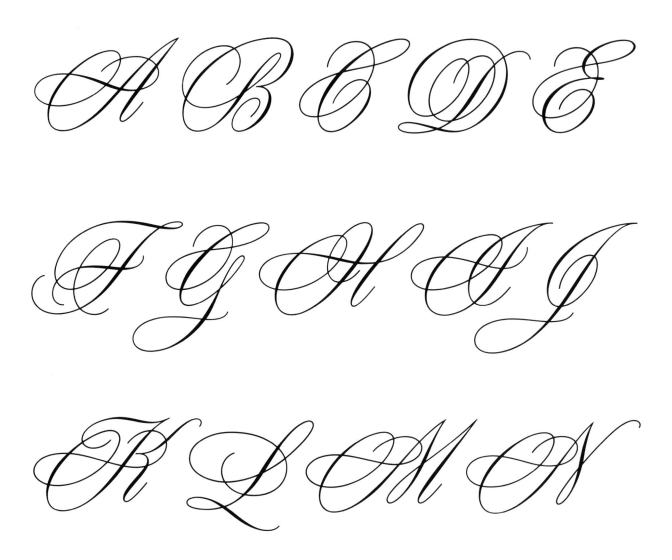

Esselte Letraset Ltd

London, England

Colin Brignall, Type Director
Doyald Young, Designer/Artist
Peter O'Donnell, Letraset, Finished Art
Phillip Kelly, Digital version for Fontek™
Young Baroque, Capitals, Premier Series

My first formal script assignment in beginning lettering from Mortimer Leach came with the directive, "Design your own capital letter." The assignment forever hooked me on formal script, and I am convinced that a lettering man's heaven is in George Bickham's eighteenth-century England.

I was smitten by the graceful flowing qualities of the letter, with its precise proportion, its replication of joining hairlines that must arc, angle, and join at the precise lateral position of the x-height. But above all I loved the freedom that could be used to add grace and shape to a word. There are no fast rules, unless you confine yourself to a particular period or national style—for there are many elegant pen scripts.

In all styles of letterform design, however, there are family characteristics that must be heeded if the font is to be of the same fabric.

The twenty-six script capitals are first married by their proportion, then by the

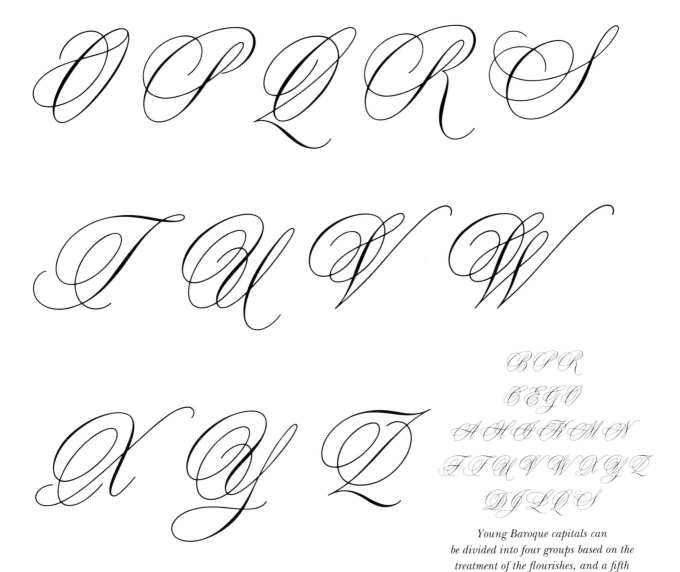

*Young Baroque capitals can
be divided into four groups based on the
treatment of the flourishes, and a fifth
group of unrelated mavericks.*

thickness and distribution of weight, but most importantly by loops, which can be either an ellipse or an oval, that make up the shapes. These can be drawn with the same degree of ellipse, or the same oval shape, or more interestingly, with a series of ovals. It must be remembered that an ellipse is a circle in perspective, and an oval is an ellipsoidal shape, symmetrical on a longitudinal centerline, and to my eye, more pleasing. The ovals may vary in proportion,

orientation, and size—all determined by one's personal esthetic. For example, Young Baroque's group of caps *B*, *P*, and *R* have less mass than the other caps, but relate because of the similarity of their ovals. A rule of thumb is to draw the loops or volutes with approximately the same volume, exercising care not to divide the shape equally (to avoid monotony) or to make small, distracting loops. Additional weight may be added to the loops, tradi-

tionally on a downstroke, but sometimes on the upstroke. There may be several different weights—all as personal choice. I think the same scheme of loops drawn on a majority of caps is often monotonous: variation and surprise are the elements of delight. It is sometimes difficult to make a design element work on prescribed groups. This font is divided into five: *BPR*, *CEGO*, *FTUVWXYZ*, *AHIKMN*, and a group of separate letters that defy categories, *DJLQS*.

YOUNG BAROQUE — DOYALD YOUNG, LETRASET PREMIER SERIES 1984

aabbccddefg

hhhijkllmm

nnoppqurkr

rsſßsttuvv

Esselte Letraset Ltd
London, England

Colin Brignall, Type Director
Doyald Young, Designer/Artist
Peter O'Donnell, Letraset, Finished Art
Phillip Kelly, Digital version for Fontek™
Young Baroque, Lowercase, Premier Series

Many formal script types have small x-heights—the standard nineteenth-century styles Palace Script, Bank Script,

Commercial Script, and Royal Script are roughly one-quarter of the cap height.

To prevent the fussiness of the lowercase from filling in in small sizes, Young Baroque was drawn with an x-height approximately one-third of the cap height, so the lowercase is almost as opulent as the caps. Looped ascenders and descenders are a natural for design variation. I began with the *h* and tested it on the *b*, *k*, and *l*. The normal script *k* was dismissed

in favor of an italic form that permitted the baroque scheme. The looped element was inverted for the *q* and applied to the *j* and *s* in an unorthodox manner.

Words that have no descenders are a bit plain for their caps and can be enlivened with the swash strokes of the *h*, *m*, and *n*, which function as descenders. The free-swinging loops of the alternate *b* and *h* are used for embellishment too. In addition to the standard character set

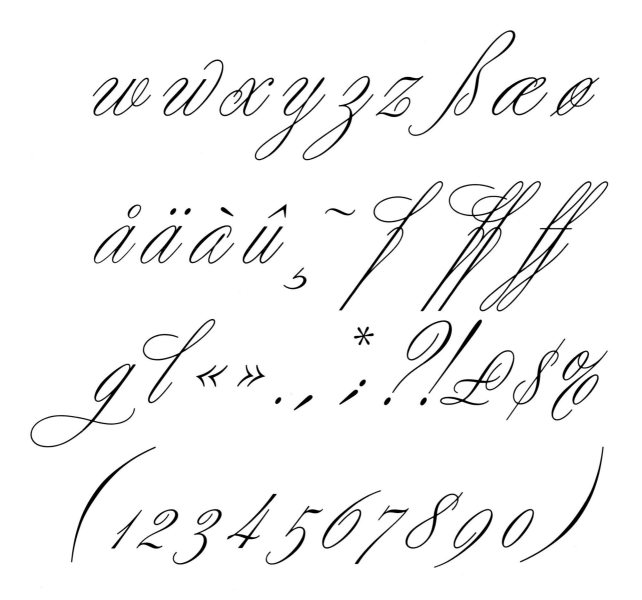

there are twenty-nine alternate letters to facilitate difficult spacing situations, all designed to create a script with a hand-lettered appeal. There are four ligatures, and the old-style figures favor the lower-case. Unlike most old-style fonts, the *4* does not descend.

Some characters and ligatures are recent additions to the newly introduced Fontek™ version, Letraset's digitized display library for the Macintosh, which is compatible with Apple's TrueType,™ and Adobe® PostScript Type 1 fonts.

Sadly, there are never enough, for there are simply too many possibilities within the twenty-six letters. In a face designed expressly for setting poetry, Jan van Krimpen drew forty-nine swash caps for his Cancelleresca Bastarda face, thirty-six special initial or terminal letters, and a bountiful twenty-one ligatures—totaling two hundred and ten characters.

Because Young Baroque is designed as a display font with a careful proportion/spacing ratio, it should not be used in very small sizes. It is best used for only a few words to suggest quality and refinement, and to relieve gray masses of type. Appropriate uses are for stationery and note papers, menus, wine and liquor labels. The caps by themselves are highly stylized shapes that are ideal for large decorative stand-up or drop-initial caps.

Above—A grid used to illustrate the relationship of the capitals and lowercase for family characteristics.
c.—*cap height,* *x.*—*x-height,* *b.*—*baseline,* *d.*—*descent.*

Below—Word sets used to demonstrate letterspacing and the use of alternate characters for an article in
How *magazine, January/February 1987, on the design of Éclat and Young Baroque.*

Esselte Letraset Ltd
London, England

Colin Brignall, Type Director
Doyald Young, Designer/Artist
Peter O'Donnell, Letraset, Finished Art
Young Baroque, Premier Series

Miscellany

Afterword

THE EXAMPLES in this chapter do not fit easily into the categories that define this book. They are varied—half of them are commissioned assignments, and the others were drawn for my enjoyment.

The group is a mix of minimal and ornate letterforms. I enjoy drawing both styles, though the more simple shapes present the greater challenge. It is no idle task to draw a beautiful, distinctive shape stripped of all decoration, because every interruption of a curve's acceleration or languor must count precisely if the concept is to be fully realized. A single-weight sans serif is a test of talent, because there are no frills to hide behind; the drawing must unequivocally be impeccable.

An ornate letter presents a different challenge. While it is desirable to draw the structure of the letter as gracefully as possible, the elaborate texture takes center stage and good design is then vital.

Whether letters are simple or ornate, both are governed by skillful drawing and a knowledge of letterforms. Only when letters are drawn over a long period of time is it then possible to discover subtleties that are not apparent in a simple drawing exercise. Lettering is a discipline that requires constant practice, analysis, persistence, and sedulous attention to detail. My enjoyment of drawing letters is derived from the basic process of learning to draw, for only rarely have I drawn them to my keenest liking.

The designs in this book demonstrate the requirements of legibility within this chosen area of commercial application. The shapes of letters cannot vary much, or else they will be perceived as abstract objects. Yet that is the intriguing challenge: to fashion distinctive shapes without sacrificing the heritage of legibility. Within this area of recognition, endless variation is possible, limited only by imagination—and exemplified by the work of Morris F. Benton, Adrian Frutiger, Jan van Krimpen, Aldo Novarese, and Hermann Zapf—heroes all.

There is scant difference in some of the most widely used fonts of today, and the classic Roman letters of the Trajan column. Yet survival in the commercial world is dependent on the demands of fashion, which are often at odds with traditional responses. Some of these design rationales are fashions of an earlier day, but many of them have held fast and, as a saturnine friend observed, are a solace in a "very fast-food world."

Advertising, industrial design, packaging, and the world of the graphic arts constantly require new forms, revivals, and marriages of existing fonts for the market and for young emerging audiences. The rules for using type will continue to evolve and repeat. This is a necessary function of design—it is not necessarily progress, but only a mirror of the demands and changing tastes and preferences of a generation, or a culture. But there will remain certain proven principles that lend grace and artistry to the printed word. These will be used in coming generations as they have been since the Romans chiseled the deeds and conquests of the Caesars into stone.

Opposite—
Detail of Bernyce Polifka
Gallery Announcement
(see page 278).

BERNYCE
POLIFKA

ABCDEFGHIJKLMNOPQRSTUVWXYZ

abcdefghijklmnopqrstuvwxyz

OPTIMA — HERMANN ZAPF, STEMPEL 1958

Bernyce Polifka
(Mrs. Eugene Fleury)
Northridge, California

Doyald Young, Designer/Artist
Gallery Announcement

Bernyce Polifka taught design and color at Art Center College of Design, Pasadena, California, for the better part of forty years, and I had a weekly luncheon with her for the better part of twenty. An individualist who always created a stir, she was a great colorist and hard-edge painter. The art critic for the *Los Angeles Times*, William Wilson, dubbed her paintings "Romantic Hard-edge"—which secretly pleased her. This lettering, designed for an announcement to fit a number ten envelope, was for her very first painting exhibition at the Paideia Gallery in Los Angeles. Based on Optima, it is almost nine inches wide. The weight is light, for Bernyce loved finesse and exquisite craftsmanship. It is all drawn freehand with the exception of the *A*'s crossbar—the only trick used here is the *KA* ligature, which seemed mandatory to lessen a massive misspacing. Bernyce made a *cause célèbre* of the Golden Section and loved taut mathematical design. This was designed for her esthetic: *BERNYCE* is half as wide as *POLIFKA*, which divided the card's height.

*A true friend of Smokey's
Leaves matches alone;
He won't burn his fingers,
Or the animals' home.*

ABCDEFGHIJKLMNOPQRSTUVWXYZ
abcdefghijklmnopqrstuvwxyz

CENTURY OLD STYLE — MORRIS F. BENTON, ATF 1906

Foote Cone & Belding

Los Angeles, California

Ralph Price, Creative Director
Judy Hersley, Art Director
Doyald Young, Designer/Artist
*USDA Forest Service and the
Advertising Council*

This is an unretouched HB pencil draw-ing that I drew one long Thanksgiving-weekend at my cabin in the Angeles Na-tional Forest. It was for a grade school poster with a magical drawing by Teresa Woodward of Smokey and his friends.

Ligatures[1] abound, and there are swash characters with a mixture of italic and roman forms that frequently de-scend. It is a Century old style defined by sturdy thins and cupped diagonal serifs at x-height. Its abundant volutes and swash letters define it as fabulist style. The letters are drawn freely, with con-cave stems that are slightly off their feet. The ascenders are softly arched and are tipped with slender teardrop termi-nals in the style of *cinquecento* calligraphy.

---

1. These ligatures stem from early attempts to fash-ion types that were imitative of the flourishes of handwriting such as the *civilité* type of Granjon and, more recently, Hermann Zapf's magnificent Zapf Civilité. Jan van Krimpen's Cancelleresca Bastarda is based on the same aspirations. His italic more close-ly parallels the styles of Italian writing masters of the sixteenth century: Arrighi, Tagliente, and Palatino.

Clock Face
Doyald Young, Designer/Artist
(unpublished)

I never cared for the typographical solution for the face of a ship's clock that I own, nor do I know why I decided that a Victorian design would be more appropriate than the design that Seth Thomas supplied with the clock. The style would not be very legible in the dim light of a ship's cabin in a roiling sea, but, then, we don't read the numbers on a clock face: we read the position of the hands. All else is decoration (several high-end mail-order catalogs now advertise a wall clock with Baskerville "numbers").

The beginnings and endings of the clock's numerals are like fat spit curls and are derived from the endings produced by a pointed flexible pen—note the *2, 3, 5, 6,* and *9*. These endings occur on many ornate nineteenth-century forms and are similar to the arabesques introduced into Venice by Moorish traders in the fifteenth century (see Calabasas Park, page 246). They form the basis for many of the fleurons originally designed for gold foil stamping on bookbindings.

These figures (as typographers prefer to call them) are called "fat face." They are part and parcel of the excesses of the Victorian age. I lovingly call them sawbuck Bodoni, for in all four corners, front and back, of United States currency, the denomination of the note is drawn in fat face. The amount is spelled out also, in caps of the same style at the bottom on both sides. ("Sawbuck" is an old slang word for a ten-dollar bill. It refers to the roman numeral X, which suggests the crossed-end supports of a sawhorse.)

There are many "fat faces:" Normandia, designed by Novarese and Buti in 1946 for Nebiolo, follows the same general design of Robert Thorne's Thorowgood design, cut around 1835 and reissued by Stephenson Blake in 1953. The basic shapes of these types are really nothing but slight variations of the weights and proportions of Bodoni and are called moderns. Ed Benguiat's admirable Modern No. 216 for ITC is a new version. Stephenson Blake's Modern No. 20 is a family assembled from a collection of sizes from different foundries in England. (In the nineteenth century some of the bold condensed versions were known as Aldine.[1]) Ultra Bodoni is an unbracketed fat face from ATF where the weighted strokes do not blend gradually into the hairline but instead hit it abruptly, almost at right angles. The formal, symmetrically distributed weight of these modern-style letters allows them to be greatly extended, both in weight and proportion, without compromising the basic structure of the letter.

The cartouche is composed of four separate overlapping designs and is contrived to bisect the cipher precisely at the baseline and dead center of the counter.

---

1. Mac McGrew, *American Metal Typefaces of the Twentieth Century*, preliminary edition (New Rochelle, New York: The Myriade Press, 1986), page 237.

MODERN NO. 216 HEAVY — ED BENGUIAT, ITC 1982

ABCDEFGHIJKLMNOPQRSTUVWXYZ
abcdefghijklmnopqrstuvwxyz
0123456789

LOGO TYPES & LETTER FORMS

LOGO TYPES &LETTER FORMS

*The book's title set in
ATF/ITC/Adobe Baskerville,
to show relative proportions.*

Design Press
Imprint of TAB Books,
Division of McGraw-Hill, Inc.
Nancy N. Green,
Vice-President, Editorial Director
Doyald Young, Designer/Artist
Book Jacket

One of the most difficult assignments is one that is directed to your own efforts. The difficulty here is lessened because a book dust jacket must perform exacting tasks. Not only must the editor and the publisher's team of marketing experts approve the design, but the international distributor's requirements must be satisfied. It should catch the eye, even when reduced to two-and-a-half inches in height for catalogs designed expressly for booksellers. At that size it must be easily read—even the subtitle must withstand a 25 percent reduction. Its competitive image is a must on the bookseller's racks; faint-hearted designs need not apply. The design should not pander to an ephemeral style, but instead the concept should be accessible to a wide variety of tastes.

Much of my early work was done for architects, industrial designers, package designers, and exacting graphic designers. Because of this, I am comfortable with layouts of organized justified type. The book's contents demand that the title be drawn by hand, though several layout arrangements were tried with Baskerville type, with little success. One is shown above that shows the proportions of the Adobe version, and vividly contrasts the proportions of the final layout.

To achieve a justified four-line layout, each word must be modified and the proportions compromised for the rectangular image. *LOGO* establishes the title's style with its near classical proportions. Drawn normally, *TYPES* is a shorter word than *LOGO*, and because spacing throughout should be visually consistent, it was enlarged to fit. To minimize large areas of space, the *TY* ligature in *TYPE* seemed a necessity. (Note the *Y*'s bracketed waist drawn to soften the letter.) The ampersand is tailored to snuggle around the *T*, *L*, and *E*.

The crossbars of the *T*s in *LETTER* admit a great amount of space and have been narrowed to create a more even color and to prevent too great a reduction of the word for the justified scheme. Because of the *M*'s extreme width, *FORMS* must be reduced, and then ever so slightly weighted for an optical match.

Serifs were originally formed by the stonecutter's attempts to dress the corners of a stem. These are not as pointed as the original incised letters. Instead, they are thin and modeled, and their tips are chopped at an angle. The serif bracket is gentle, though the weight flows gradually into the stem and creates an optically widened ending. While the general style of the title is classical, the round forms, *G*, *P*, *R*, and *O*, have a modern weight distribution with a vertical centerline. The face pays homage to classical styles with a height-to-thickness ratio of almost 1:13; the Trajan capitals are 1:12. Both the *E* and *R* are similar to Hermann Zapf's classic Palatino and Michelangelo faces.

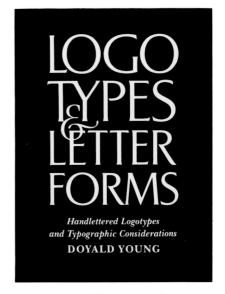

*A livelier ampersand
was tried with softer shapes and a
flourish with a pronounced horizontal
curve that underscores
the **Y** in **TYPES**.
Considered initially to fill the
space between the **TY**, it succeeds
only as a space filler and lacks the
legibility of the final version.
The subtitle was changed to three
even lines for a more
simplified shape.*

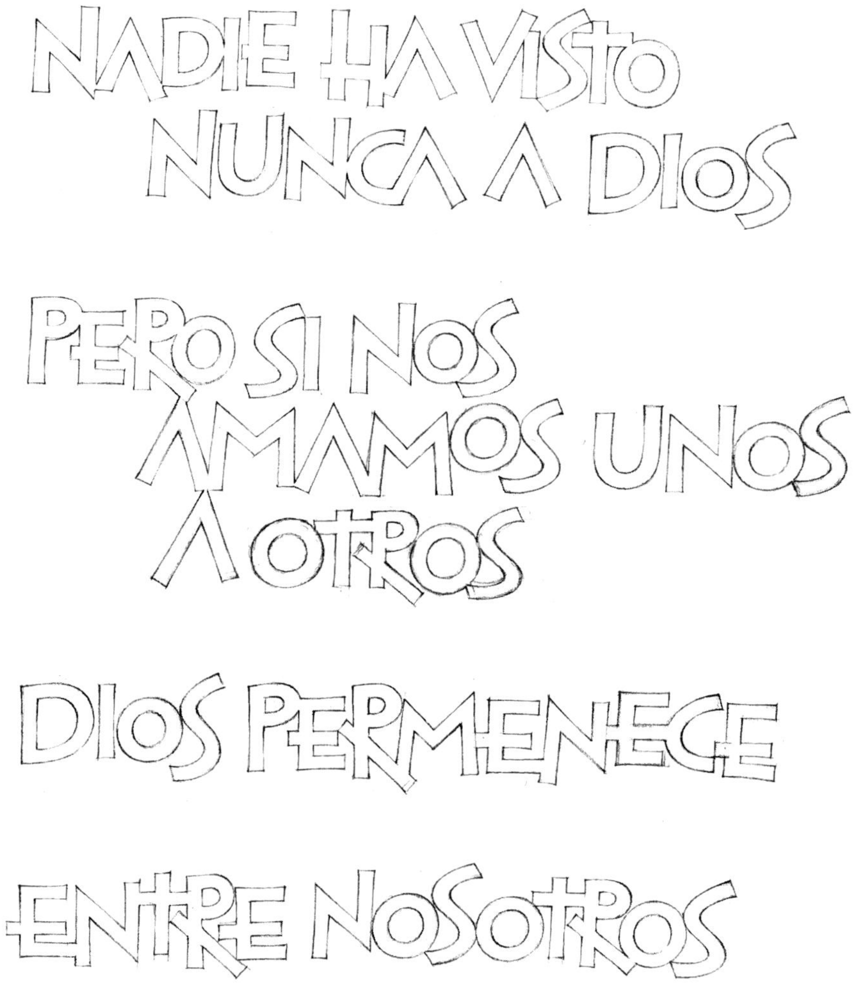

NADIE HA VISTO
NUNCA A DIOS

PERO SI NOS
AMAMOS UNOS
A OTROS

DIOS PERMENECE

ENTRE NOSOTROS

Nadie ha visto

Cuernavaca, Mexico

Designer and author unknown
Doyald Young, Artist
Cloisters Plaque

This sketch (opposite) is reminiscent of early religious graffiti written hurriedly and furtively on walls. Originally, forms similar to these were incised with a pointed stylus into clay, which produced a single-weight letter. The style is also reminiscent of the single-weight writing on Greek vases that was produced by a slightly blunted brush. In the same manner, Rudolf Koch desired a more intimate relationship with his metal font Neuland and cut it directly into metal, forsaking the elaborate and pains-taking drawings that were pantographed to produce a punch.

In a Greco-Roman vein, the ATF Pericles font shown below, designed in 1934, is a forerunner of a recent sans serif design named Lithos—a family of five weights drawn by Carol Twombly at Adobe Systems.

In the preliminary tissue, the *S*s are overbalanced, the ending stroke of the *N* reaches highly, and the *O*s tumble and are warped. The middle crossbar of the *E* is low and crosses the vertical stem. The letters are of different sizes, often list to the right, and rest casually on the base-line. Frequently they are joined, and some tuck beneath crossbars. Easily read, the *A* drops its crossbar, while the *R* departs radically from conventional forms.

The tissue is derived from a photo-graph I took of an inscription in the cloisters of a cathedral in Cuernavaca, Mexico (below). Painted in black on a four- by three-foot gold-leafed plaque, the casual, somewhat angular sans serif letters were original, unsophisticated, vigorous, yet drawn with great authority. The piece was not signed, nor was there any information about it. I was moved by the sentiment, and one day I plan to finish it, along with my translation of it: *"No one has ever seen God, but if we love one another, God abides forever among us."*

ABCDE**Ɛ**FGHIJKLMNOPϘ
ꓤꓤSTUVWXYZ&

ABCDEFGHIJKLMNOPQRSTUVWXYZ
1234567890

Type Classification

Reprinted by permission from Jaspert, Berry & Johnson's *Encyclopaedia of Type Faces,* fourth edition. London: Blandford Press, 1970, page xiv. (Extracts from British Standards 2961:1967.)

The names of groups of type faces now in general use have grown haphazardly over the past 150 years. Some of the names are descriptive but others are historical and, except to those well versed in the history of printing and type design, have little meaning. Since the end of the last century, several attempts have been made to evolve a classification of type faces, but none has found really wide acceptance. It has become increasingly evident, especially during the last ten years, that there is a real need for classification which can be accepted nationally, and preferably internationally, and which will facilitate discussions between type face designers and printers, printers and print-buyers, and teachers of typography and their students.

In 1954, Maximilian Vox, in France, published some proposals which were simpler than any of the earlier attempts. While they were generally welcomed, they were also criticized and were amended later. In 1959, a draft German Standard was issued, giving a classification which related to the principles adopted by Vox, but which was considerably more complex. After considering the comments which they received on this draft, the Deutscher Normenausschuss published a revised classification (DIN 16518) in 1964, which was almost identical to the Vox classification. The Vox classification is widely used in many European countries.

The difficulty arises that if the categories are rigidly defined and limited to a practical number, many type faces elude classification. On the other hand if the categories are loosely defined, each may contain type faces which are fundamentally different although having certain, perhaps arbitrary, factors in common. This classification attempts to limit the possibilities of confusion.

The actual nomenclature must, of course, differ in different countries according to language. The classification in the British Standard is based on the concepts of English-speaking countries.

The following are my versions of the definitions, and the typeface examples were selected from those used in this book.

Humanist—Formerly Venetian. Diagonal axis. Slight contrast between thick and thin. Heavily bracketed serifs. Ascenders often taller than caps with oblique serifs. Cross-stroke of *e* is oblique.
Centaur, Plantin 110.

Garalde—Formerly old style. More refined than humanist but still with diagonal axis. Oblique serifed ascenders.
Adobe Original Garamond, Caslon.

Transitional—Vertical axis. Thins more finely modeled. finely modeled serifs. Cross-stroke of the *e* is horizontal.
Baskerville, Lutetia.

Didone—Formerly modern. Vertical axis and abrupt contrast between thick and thin strokes. Usually unbracketed, horizontal hairline serifs. Based on Bodoni and Didot forms.
Bodoni, Didot, Torino.

Slab-serif—Faces with heavy square-ended serifs, with or without brackets.
Serifa, Guts.

Lineale—Formerly sans serif. Typefaces without serifs.
a. Grotesque—Nineteenth-century origins. Slight contrast between thick and thin strokes. Squarish curves and curling close-set jaws. Curved ending strokes are usually horizontal.
Franklin Gothic, Venus.

b. Neo-Grotesque—Derived from the Grotesques. Stroke contrast is near monotone. Curved ending usually oblique and more open. More regular in proportion and design.
Frutiger, Helvetica, Univers.

c. Geometric—Simple geometric letters, circle or rectangle. Usually monotone or with single-story *a* and *g*.
Futura, Eurostile, Microgramma.

d. Humanist—Based on proportions of the humanist or classical roman letter. Thick and thin qualities. Two-story **a, g**.
Gill Sans, Optima.

Glyphic—Letters that are chiseled rather than calligraphic shapes.
Friz Quadrata, Serif Gothic.

Script—Imitative of handwriting or flowing cursive forms, joined or separate.
Coronet, Murray Hill, Young Baroque.

Graphic—Characters that suggest that they have been drawn instead of written.
Hobo, Topic, Open Roman Capitals.

Note—*The impossibility of placing every typeface into one of the categories above is recognized. In cases of difficulty the use of a compound term,* e.g. *Humanist/Garalde, is suggested.*

Glossary

Note—Depending on the source, the usage may vary for terms given here, which are the ones used in this book.

agate—1. Originally, an English typeface whose body size was 5.5 points. **2.** A 5.5 point size of type used primarily in newspaper advertising. **3.** A unit of the same measure used to measure depth in newspaper advertising.

alphabet—A set of letters in which a language is written.

ampersand (&)—The symbol for "and." A contraction of "and per se and." It derives its form or shape from the Latin word *et*, meaning "and."

arm—A horizontal extension from the vertical stem of an *E*, *F*, *L*, and *T*.

ascender—The portion of a letter that extends above the body or x-height of a lowercase letter, as in *b,d,f,k,l*, and *t*.

ballot box (□)—An outline square. For use primarily as a device in which to indicate a preference. Also used in place of a center dot or square dot.

baseline—The horizontal base alignment of capital letters and the lowercase letters that do not descend.

beard—The bottom sloping edge of handset type between the face baseline and the shoulder.

beak—The triangular shape usually found on the **s**, **z**, **C**, **E**, **F**, **L**, **T**, and **Z**.

biform—Same-height caps and lowercase without ascenders or descenders.

black letter—Style of writing used in the medieval period. Sometimes called *lettre de forme, textura,* or *fraktur*. A flat-sided and pointed letter. Type used in the Gutenberg Bible.

Bodoni dash—A horizontal swelled stroke tapering to hairlines at both ends. Used to denote an ending or sometimes to separate different items of copy.

body matter—The reading text of an ad or other copy, also known as body copy, body text, or reading matter.

boldface—1. A heavy-weight typeface. **2.** In machine type some fonts contain the regular letter and either the boldface or italic companion on the same matrix and called duplex.

bowl—The upper portion of the lowercase *g*, in serif faces and some sans serif faces, *e.g.,* Gill Sans.

bracket—1. The filled-in area that connects the serif to a stroke on capital and lowercase letters. Also called *fillet*. **2.** [ ] Brackets are used to set off a phrase within a parenthetical phrase.

branch—The curved stroke that connects to the stem on lowercase letters such as *h,m,n*, and *u*.

brass—A one-point-wide spacing unit in handset (metal) type.

calligraphic type—Type that derives its form from letters written with a brush, quill, flat pen, or a chisel instrument held at a slight angle from the horizontal. Examples are Palatino and Trump.

cap height—Exclusive of accent marks, the vertical measurement of caps. In many old-style fonts, the caps are not as tall as the ascenders. The caps and ascenders of most modern fonts are the same height.

caps and small caps—1. Originally, two different sizes of capitals cast on the same-size type body. **2.** Caps set with small caps that are same size as the lowercase body.

center dot (·)—Also called a *bullet,* and usually round, a dot that centers vertically on the x-height of the lowercase. Primarily used to set apart phrases or listings. The weight used is usually balanced to the weight of the type.

chancery script—A style of writing developed by papal scribes in the fifteenth century, and the model for many early italic types.

character—Any letter, figure, punctuation, mark, symbol, or space.

cipher—The figure **0** (zero).

civilité—A French Gothic cursive type of the sixteenth century, based on the handwriting of Robert Granjon. Zapf Civilité typeface is an example.

color spacing—The addition of spaces to congested areas of words or word-spacing to achieve a more pleasing appearance after a line has been set normally. Color additionally refers to the length of the ascenders and descenders. If they are long, a page will color lighter than if they are short.

column gutter—The space between two columns of type.

condensed type—Type that is compressed horizontally—Empire, Onyx, Tower, Helvetica Condensed, Franklin Gothic Condensed, etc. (Called *elongated* in England.)

copper—A spacing unit in handset type that is .5 point wide.

counter—1. The area, including the shoulder, surrounding a letter, figure, punctuation mark, or symbol in metal type below the face or printing surface. **2.** The enclosed lobe or interior spaces of letters: *a,b,d,g,o,p,q,A,B,D,O,P,Q,R*.

crossbar—The horizontal stroke on the cap *A*, and the lowercase **e**, *f*, and *t*.

cupped—1. Refers to slightly arched serifs, to the top of the lowercase *t*, and sometimes to the top of the cap *A*. **2.** A design feature in some sans serif stems. An example is Erasmus (see page 248).

cursive—Literally: running. Possessing a flowing quality. Formal scripts are cursive. The fifteenth-century chancery hand is described as cursive.

curved stem—The heavy portion of curved letters, either serif or sans serif.

dagger (†)—**1.** A mark used for a reference. **2.** Symbol meaning "deceased." Also called *diesis*.

descender—The portion of a lowercase letter that descends below the baseline, as in *g,j,p,q*, and **y**. In some old-style fonts, the cap *J* descends.

diagonal hairline—The thin portions of the **A,K,M,V,W,X,Y, k,v,w,x,** and **y**.

didoni—Didot and Bodoni combined. See *Didone* in "Type Classification," page 286.

diphthong ligature—Two vowels joined together, for example æ.

display faces—Type used for headings and titles and generally larger than 14 point, as opposed to text faces, and often spaced tightly for visual impact.

ear—The projection from the righthand side of the bowl of the lowercase *g*.

Egyptian types—Originally, from 1815 on, bold faces with heavy slab or square serifs (though Caslon drew a sans serif in the eighteenth century that he named Egyptian). Lighter versions are Beton, Cairo, Clarendon, Egyptian Expanded, Fortune, Graph, Stymie, Memphis, and Rockwell. (See "Type Classification," page 286.)

elite—A typewriter face size which contains twelve characters to the linear inch, and six to the vertical inch (*see also* pica).

em—The square of any point size of type. Also, 3-em and 4-em spaces or ⅓ and ¼ of an em are commonly used as word spacing. Em is sometimes called *mutton* or *mutt.*

en—Half the width of any point size of type. Also called *nut.*

extended type—Typefaces whose proportions are wide horizontally, such as Egyptian expanded, Hellenic, Latin wide, Microgramma extended, Standard extended, Univers 53 and 63.

eye—The enclosed portion of an *e*.

face—Any style of type. Also, in letterpress, that portion of type that creates the printed impression.

fat faces—A style from the late nineteenth century and based on the modern forms of Bodoni and Didot. Extremely bold and often extended. Normandia and Thorowgood are examples.

figures—Numbers or numerals.

fleurons—Ornaments resembling flowers or leaves. Also called *flowers.*

flush left—Copy that is aligned vertically on the lefthand side.

flush right—Copy that aligns vertically on the righthand side.

folio—A page number. Lefthand pages are even numbered, righthand pages are odd numbered.

font—The complete set of characters, figures, punctuation marks, and symbols of a typeface.

foot—**1.** In some faces, the horizontal serif or stroke that appears at the bottom of the lowercase *a* and *t.* **2.** The bottom of metal type. (When the expression "off its feet" is used, it means the type is not standing square and only part of the letter or letters will print.)

foundry type—A bas-relief letter cast in reverse on a block of metal. Block height to paper is .918 inch. Set by hand and justified in a composing stick; usually 6- to 72-point. Also called *hand type.*

grotesque—European for sans serif (often round faces, *i.e.,* Helvetica normal).

Gothic—**1.** A widely accepted name for sans serif faces—Helvetica, Futura, News Gothic, etc. **2.** More traditionally, the German black letter and Old English, such as Goudy Text, Engraver's Old English, American Text, etc.

hairline—**1.** The thin portion of a two-weight roman letter. **2.** A ¼-point or thinner rule. **3.** Small pieces of metal (sometimes called *fins*) that appear between letters when matrices on metal line-casting machines become worn.

head—A line or lines of copy set in a larger face than the body copy. Short for headline or headings.

hung punctuation—Punctuation that is set wholly or partially beyond the left or right margins of the text to create a more optically even margin.

horizontal serifs—On most lowercase straight stems, mostly at the baseline, though on **k, v, w, x, y,** in old-style fonts, (the rest of the serifs are usually cupped). At the baseline and x-height of modern fonts such as Bodoni, Fenice, Walbaum.

inferior figures or letters—Small figures or letters at the bottom of type for reference notes, mathematical and chemical symbols.

initials—Large or decorative letters, usually caps, used at the beginnings of paragraphs or important sections. "Stand-up" initials align at the baseline of the first line of text. "Drop" or "sunken" initials align at top with the ascenders of the first line. Except for the first line, text is indented flush around the initial.

italic—**1.** A cursive letterform designed to complement or be compatible with a companion roman typeface. **2.** Term loosely used in the printing trade to describe any slanted or leaning letter (*see also* oblique).

justified type—Type that aligns vertically on both the left- and righthand sides.

kerned letters—**1.** In foundry type, letters that partially extend beyond the edge of the body for better spacing, including diagonals that admit too much space. In computer fonts, letters that intrude on another matrix: *TA, AT, WA, LT, LY,* etc. **2.**—Letters fitted together to reduce unwanted space between them.

leader—Line of dots or dashes across the page to separate copy.

leading—The vertical space between lines of type. Also called line spacing.

ligature—Two or more connected letters: *ff, fi, fl, ffl*. Formerly, in metal type, the same letters cast on one piece of metal (*see also* logotype).

lobe—An enclosed projection of a letter, either rounded or flat, as in *B, D, P, R, a, b, d, p,* and *q*.

logotype—**1.** An identifying name. **2.** A symbol or mark. **3.** Separate letters cast on one piece of metal to avoid open letterspacing—*TA, TO, VA, WE,* and *QU*.

loop—The lower portion of the lowercase *g* in most serifed faces and in some sans serif faces.

machine composition—Type set by a machine, such as Intertype, Linotype, or Monotype, which casts type in metal.

majuscule—Capital letter.

masthead—The name of a periodical; also staff credits of the publication.

minuscule—Lowercase letter.

modern style—Type that originated in the late eighteenth century. Characterized by a vertical stress and extreme contrast between the thick and thin strokes. Serifs are usually horizontal and mostly unbracketed. Examples are Bodoni, Corvinus, De Vinne, Didot, Scotch Roman, Torino.

modern-style figures—Figures that are the same size as the caps (in many faces) and align at the top as well as with the baseline: 1234567890. Also called *lining*.

oblique—A slanted letter of the same form as the roman version—often sans serif (such as Futura and Romulus).

oblique serif—*See* triangular serif.

ogee curve—A reverse curve. Found on the tail or loop of the *g, s, S,* and sometimes on the tail of the cap *R* and some swash caps.

old style—Letters with slight differentiation between the thick and thin strokes. The rounded forms possess a diagonal axis. Examples are Berkeley, Caslon, Centaur, Garamond, Kennerly. Generally, based on sixteenth-century Italian forms. (See "Type Classification," page 286.)

old-style figures—Forms derived from the Hindi and Arabic alphabets: 1234567890. The 1, 2, and 0 are the same height as the lowercase body. The 3, 4, 5, 7, and 9 align with the x-height and descend below the baseline. The 6 and 8 align with the baseline and ascend above the x-height. (Bodoni old style does not follow this pattern exactly.)

photocomposition—Type set by reproducing on film or photographic paper letters from a master alphabet on film or paper.

pica—**1.** A measuring unit of type equal to 12 points. Approximately one-sixth of an inch. **2.** A typewriter face size with ten characters to the inch. **3.** A 12-point English typeface. See "Type Sizes," page 290.

point—A measurement used for type sizes and letterspacing and line leading. There are twelve points to a pica, and six picas to the inch, or seventy-two points to the inch.

pothook—Initial curved hooks on some lowercase italic faces, such as Torino, Century expanded, Modern No. 216, etc.

proportion—The width to height ratio of any given typeface.

quad—A metal space that is one en or more in width (em quad, etc.).

return stroke—Lefthand side of the *g*'s loop.

rivers—Word spaces that create irregular vertical lines of white space in body type. These occur when lines of type have been set with excessive word spacing, with little or no hyphenation in justified copy only.

roman—**1.** A letter modeled after the classic Roman letter. **2.** An upright letter, as opposed to a slanted one.

rule—Lines in varying point-size thicknesses. Used for borders and also to separate copy blocks or columns.

runaround—Type that is set to fit the contour of an illustration, photo, ornament, or initial.

run-in—Heads that are set in a different style from the text, which follows on the same line. Also called *lead-in*.

sans serif—Letters without serifs. Commonly called *Gothics*.

script—Connected letters resembling pen handwriting. May be upright or slanted to the left or right. Some classifications include separated letters.

serif—A short line stemming from and at an angle to upper and lower ends of the strokes of a letter. Sometimes oblique.

set—The basis for determining the width of all characters or individual letters of a given font.

shoulder—**1.** The top left or right side of a round letterform. **2.** In metal type, the counter beneath a descender that prevents the descenders of a line of type from touching the ascenders of the following line when the lines have been set solid (zero leading).

single-story—Describes the *a* in most italics. Many sans serifs have both a one-story roman and italic *a*. See Erbar, Futura, Kabel, Metro, Spartan, and Tempo.

small caps—Capitals, usually the same height as the x-height of the lowercase. Usually drawn in a wider proportion and a weight to match the lowercase. Sometimes named "expert" in PostScript fonts. Usually includes fractions, fleurons, and odd characters.

solid—Lines of type with no line leading. Also called *unleaded*.

sort—**1.** An individual piece of type, whence the expression "out of sorts." **2.** A special character or symbol not usually included in a font of type or matrices.

specimen sheet—A sheet or brochure from a type maker, usually showing the complete font and reading matter set in the same face in available sizes.

spine—The reverse curve of the *S*.

spur—In many serifed faces, the triangular extension at the top of the beaks of some letters, as in *s, C, G, S,* and sometimes *T* and *Z*.

square spot—A solid square used in place of a center dot as an accent or lead-in to paragraphs or listings. Usually drawn to align with the x-height.

stem—The vertical, diagonal, or curved weighted stroke of a letter.

TYPE SIZES

Before the point system was invented by Pierre Simon Fournier in 1736, type sizes were named instead of numbered.

	POINTS
Diamond	4.5
Large English Pearl	5
Agate	5.5
Nonpareil	6
Minion	7
Brevier	8
Bourgeois	9
Long Primer	10
Small Pica	11
Pica	12
Great Primer	18
Paragon	20
2-Line Pica	24
2-Line English	28
2-Line Great Primer	36
2-Line Double Pica	44
Canon	48

stroke—The lines of a letter, horizontal, vertical, curved, diagonal, thick, or thin.

subhead—A secondary phrase following a headline. Display line(s) of lesser importance than the main headline(s).

superior figures or letters—Small raised figures or letters next to type, used for reference, such as footnotes, bibliographical composition, or mathematical and chemical symbols.

swash letters—Capitals or lowercase letters, roman or italic, embellished with flourishes, often ending with a teardrop or circular shape. From early sixteenth-century writing masters Arrighi, Palatino, and Tagliente. Jan van Krimpen's Cancelleresca Bastarda is an example.

swelled stroke—The reverse curve of one side of the italic *h,m,n,u,* and sometimes *v, w,* and *y.* Also, the script versions of these letters.

tail—The curved stroke at the bottom of the lowercase *a* and *t.* Also, the curved or horizontal stroke at the bottom of the *Q* and the diagonal stroke attached to the lobe of the cap **R.**

terminals—In most serifed faces, the circular, teardrop, or wedge-shaped endings occurring on the lowercase letters *a, c, f, j ,r,* and *y,* and on swash extensions of some capitals, mostly italic.

thins—The thin portions of a letter, sometimes referred to as hairlines.

titling faces—Capital letters without a corresponding lowercase, which occupy almost the full point size (minus the shoulder) of the type. Examples are Adobe Original Garamond Titling, Perpetua Titling, Michelangelo Titling, Microgramma, Trajan, Bauer Text.

transitional—Letters with greater contrast between thick and thin strokes than in old style. Curved forms usually possess a vertical axis. In classification, can be regarded as a transition from Garalde to Didone. Some examples are Baskerville, Bulmer, Caledonia. (See "Type Classification," page 286.)

triangular serif—Found on the lowercase ascenders and tops of the straight stems of many old-style fonts. Sometimes referred to as *oblique.*

two-story—Lowercase **a** with a small lobe, opposed to a single-story *a* whose lobe occupies the full x-height.

type—A letter or character, originally in bas-relief, from which an inked impression is made.

typeface—Type of a single design, regardless of size. In letterpress, its printing surface (also type).

type family—A group of typefaces of the same design but with different weights and proportions. Examples are Bodoni, Century, Helvetica, Futura, Univers.

type series—A range of sizes of one basic typeface, usually from 6- to 72-point, in machine faces, and 4- to 600-point in computer fonts.

uncial—Lettering style freely written by quill or flat pen. Uncial capital letters sometimes assumed the shape of lowercase letters and served as a basis for our present lowercase alphabet. Fourth to eighth century.

vertical serif—Found on the center arm of the *E* and *F.*

waist—The narrow part of a *K, X,* or *R,* or the convergence of the *Y*'s diagonals.

weight—The thickness of a letter stroke, characterized as light, extra light, regular, medium, demi-bold, bold, extra bold and ultra bold.

weighted diagonal—The thick strokes of the letters *A, K, M, N, R, V, W, X, Y, Z,* k, v, **w, x, y,** and **z.**

widow—An undesirably short line, word, or part of a word that occurs at the top of a page or column; called an *orphan* when it occurs at the bottom of a page or column.

x-height—The height of the lowercase **x.** Sometimes *body height.*

Bibliography

A LONG LIST OF BOOKS in a bibliography can be daunting to a reader. Here are the books that have pleased me most, and the ones that I have found rewarding and useful. They include the history of letters and specimen catalogs, but unfortunately not many have dealt with the esthetic reasons for the legibility factors in the actual drawing of a letter. In first learning to draw letters, I tried desperately to understand the rules. At times I found that the rules varied but mostly were based on empirical reasons.

The first reference work that I tackled was Daniel B. Updike's formidable *Printing Types: Their History, Forms, and Use*, valuable for its historical and regional examples. The biographies are short and informative. Alexander Lawson's *Anatomy of a Typeface* is an indispensable history of type: its reasons, use, fashion. It is learned and accessible, a certifiable classic with the most complete bibliography that I have encountered. Mac McGrew's *American Metal Typefaces of the Twentieth Century* is published in a preliminary edition and offers much scholarly information found only in this work. Oliver Simon's *Introduction to Typography* is an absolute gem, because it explains how to use type, with valid rules that every young designer should know. Jan Tschichold's *Asymmetric Typography* simply has not been improved upon. For editing, and the parts of a book, *The Chicago Manual of Style* is a must-own. The *American Type Founders Specimen Book and Catalog 1923* edition is an old friend. *Berthold Fototype* and *Body Types E2* are two volumes that contain a superb and extensive library of 577 text faces and 1400 headline faces in a very handsome format. Monotype's specimen catalogs are a collection of fonts that record their illustrious history—their *Newsletter* and *Recorder* are great sources of information. In Los Angeles, Andresen Typographic's monumental five-volume specimen catalog is a collection of six thousand fonts: two volumes of text faces, and three volumes of "heads" (display faces). Jaspert, Berry, and Johnson's *Encyclopaedia of Type Faces* is a constantly used reference work—and for sheer delight, John Ryder's *A Suite of Fleurons* is one of my most prized possessions. I have listed most of Prof. Zapf's books; his work has greatly influenced me, and I find him inspirational. Because I love script, George Bickham's *The Universal Penman* is well worn. John Dreyfus's *The Work of Jan van Krimpen* is a beautiful and informative homage—it explains much about type design. Both Sebastian Carter's *Twentieth Century Type Designers* and Walter Tracy's *Letters of Credit* are scholarly accounts of the complexities of type design. *Fine Print on Type* is a superb and thoughtful selection of essays by contributing experts from their past issues.

American Type Founders
Specimen Book and Catalogue
Jersey City, New Jersey:
American Type Founders Company, 1923

Book of American Types Standard Faces
Jersey City, New Jersey:
American Type Founders Sales Corporation, 1934

Andersch, Martin
Symbols Signs Letters
About Handwriting, Experimenting with Alphabets,
and the Interpretation of Texts
New York: Design Press, 1989

Anderson, Donald M.
The Art of Written Forms
The Theory and Practice of Calligraphy
New York: Holt, Rinehart and Winston, Inc., 1969

Andresen Typographics
Text and Heads (5 vols.)
Los Angeles: Andresen Typographics, 1990

Berthold Fototypes E2 Body Types
erl. u. zgest. von Gotz Görisson
Vol. I, Layouts, 577 Typefaces
Berlin: Berthold; München: Callwey, 1980

Berthold Headlines (E3)
erl. u. zgest. von Gotz Görisson
1400 Headlines Faces Arranged According to Similarity
Berlin: Berthold; München: Callwey, 1982

Bickham, George
The Universal Penman
1743
Reprint, New York: Dover Publications, 1941

Bigelow, Charles,
Paul Hayden Duensing, and
Linnea Gentry, eds.
Fine Print on Type
The Best of *Fine Print* Magazine on Type and Typography
San Francisco: Fine Print/Bedford Arts, 1989

Blumenthal, Joseph
Bruce Rogers: A Life in Letters 1870–1957
Austin: W. Thomas Taylor, 1989

Carter, Sebastian
Twentieth Century Type Designers
New York: Taplinger Publishing Company, 1987

Character Code Standard
Xerox System Integration Standard
Sunnyvale, California: Xerox Corporation, 1987

The Chicago Manual of Style
Thirteenth Edition
Chicago and London:
The University of Chicago Press, 1982

De Vinne, Theodore Low A. M.
The Practice of Typography: Plain Printing Types
A Treatise on the Processes of Type-Making,
The Point System, The Names, Sizes and Styles of Type
New York: Oswald Publishing Company, 1925

Dreyfus, John
The Work of Jan van Krimpen
A Record in Honor of His Sixtieth Birthday
Haarlem: Joh. Enschedé en Zonen, 1952

Dwiggins, William A.
WAD to RR, a letter about designing TYPE
Cambridge, Massachusetts:
Harvard College Library
Department of Printing
and Graphic Arts, 1940

Fairbank, Alfred
A Book of Scripts
New York: Penguin Books, 1955

Frutiger, Adrian
Type Sign Symbol
Zurich: ABC Verlag, 1980

Gottschall, Edward M.
Typographic Communications Today
International Typeface Corporation,
Cambridge: The MIT Press, 1989

Goudy, Frederick W.
The Capitals From the Trajan Column at Rome
With Twenty-five Plates Drawn and
Engraved by the Author
New York: Oxford University Press, 1936

Haley, Allan
ABC's of Type
A Guide to Contemporary Typography
New York: Watson-Guptill, 1990

Typographic Milestones
New York: Van Nostrand Reinhold, 1992

Hlavsa, Oldrich
A Book of Type and Design
Prague: SNTL,
Publishers of Technical Literature, 1960

Jaspert, W. Pincus,
W. Turner Berry, and
A. F. Johnson
The Encyclopaedia of Type Faces
London: Blandford Press, 1983

Johnston, Edward
Writing and Illuminating & Lettering
London: Pitman, 1906

Lawson, Alexander
Anatomy of a Typeface
Boston: David R. Godine, 1990

Leach, Mortimer
Lettering for Advertising
New York: Reinhold Publishing Corporation, 1956

Lindegren, Erik
ABC of Lettering and Printing Types (3 vols.)
Askim, Sweden: Erik Lindegren Grafisk Studio, 1964

Ludlow Typefaces
Chicago: Ludlow Typograph Company, n.d.

Martin's Complete Ideas for Signmen,
Artists, Displaymen
Galesburg, Illinois: Dick Blick Co.
(IDEA-BOOK), 1960

McGrew, Mac
American Metal Typefaces of the Twentieth Century
Preliminary Edition
New Rochelle, New York:
The Myriade Press, Inc., 1986

McLean, Ruari
Jan Tschichold: typographer
Boston: David R. Godine, 1975

Merriman, Frank
A.T.A. Type Comparison Book
New York: Advertising Typographers Association
of America, Inc., 1965

Morison, Stanley
On Type Designs, Past and Present
A Brief Introduction (New Edition)
First Published by the Fleuron, 1926
London: Ernest Benn, 1962

A Tally of Types
With Additions by Several Hands
Edited by Brooke Crutchley
Cambridge: at Cambridge University Press, 1973

Selected Essays on the History of Letter-forms in
Manuscript and Print (2 vols.)
Cambridge: Cambridge University Press, 1981

Pardoe, F. E.
John Baskerville of Birmingham
Letter-Founder & Printer
London: Frederick Muller Limited, 1975

Ryder, John
A Suite of Fleurons; or,
A Preliminary Enquiry into the history &
combinable natures of certain printers' flowers
conducted by John Ryder
Liverpool: Tinglings of Liverpool;
London: Phoenix House Ltd., 1956

Printing for Pleasure
Chicago: Henry Regnery Company, 1977

The Case for Legibility
London: Moretus Press, 1979

Simon, Oliver
The Fleuron
Edited by Oliver Simon (1923–25)
and Stanley Morison (1926–30)
(7 vols.) 1923–30
Reprint, Westport, Connecticut:
Greenwich Reprint Corporation, 1960

Introduction to Typography
Edited by David Bland
London: Faber and Faber, 1963

Specimen Book of Monotype Printing Types (2 vols.)
Salfords, Redhill, England:
Monotype Corporation Limited, 1970

Specimen Book of Monotype Non-Latin Faces
Salfords, Redhill, England:
Monotype Corporation Limited, 1970

Specimen Book of Monotype Filmsetter Faces
Salfords, Redhill, England:
Monotype Corporation Limited, 1970

Standard, Paul
Calligraphy's Flowering, Decay & Restoration
Chicago: The Society of Typographic Arts, 1947

Three Classics of Italian Calligraphy
An Unabridged Reissue of the Writing Books of
Arrighi, Tagliente and Palatino
New York: Dover Publications, Inc., 1953

Tracy, Walter
Letters of Credit: A View of Type Design
Boston: David R. Godine, 1986

Tschichold, Jan
Asymmetric Typography
New York: Reinhold Publishing Corporation;
Toronto: Cooper & Beatty, Ltd., 1967

Timperley, C. H.
William Bulmer and the Shakspeare Press
A Biography of William Bulmer from a
Dictionary of Printers and Printing
1839
Reprint, with introductory note by Laurance B. Siegfried,
Syracuse: Syracuse University Press, 1957

Updike, Daniel Berkeley
Printing Types: Their History, Forms, and Use
A Study in Survivals
(2 vols.)
Cambridge, Massachusetts: *Harvard University Press, 1937*

van Krimpen, Jan
J. van Krimpen on Designing and Devising Type
New York: The Typophiles, 1957

A Letter to Philip Hofer on Certain Problems
Connected with the Mechanical Cutting of Punches
Cambridge, Massachusetts, Harvard College Library;
Boston: David R. Godine, 1972

Whalley, Joyce Irene
English Handwriting 1540–1853
An Illustrated Survey based on Material in the
National Art Library, Victoria and Albert Museum
London: Her Majesty's Stationery Office, 1969

Zapf, Hermann
Pen and Graver
Alphabets & Pages of Calligraphy by Hermann Zapf
Cut in Metal by August Rosenberger
New York: Museum Books, 1952

Manuale Typographicum
Frankfurt: Stempel AG, 1954

About Alphabets
Some Marginal Notes on Type Designs
New York: The Typophiles, 1960

Hermann Zapf
Calligrapher, Type-designer and Typographer
Cincinnati: Contemporary Arts Center, 1960–61

Typographic Variations
Designed by Hermann Zapf on Themes in
Contemporary Book Design and Typography
New York: Museum Books, 1964

Hunt Roman: The Birth of a Type
Commentary and Notes by Hermann Zapf
and Jack Werner Stauffacher
Pittsburgh: The Pittsburgh Typophiles, 1965

Manuale Typographicum
100 Typographical Arrangements with
Considerations about Types, Typography and the
Art of Printing Selected from Past and Present
New York: Museum Books, 1968

Hora Fugit, Carpe Diem
Hamburg: Maximilian-Gesellschaft, 1984

Creative Calligraphy
Instructions and Alphabets
A New Instruction Manual for Learning
the Art of Calligraphy
West Germany: Rotring·Werke Riepe KG, 1985

Hermann Zapf and His Design Philosophy
Selected Articles and Lectures on Calligraphy and
Contemporary Developments in Type Design
Chicago: Society of Typographic Arts, 1987

Index of Typefaces Illustrated

Index of Type Designers

Index of Clients

Index

A NOTE ON THE TYPE
in which this book is set

J OHN BASKERVILLE, who designed the
type in which this book is set, was a contemporary of William Hogarth, and his first book,
a Latin Virgil, published in 1757, established
his reputation. Despite their admiration,
critics of his day, accustomed to the sturdy
types of Caslon, groused that his finer forms
were fatiguing to the eye. Notwithstanding,
Daniel Berkeley Updike, the great printer
and type historian, in his *Printing Types: Their
History, Forms, and Usage,* quotes Pierre Simon
Fournier le Jeune, illustrious printer and type
designer of eighteenth-century Paris: "One
cannot deny that they are the most beautiful
things to be seen in this sort of work."

In 1978, Linotype released this version
designed by George W. Jones, which included three additional weights and their italics.
Avowed to be a faithful interpretation of Mr.
Baskerville's original forms, it was licensed
by International Typeface Corporation from
Mergenthaler Linotype Company in 1982 and
dressed up with a new name, ITC Baskerville.

Formatted in PageMaker 4.01 by the author.

Printed and bound by
Toppan Printing Company, (H. K. Limited)
Text is 128 gsm Kinmari matte Artpaper
Endpapers are printed on 157 gsm Kinmari Artpaper
Silver-foil stamped on Excelin cloth over 3mm board
Jacket printed on 157 gsm gloss Artpaper
with gloss film lamenation.

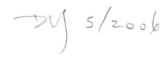